The Geographical Dimensions of Terrorism

THE GEOGRAPHICAL DIMENSIONS OF TERRORISM

EDITED BY
SUSAN L. CUTTER,
DOUGLAS B. RICHARDSON,
AND THOMAS J. WILBANKS

ROUTLEDGE
NEW YORK AND LONDON

Published in 2003 by
Routledge
29 West 35th Street
New York, NY 10001
www.routledge-ny.com

Published in Great Britain by
Routledge
11 New Fetter Lane
London EC4P 4EE
www.routledge.co.uk

Library of Congress Cataloging-in-Publication Data

The geographical dimensions of terrorism/ edited by Susan L. Cutter, Douglas B. Richardson, and Thomas J. Wilbanks.
     p. cm.
  Includes bibliographical references and index.
    ISBN 0-415-94641-7 (alk. paper)—ISBN 0-415-94642-5 (pb.: alk paper)
  1. Terrorism. 2. Terrorism-Prevention. 3. Geography. 4. Geographic information systems. 5. Emergency management. 6. Risk assessment. I. Cutter, Susan L. II. Richardson, Douglas B. III. Wilbanks, Thomas J.

HV6431.G463 2003
363.3'2—dc21
                                    2003040923

CONTENTS

LIST OF FIGURES

LIST OF TABLES

LIST OF ISSUE BOXES

ACKNOWLEDGMENTS

This is truly a collaborative effort, one that was made possible by the generous support of colleagues, the Association of American Geographers (AAG), and funding provided by the Geography and Regional Science Program of the National Science Foundation (BCS-0200619). We are especially grateful for the encouragement provided by Tom Baerwald and Richard Aspinall at the National Science Foundation, who saw the potential for this effort and who provided excellent feedback at crucial times during its evolution and completion. Ronald F. Abler and the AAG Central Office staff were instrumental in planning and executing the January 2002 workshop held in Washington, D.C., a task that is complicated at the best of times, but with our short timeframe (less than eight weeks), these efforts bordered on the heroic. We are especially indebted to Misty Allred, who kept everything moving (e-mails, travel plans, white papers, etc.).

The development of the research agenda and this book that supports it has been a community-wide effort. Critical feedback from geographers was solicited via the AAG's website and newsletter, special sessions at the AAG annual meetings in Los Angeles, numerous regional conferences, Congressional briefings, public agencies and private sector firms, related disciplines, email listserves, and elsewhere. Joel Morrison (Ohio State University) and Jack Shroder (University of Nebraska-Omaha) read a draft of the book in record time and provided important constructive criticisms and comments that helped improve the text. We are appreciative of our editor at Routledge, David McBride, who also saw the potential of this book and significantly shortened the production schedule to accommodate our desire to get the material into print as quickly as possible.

As is the case with all large and time dependent projects, we are especially grateful to our families who put up with physical absences and mental inattentiveness as we tried to complete the manuscript. As co-editors, we share equally in errors of omission or commission and any kudos that may be derived from this publication. We will have achieved our goal, however, if this volume stimulates new thinking and applications of knowledge to secure the future of the world's children and grandchildren in these uncertain times.

Susan L. Cutter, Douglas B. Richardson, Thomas J. Wilbanks
December 2002

FOREWORD

JOHN H. MARBURGER

During the months following the heinous terrorist attacks of September 11, 2001, many of us began to ponder the dimensions of terrorism. I voiced my uneasiness in an address to a symposium organized by the American Association for the Advancement of Science: "When President Bush introduced the notion of a War Against Terrorism, my first thought was how a map for such a war would differ from a conventional battle map. Conventional wars are fought for territory, easily measured on a chart with latitude and longitude, but the fronts in the war against terrorism cover multiple dimensions. How can we detect an unprotected flank in this complex territory? How do we measure progress?"

Who better qualified to respond to such questions than geographers? And who better equipped to instruct others charged with defending not only our territory, but the complex physical and conceptual systems of daily life? Geography gives us tools to visualize, organize, and assess the real world data that inundate essential information with a deluge of detail. Among the sciences, geography has the longest history of relating facts to visualizable, and therefore inevitably spatial, structures. Its tools apply, however, not only to concrete earthbound spaces of breadth and length and elevation, but also to the abstract spaces that exploding technology has made such an important part of our daily infrastructure, of which the most familiar is "cyberspace."

Terrorism, an ancient practice, is newly significant because technology has magnified the destructive power of individuals and small groups. The most ominous vulnerabilities to terrorist disruption occur in the systems that serve the largest populations, and these are necessarily extensive systems. They possess patterns of links and nodes, with corresponding spatial as well as functional distributions, and hierarchies of significance. Some of them, such as the system of energy distribution, are well mapped. Others are not. The systems for disseminating necessary or hazardous materials, food, water, and information are all arguably at risk, but none is usefully characterized in a form readily accessible to planners or emergency responders. At each stage of planning, implementing, assessing, and perfecting strategies for preventing, mitigating, and responding to terrorism, detailed geographical information is essential.

While technology has aided terrorism, it is to technology that we must turn for tools to counter terrorism. Revolutionary enhancements in computing power, data handling, and communications—accompanied by instruments of unprecedented power for detecting, measuring, and manipulating all kinds of physical phenomena—are bringing new tools to all the sciences, not least to geography. Practical geographical information systems, for example, would be impossible without modern computing and display technology, and the rapid mapping capabilities of satellite based global positioning devices. New forms of organizing and displaying data, based on techniques long employed in geography but newly extended to abstract spaces, are now assisting managers of complex industrial processes, engineering designers, economists, and policy experts.

This timely volume confirms the value of the geographical perspective for grappling with the complex issues of terrorism. It touches upon nearly every aspect of the modern terrorism phenomenon, and demonstrates the kind of interdisciplinary approach necessary for any practical engagement with these difficult issues.

INTRODUCTION[1]

Philip Rubin

As is true for other national or regional crises like natural disasters and industrial accidents, terrorism has enormous impacts beyond the immediate destruction, injury, loss of life, and consequent fear. These impacts span the personal, organizational, and societal levels and can have profound psychological, economic, and social consequences. The social and behavioral sciences must provide the knowledge, tools, techniques, and trained scientists that are needed if we are to be prepared to understand, prevent, mitigate, and intervene where required in events related to such crises. Lessons learned from previous research and development efforts are diverse and numerous. For example, research on the mental health consequences of disasters like the Oklahoma City bombing has produced a better understanding of the course of disruptive and disabling symptoms of distress, who is at risk of developing a serious mental illness, and helpful interventions to reduce trauma-related distress, including depression and anxiety disorders. Basic economic research on how markets work was used by government economic advisors to devise policies that would provide the right incentives and not interfere with transitions in industries most affected by the changed security situation after September 11, 2001.

Tragically, there are times when researchers must respond quickly to unanticipated events of horrific proportions. September 11 was just such an event, when fundamental perceptions, systems, structures, and behaviors that had been taken for granted were suddenly questioned. How will we cope with our shock and grief? Will we ever feel safe again? How can we better understand terrorism and its root causes?

What can we do as scientists and citizens to improve the readiness of our nation should another attack occur?

As a Federal research-funding agency, the National Science Foundation (NSF) struggled to cope with such events. At both personal and institutional levels, NSF staff thought it was our obligation to provide funding vehicles and opportunities, where and when possible, to help answer the kinds of questions posed above and to help make our nation safer. To some degree, the present volume was a result of such a funding opportunity. NSF's Small Grants for Exploratory Research (SGER) often are appropriate for the kind of quick response required in situations of great urgency. SGER awards provide support for small-scale, exploratory, high-risk research in the fields of science, engineering, and education. Such research generally can be characterized as preliminary work on untested and novel ideas; a venture into emerging research ideas; an application of new expertise or new approaches to "established" research topics; having a severe urgency with regard to availability of, or access to data, facilities or specialized equipment, including quick-response research on natural disasters and similar unanticipated events; or an effort of similar character likely to catalyze rapid and innovative advances.

Sometimes rapid response is in terms of emergency services or immediate, on-site research. The present volume emerged from another form of rapid response, as members of the geographic community rapidly came together to ask: "What can we do together as a community?" Douglas B. Richardson, Susan L. Cutter, and Thomas J. Wilbanks quickly crafted a proposal entitled "The Geographical Dimensions of Terrorism: A Research Agenda for the Discipline," which was submitted in October 2001. The review and award process normally takes six months or more, but was expedited by NSF Geography and Regional Science Program Directors Richard J. Aspinall and Thomas J. Baerwald. The result was a workshop, a brochure, the present volume, and most importantly, a national research agenda.

Research in the social and behavioral sciences can help us prepare for, understand, mitigate the effects of, and, in some cases, predict and prevent a variety of hazards and other extreme events. Moreover, statistical and computational modeling of longitudinal demographic, economic, and health-related data, emergency response information, geospatial, cultural, linguistic, and political data will yield enormous benefits for the development of the necessary research infrastructure to lessen the impacts of extreme events. There is a need to consider a more holistic approach for understanding our vulnerabilities and resiliencies. A major research effort is needed to develop the basic data, models, and methods for conducting vulnerability assessments at all spatial scales. Rapid access to and analysis of geographic, spatial imaging, and ancillary data that capture the range of social and economic changes caused by crisis or emergencies, such as combining geographical information science with regional health data, would be extremely useful in this regard. Preparedness requires improved vulnerability science and hazards research to address the consequences of a variety of emergencies and other extreme events. Research in the social and behavioral sciences can aid in the development of an effective response strategy to such crises by helping us to assess and understand their "costs", and to design interventions to mitigate against their negative consequences, and take advantage of their positive effects, for example, increased social cohesion.

Strengthening our national, homeland, and economic security requires the creation and use of critical social and behavioral resources. Infrastructure development efforts must focus on wider access to, and integration of, a variety of information including longitudinal demographic, economic, and health-related data, emergency response information, geospatial, cultural, linguistic, and political data. There is a tension between the desirability of free and open access to data and the potential security issues raised by access to certain information. Also of great concern are issues related to privacy and confidentiality. These are difficult matters that must be carefully discussed and considered. Science and security must not unduly impinge on our civil liberties—we must retain a nation that is worthy of defending. Sensitivity and thoughtfulness are also required for a host of other social and behavioral issues related to terrorism and other crises. These issues span multiple scales. They are domestic and international, regional and national. They are also broadly contextual, encompassing social, cultural, behavioral, economic, political, and other concerns. Policy related to these questions must be informed by the best science. Often this is basic research, whose payoff is not immediate and whose application is not always obvious. Experience has shown that investments in fundamental research can have long-term benefits with enormous and profound impact. Investments in basic research must be coupled with attention to infrastructure and data resource development, and with a clear and well-reasoned agenda.

The papers in this volume explore the geographical dimensions of terrorism and other extreme events. The vulnerabilities in our world are discussed and solutions are proposed that will help us to begin to build "a safer but open society." At the heart of this discussion is the need to design and start implementing a geographic research agenda. This volume provides that start.

CHAPTER 1

The Changing Landscape of Fear

SUSAN L. CUTTER, DOUGLAS B. RICHARDSON,
AND THOMAS J. WILBANKS

In the days following September 11, 2001, all geographers felt a sense of loss—people we knew perished, and along with everyone else we experienced discomfort in our own lives and a diminished level of confidence that the world will be a safe and secure place for our children and grandchildren. Many of us who are geographers felt an urge and a need to see if we could find ways to apply our knowledge and expertise to make the world more secure. A number of our colleagues assisted immediately by sharing specific geographical knowledge (such as Jack Shroder's expert knowledge on the caves in Afghanistan) or more generally by assisting rescue and relief efforts through our technical expertise in Geographic Information System (GIS) and remote sensing (such as Hunter College's Center for the Analysis and Research of Spatial Information and various geographers at federal agencies and in the private sector). Still others sought to enhance the nation's research capacity in the geographical dimensions of terrorism (the Association of American Geographers' Geographical Dimensions of Terrorism project). Many of us have given considerable thought to how our science and practice might be useful in both the short and longer terms. One result is the set of contributions to this book.

But, we fail in our social responsibility if we spend our time thinking of geography as the <u>end</u>. Geography is not the end; it is one of many <u>means</u> to the end. Our concern should be with issues and needs that transcend any one discipline. As we address issues of terrorism, utility without quality is unprofessional, but quality without utility is self-indulgent. Our challenge is to focus not on geography's general importance but on the central issues in addressing terrorism as a new reality in our lives in the United States (although, unfortunately, not a new issue in too many other parts of our world).

The September 11, 2001 events have prompted both immediate and longer-term concerns about the geographical dimensions of terrorism. Potential questions on the very nature of these types of threats, how the public perceives them, individual and societal willingness to reduce vulnerability to such threats, and ultimately our ability to manage their consequences require concerted research on the part of the geographical community, among others. Geographers are well positioned to address some of the initial questions regarding emergency management and response and some of the spatial impacts of the immediate conse quences, but the research community is not sufficiently mobilized and networked internally or externally to develop a longer, sustained, and theoretically informed research agenda on the geographical dimensions of terrorism. As noted more than a decade ago, "issues of nuclear war and deterrence [and now terrorism] are inherently geographical, yet our disciplinary literature is either silent on the subject or poorly focused" (Cutter 1988: 132). Recent events provide an opportunity and a context for charting a new path to bring geographical knowledge and skills to the forefront in solving this pressing international problem.

PROMOTING LANDSCAPES OF FEAR

Terrorists (and terrorism) seek to exploit the everyday—things that people do, places that they visit, the routines of daily living, and the functioning of institutions. Terrorism is an adaptive threat which changes its target, timing, and mode of delivery as circumstances are altered. The seeming randomness of terrorist attacks (either the work of organized groups or renegade individuals) in both time and space increases public anxiety concerning terrorism. At the most fundamental level, September 11, 2001 was an attack on the two most prominent symbols of U.S. financial and military power: the World Trade Center and the Pentagon (Smith 2001, Harvey 2002). The events represented symbolic victories of chaos over order and normalcy (Alexander 2002), disruptions in and the undermining of global financial markets (Harvey 2002), a nationalization of terror (Smith 2002), and the creation of fear and uncertainty among the public, precisely the desired outcome by the perpetrators. In generating this psychological landscape of fear, people's activity patterns were and are being altered, with widespread social, political, and economic effects. The reduction in air travel by consumers in the weeks and months following September 11, 2001 was but one among many examples.

WHAT ARE THE FUNDAMENTAL ISSUES OF TERRORISM?

There are a myriad of different ways to identify and examine terrorism issues. Some of these dimensions are quite conventional, others less so. In all cases, geographical understanding provides an essential aspect of the inquiry. There are a number of dimensions of the issues that seem reasonably clear. For instance, one conventional way of looking at the topic is to distinguish four central subject-matter challenges:

1) *Reducing threats*, including a) reducing the reasons why people want to commit terrorist acts, thereby addressing root causes, and b) reducing the ability of potential terrorists to accomplish their aims, or deterrence.
2) *Detecting threats* that have not been avoided, using sensors and signature detection to spot potential actions before they happen and interrupt them.
3) *Reducing vulnerabilities to threats*, focusing on critical sectors and infrastructures, hopefully without sacrificing civil liberties and individual freedoms.
4) *Improving responses to terrorism*, emphasizing "consequence management," and also attributing causation and learning from experience (for example, forensics applied to explosive materials and anthrax strains).

A different way of viewing terrorism is according to time horizons. Immediately after September 11, 2001, governmental leaders told us that the nation was now engaged in a new "war on terrorism" that will last several years, and that our existing knowledge and technologies are needed for this war. Early estimates of the overall U.S. national effort are very large—in the range of $30 to $40 billion per year—including the formation of a new executive department, the Department of Homeland Security. Early priorities include securing national borders, supporting first responders mainly in the Federal Emergency Management Agency (FEMA) and the Department of Justice, defending against bioterrorism, and applying information technologies to improve national security.

Beyond this, we know that better knowledge and practices should be put to use in the next half decade or so, as we face a challenge that is more like a stubborn virus than a single serial killer. To address this type of need, attention often is placed on capabilities where progress can be made relatively quickly if resources are targeted carefully. Some of our GIS and GIScience tools are especially promising candidates for such enhancements, which have both positive and negative consequences (Monmonier 2002). The use of such technologies surely will help secure homelands, but at what price, the loss of personal freedoms or invasion of privacy?

There are other dimensions as well. For instance, one dimension concerns boundaries between free exchanges of information and limited ones, between classified work and unclassified work. Another differentiates between different types of threats: physical violence, chemical or biological agents, cyberterrorism, and the like. Still other themes are woven through the material that follows.

THE CHALLENGE AHEAD

The greatest challenge to geographers and our colleagues in neighboring fields of study is to stretch our minds beyond familiar research questions and specializations so as to be innovative, even ingenious, in producing new understandings that contribute to increased global security. Clearly, the most serious specific threats to security in the future will be actions that are difficult to imagine now: social concerns just beginning to bubble to the surface, technologies yet to be developed, biological agents that do not yet exist, terrorist practices that are beyond our imagination. A core challenge is to improve knowledge and institutional capacities that prepare us to deal with the unknown and the unexpected, with constant change calling for staying one step ahead instead of always being one step behind. When research requires, say, three years to produce results and another two years to communicate in print to prospective audiences, we need to be unusually prescient as we construct our research agendas related to terrorism issues, and we need to be very perceptive and skillful in convincing non-geographers that these longer-term research objectives are, in fact, truly important.

The topic of combating terrorism is not an easy one. It calls for us to stretch in directions that may be new and not altogether comfortable. It threatens to entangle us in policy agendas that many of us may consider insensitively conceived, even distasteful. It may endanger social cohesion in our own community of scholars. On the other hand, how can we turn our backs on a phenomenon that threatens political freedom, social cohesion far beyond our own cohorts, economic progress, environmental sustainability, and many other values that we hold dear, including the future security of our own children and grandchildren?

More fundamentally, geographers are not concerned only with winning the war on terrorism in the next two years or deploying new capabilities in the next five or ten. We are concerned with working toward a secure century, restoring a widespread sense of security in the global society in the longer term without undermining basic freedoms. This is the domain of the research world; assuring a stream of new knowledge, understandings, and tools for the longer term, and looking for policies and practices that—if they could be conceived and used—would make a significant difference in the quality of life.

As we prepare to create this new knowledge and understandings, what we are trying to do, in fact, is to create the new twenty-first-century utility—not a hardened infrastructure such as for power or water, but rather a geographical understanding and spatial infrastructure that helps the nation understand and respond to threats. The effort required to create this new utility to serve the nation has an historical analogy in the creation of the Tennessee Valley Authority (TVA), under Franklin Roosevelt's New Deal. The Appalachian region the southeastern United States had a long history of economic depression and was among those areas hardest hit by the Great Depression of the 1930s. The creation of the TVA, a multipurpose utility with an economic development mission, constructed dams for flood control and hydroelectric power for the region in order to: 1) bring electricity to the rural areas that did not have it; 2) stimulate new industries to promote economic development; 3) control flooding, which routinely plagued the region; and 4) develop a more sustainable and equitable future for the region's residents. This twenty-first-century utility must rely on geographical knowledge and synthesis capabilities as we begin to understand the root causes of insecurity both here and abroad, vulnerabilities and resiliencies in our daily lives and the systems that support them, and our collective role in fostering a more sustainable future, both domestically and globally.

Much of the content of this book is aimed at this longer term, and it is important for geography to join with others in the research community to assure that the long term is not neglected as research support is directed toward combating terrorism and protecting homelands in the short run. This is why the Association of American Geographers and some of its members have joined together to produce the perspectives and insights represented in this book. It is only a start, we still have a long way to go, and there are daunting intellectual and political hazards to be overcome. But if many of us will keep a part of our professional focus on this global and national issue, we have a chance to make our world better in many tangible ways.

CHAPTER **2**

Societal Responses to Threats

INTRODUCTION

Hazards arise from a multitude of sources such as natural events, technological failures, social violence, biological agents, and chronic or globally significant conditions. Hazards research is an interdisciplinary endeavor and spans the divide between the social, natural, engineering, and health sciences. While approaching the field from different perspectives, the hazards research community has one thing in common: a focus on the human environmental dimensions of extreme events caused by natural sources, technological failures, or human agency.

Hazards research and applications have a long and distinguished tradition within the discipline, stretching back more than half a century (Barrows 1923, White 1964). Hazards geographers examine how society amplifies risks (Kasperson et al. 1988), how human occupance of hazard zones is delineated and mapped (Hewitt and Burton 1971, Monmonier 1997), how individuals and society respond to and cope with hazards (Burton et al. 1993), how underlying social conditions create hazard vulnerability (Blaikie et al. 1994), and finally what factors influence the variability in hazardousness from place to place (Kasperson et al. 1995, Cutter 2001).

The papers in this chapter demonstrate the continuing relevance of hazards perspectives to homeland security and terrorism in theory and in practice. Deborah Thomas examines the interplay between public health, law enforcement, and emergency management in response to terrorism and describes key spatial concepts that emerged from these fields: geographic profiling, geographic intervention, and risk management. Ken Mitchell's paper argues for a different approach in combating terrorism by moving away from risk or threat reduction

7

to placing more emphasis on reducing societal vulnerability, especially in urban areas. Gerry Galloway's paper draws on his personal experiences in evaluating disaster preparedness and response, and examines the use of geographical information in the emergency response to the World Trade Center attack. Finally, the challenges faced in managing future disasters, especially those in regions with multiple political jurisdictions, provide the focal point for the paper by Richard Wright, Paul Ganster, and David Dow. These four papers provide a rich sampling of how the geographical community assists in emergency management efforts and how geographical hazards analysis helps inform our understanding of how society responds to natural, technological, and human-induced threats, including terrorism.

2.1

PUBLIC HEALTH, LAW ENFORCEMENT, AND HAZARDS MANAGEMENT

Deborah S. K. Thomas

WHILE HAZARD MANAGEMENT, public health, and law enforcement each has a unique role and mission in society, they become integrally linked when a disaster strikes. Regardless of the type of disaster—from tornadoes to hazardous materials spills to bombings—public health officials, law enforcement, and emergency responders all work together toward the common goal of minimizing death and injury; a relationship clearly demonstrated by the events of September 11, 2001. Preparation for, and response to, terrorism necessitates even closer linkages between these three professional communities because of the unique nature of the terrorist threat. Yet how can those linkages be achieved?

Geography functions as the basis for integration between all organizations charged with hazard risk management, particularly with regard to terrorism, especially bioterrorism. For example, geographic approaches in law enforcement, public health, and hazard management are similar even though the focus and terminology differ slightly between disciplines. This paper explores these commonalities and the potential for creating stronger linkages between public health, law enforcements, and hazards management.

GEOGRAPHIES OF HAZARD MANAGEMENT, PUBLIC HEALTH, AND LAW ENFORCEMENT

Hazards geography has a long tradition in the United States and focuses on a core set of questions centered on finding where hazards are located, identifying the range of adjustments available, and highlighting the choices that individuals and communities make to mitigate

9

impacts. Geographers not only seek to understand what the hazard is, but also who is vulnerable and why. In a similar fashion, public health and medical geography attempt to understand how disease relates to geographic space. Professionals track diseases through surveillance systems in order to identify unusually high incidence rates in certain locations, endeavoring to uncover what environmental conditions may contribute to unhealthy individuals. The integration of geographic approaches and techniques is wide-ranging (Gatrell 2002), and includes everything from trying to establish links between environmental pollution and health outcomes (Vine et al. 1998), to the impact of access to health care on people's selection of medical providers (Albert et al. 2000). Law enforcement also utilizes geographic approaches in crime analysis to identify unusual patterns and areas with high crime rates, and to uncover linkages between policing activity and criminal behavior (Weisburd and McEwen 1997, Camp 2000, Hirschfield and Bowers 2001).

Fundamentally however, all three disciplines ask nearly the same set of geographic questions with regard to hazards, disease, and crime: where are there potential problems, why does the geographic pattern manifest itself in that way, and what can be done to reduce the negative impacts on people? If the ultimate objectives are similar, then it stands to reason that they can effectively come together for anticipating, responding to, and ultimately managing hazards and risk, including terrorism.

SUPPORTING HAZARD AND RISK MANAGEMENT

The goal of hazard risk management is broader than emergency management (UNISDR 2002). Emergency management efforts focus on disaster response, in essence, preparing for crisis management. These efforts coordinate government functions and other private and public relief efforts for rescue, relief, and reconstruction after an event occurs (see Galloway, this chapter). Hazard management includes these functions, but also incorporates risk reduction strategies into the process in order to avoid or minimize present and future losses. In other words, hazard risk management acts as an overarching framework for structural and non-structural approaches aimed at minimizing the impacts of hazards.

Public health and law enforcement are linked with response efforts before, during, and after a hazard. Each has a particular function as codified in the Federal Response Plan for emergencies, yet both contribute expertise to the protection of human life. Most often, police officers and firefighters are first responders to a disaster. The high death tolls of these groups in the aftermath of the World Trade Center attack emphasized this critical role in being the first at the disaster site. Medical and public health professionals play a large role in disaster response efforts as well. Health disaster managers attempt to assess the health effects of an event in order to allocate resources effectively and appropriately (Noji 2002). In addition, public health workers evaluate the longer-term potential for adverse health outcomes related to an event, such as respiratory illness from breathing the smoke at the World Trade Center site or the possibility for cholera outbreaks following a hurricane or flood.

Within the context of hazard risk management, law enforcement and public health professions perform a broader function, contributing to mitigation, prevention, and early intervention efforts. This is especially true when considering terrorism and bioterrorism, particularly through surveillance systems, which detect a potential problem early enough so that intervention activities can occur to either minimize or eliminate the threat. Law enforcement activities also add a key element to preparedness and mitigation through intelligence gathering and monitoring the patterns of criminal activities.

ROLE OF GEOGRAPHIC TECHNOLOGIES

Both hazards and public health point to John Snow's cholera mapping in London in the late 1800s as being one of the earliest examples of mapping an environmental health hazard. Even though he did not use computers, Snow's hand-drawn map was the precursor to computer mapping in these disciplines. The emergence and proliferation of Geographic Information Systems (GIS) throughout public health, crime analysis, and hazard management in the 1990s vastly expanded the possibilities for examining criminal activity, disease patterns, and hazards in a spatial context. With the ease of desktop GIS systems, the possibilities for exploring geographic questions in crime and health applications became much more accessible to a broader audience. GIS made exploring geographic questions easier for non-geographers.

The recognized value of GIS and related technologies for hazard management is well established, not only in emergency response, but for mitigation efforts as well. Hazard and vulnerability assessments identify where risky places intersect with vulnerable infrastructure or populations (Morrow 1999, Cutter et al. 2000). Maps produced from GIS are commonly used for risk communication, and for prediction and warning capabilities. After an event, maps are important tools for coordinating response efforts and conducting damage assessments (Hodgson and Cutter 2001). For example, the immediate postevent mapping efforts by the New York Fire Department's Phoenix Group illustrated this capacity. They produced real time or near real-time maps of the World Trade Center site to minimize the risk to first responders and to improve search and rescue efforts.

Techniques from crime mapping can be incorporated into a GIS for hazard management, particularly when related to urban hazards or first response efforts. Computer aided dispatch systems (CAD) often have mapping capabilities integrated into them, and are used for routing emergency vehicles or tracking resource allocation. In a disaster situation, access to this system for emergency management would be quite useful. Crime mapping is applied to a number of other broad areas in law enforcement, including crime prevention, criminal intelligence, and interaction with the public (Hirschfield and Bowers 2001). Map use for crime prevention is quite similar to disease surveillance; the objective is to detect areas of concern, design intervention activities, and then assess changes. One emerging area within crime analysis that may be useful for combating terrorism is geographic profiling, especially for investigative purposes. The underlying geographic relationship of a series of crimes is used to determine probable locations of criminal residence (Clark 1999). Currently, this technique is not highly refined, but could someday provide the basis for monitoring terrorist activities.

Increasingly, the public health community is utilizing GIS to answer spatial questions in a variety of health-based applications. GIS systems provide the quick response needed for public health decision making, and aid in a range of activities, from disease surveillance to emergency response (Cromley and McLafferty 2002). Disease surveillance is one of the most common uses, particularly in the creation of simple maps of various diseases or disease rates. For example, maps of mortality rates, cancer rates, and birth rates are frequently displayed on the Internet or in atlases (Pickle et al. 1996). GIS can produce maps and integrate with spatial statistics to identify risk areas, calculate time and distance to health care facilities which have the necessary equipment to treat a specific case, or track in real time the location of emergency crews and equipment. The application of GIS and remote sensing for infectious disease mapping also has become more common (Albert 2000). For example, the spread of West Nile was geographically documented using maps (National Atlas of the United States and CDC 2002).

In the public health arena, geographic technologies have direct applications to bioterrorism. The Federal government has identified aerosol exposure, food contamination, and release into the water supply as possible scenarios, all of which can be monitored and modeled with a GIS. Affected people would likely manifest symptoms at a later time than the exposure, and numerous medical facilities would provide treatment. The common location of contact or source of exposure would not be readily apparent. Surveillance systems that account for space could uncover the source of exposure by modeling past activity patterns of patients, or at the very least identify elevated rates at individual treatment centers.

There are several overarching themes between these uses of GIS, a point that emphasizes the need and potential for integrating public health and crime analysis with hazard management for addressing terrorism and bioterrorism. All attempt to integrate data from a variety of sources, although not necessarily between one another. Maps are used in all of three of these professions for hypothesis generation, surveillance, intervention, and education and public outreach. Geography, through GIS, could act as a coordinating force.

ISSUES AND REQUIREMENTS

In theory, the combined contribution of public health, crime analysis, and hazard management to terrorism and homeland security seems quite logical. In reality, these three professional and research communities have not worked closely together. All too often, approaches developed in one discipline have not been incorporated into others, not because they were inadequate, but rather due to the resistance of the community. Facilitating geographical linkages between law enforcement, public health, and hazards management entails several challenges.

The first hurdle is to develop uniform and consistent terminology that reflects similarities in approaches and goals. Hazards management, for example, commonly uses the terms *vulnerability* and *hazardous areas*. Crime analysis uses *prevention*. Public health uses *surveillance* and *intervention*. In fact, the underlying meanings of all of these are similar. Within the context of homeland security, the terms and jargon should not get in the way of intent and interpretation.

There is little doubt that these three disciplines and professions operate independently of one another in day-to-day activities, and have different professional and organizational cultures. Integration of organizational activities is no small task in the face of a disaster, and requires special attention to the roles that organizations play during an emergency. The current discussion suggests the need for the integration beyond the crisis management moment in order to better perform prevention and detection of terrorist activities, a task with even greater challenges than most natural disasters. Geographic analysis and data integration in a GIS environment could act as a catalyst for cooperation.

GIS is, by its very nature, data intensive, which means that integrating data from a variety of sources creates unique challenges, many of which are discussed elsewhere in this book. For the purposes of health, crime, and hazard management, a few unique issues arise. Health data often have strict confidentiality restrictions to protect patient identity. Some subsets of crime intelligence information are not public and generally not shared with those outside of law enforcement agencies. Some data are even classified, particularly when it concerns terrorism. So, security clearance issues restrict access.

There is a distinct need to integrate GIS techniques with spatial statistics for addressing terrorism and bioterrorism. Spatial statistics enable cluster detection and show patterns based on location and time (Haining 1998). The difficulty is that many of these techniques, particularly for the analysis of human exposure data, are not fully integrated within existing GIS systems. Consequently, end users (some of them geographically trained, others less so) must be familiar with several different software programs, limiting the potential for real-time detection because the analytical procedures are not seamless. Still, the potential remains for combining these techniques within surveillance systems to facilitate real-time detection and response. The most important element is integrating mapping systems into comprehensive preparedness and response plans for terrorism and bioterrorism, in order to detect the geographical patterns in the information.

Within the context of hazard risk management, there is little doubt that maps can support the decision-making process for a variety of end users. However, this also requires the creation of easily accessible map products that meet the needs of those who will use them. What type of geographic information might a first responder need? What about the emergency manager in the emergency operations center? How about the differences between the needs of a hazard mitigation planner and a public health official? The significance of designing and constructing maps for effective risk communication cannot be overlooked.

CONCLUSIONS

Public health and law enforcement are linked to hazards management, but the threat of terrorism emphasizes the need to strengthen the ties between organizations. Geographic approaches, accessible through GIS, provide a mechanism for sharing information between them, which is crucial for preparedness and prevention. Homeland security requires integration of these efforts more completely throughout all hazard management phases, not just emergency response efforts. To accomplish this effectively, mapping systems must be incorporated into preparedness and response plans for terrorism and bioterrorism. The by-product of closer associations between public health, law enforcement, and emergency management benefits localities no matter what the source of the hazardous threat. Improved links using geographical analyses and technologies enables communities to prepare for, and respond to, events of any kind.

2.2

URBAN VULNERABILITY
TO TERRORISM AS HAZARD

James K. Mitchell

NONTERRORISTS ACTIVELY CONSTRUCT the conditions that make human societies vulnerable to terrorism; any strategy for responding to terrorism that fails to take account of this fact runs serious risks of failure (Mitchell 2003). This does not mean that victims, bystanders, and other innocent groups should be *blamed* for contributing to the collective burden of terrorism. It simply recognizes that terrorists typically seek to exploit the mundane circumstances of everyday life, the taken-for-granted routines of individuals and institutions, the accepted practices that shape the fabric of human settlements, and the uses to which such places are put.

Terrorists are assisted in pursuit of their goals by widespread public misunderstandings of vulnerability as a policy problem, especially compared with the exaggerated importance that is attached to processes and agents of threat or risk. Environmental hazards, including terrorism, are always a joint product of risks (agents with the potential to inflict harm) and vulnerabilities (degrees to which risk-affected populations are likely to suffer loss). Vulnerability is, in turn, a function of exposure to risk, resistance to risk, and resilience in the face of disaster. The relationship between risks and vulnerabilities is usually dynamic and highly reflexive. For example, early efforts to reduce flood risks in the United States by building dams and levees were undercut by unanticipated shifts in vulnerability, as more people occupied nominally protected floodplains.

At present, U.S. public policy on terrorism is heavily committed to risk-reduction measures involving the neutralization of terrorists, the control of potential weapons, and the improvement of emergency response capabilities. Vulnerability-reduction policies are largely confined to making safety modifications of key buildings, infrastructures, and other facilities. What is missing from this picture is a broad-based understanding of vulnerability as an intrinsic, pervasive, but malleable property of all societies; a product of deliberate human choices about a myriad of commonplace decisions, many of which are only loosely connected to formal issues of risk, safety, and security. If humans are to create environments that are safer from terrorism, then risk and vulnerability need to be addressed together in a comprehensive way from the outset.

Although all sectors of advanced societies and all types of communities are potentially vulnerable to terrorism, vulnerability is worst in urban areas, where the majority of the world's people increasingly live, work, and spend their recreational time (Savitch and Ardashev 2001). In view of this situation, a comprehensive and nuanced analysis of urban vulnerability to terrorism should be a high priority on the terrorism research agenda of governments and other institutions.

HAZARDS RESEARCH AS A PARADIGM FOR STUDYING TERRORISM

Geographers who study hazards often emphasize the ecological dimensions of human responses to extreme events. This approach offers certain advantages for the study of terrorism. First, terror events bear striking similarities to the kinds of geophysical, biological, and technological risks that are commonplace objects of study in hazards research. Second, by supplying an intellectual paradigm that situates extreme events in large societal contexts and structures, hazards research neatly bypasses the criticism that terrorism is merely an epiphenomenon (a superficial layer of symptoms that conceals more fundamental causal processes). Third, hazard researchers possess a repertoire of skills for extracting and assessing emergent, fuzzy, and perishable information from complex situations that are similar to those that commonly involve terrorism events. Fourth, hazards researchers are experienced in the practice of taking their study problems from—and applying their findings to—the domain of public policy, while at the same time continuing to develop broader theoretical notions such as the role of uncertainty in human affairs. If researchers are to make a sustained contribution to the management of terrorism, a similar mix of theory and praxis will be essential in the coming years.

Just as hazards research is an appropriate paradigm for investigating terrorism, so too is a terrorism study agenda valuable to hazards researchers. This is especially true because of the intellectual challenges that it raises, many that lie along the current research frontier of hazards research. By casting light on acute hazards that are entirely generated by human agency, studies of terrorism encourage the development of a more integrated approach to all types of environmental hazards—natural, quasi-natural, and human-caused. Moreover, research on terrorism will undoubtedly open new windows on issues of instrumentality and surprise that rank high among the unsolved problems of hazards research (Mitchell 2002a). For example, most research on hazards has treated them as unwanted occurrences that call for human intervention or control, despite copious evidence that other interpretations are possible. The deliberate use of hazards as instruments to affect a desired end is one such case.

IMPACTS OF 9/11 ON PROSPECTS FOR TERRORISM RESEARCH

There is no doubt that terrorism has moved to the top of the national agenda in the United States, and has become a "hot" research topic. While the will to do something about terrorism, particularly as a public policy issue, is clear, important problems that retarded previous research on this subject still exist, so there is a need for careful crafting of any new research agenda. In addition, it is unclear whether public policy makers, and those who set the research agenda, are fully informed about the nature of the hazard that is being addressed.

The impact of 9/11 on national public policy in the United States has been extraordinary. At a single stroke, fighting terrorism has become a central concern of military services and civilian hazard management agencies, and to a significant degree, it has elbowed aside the existing priorities of both. Not only have military forces joined hot wars against terrorist suspects in Afghanistan, the Philippines, and possibly elsewhere;[1] but their leaders have begun far-reaching reassessments of military strategy and tactics that are designed to put the country's armed forces on a new footing for the twenty-first century. The reorganization of civilian agencies has been even more far-reaching, especially in the form of the new cabinet-level Department of Homeland Security and a proposed budget of $37.7 billion for terrorism-related supporting activities (U.S. Office of Management and Budget 2002).

The announced priorities and funding allocations for Homeland Security suggest how the problem of terrorism within the United States is being interpreted and conceptualized by national leaders. Some have viewed the $38 billion budget as a giant opportunity for business to sell new products to government agencies that will be charged with carrying out most of the Homeland Security mandate (*New York Times* 2002). Indeed, a considerable amount of emphasis is being placed on sophisticated technologies to identify and monitor suspects and to check for suspected weapons. But will these priorities make Americans any more secure against terrorism? Or will they make them better prepared to face other kinds of risks? The answers to both questions are not encouraging. In the first case, the kind of spending contemplated in the budget request is primarily designed to protect technologies rather than people. Most of the things that would be protected are critical infrastructures, such as those that deliver water and energy utilities, computerized information networks, transportation hubs, and emergency services. These are certainly important assets of any society and their destruction or contamination would impair the functioning of large communities by denying services or infrastructure disruptions would impose heavy economic losses, or kill or injure an unknown number of system users. But, protection of these systems does not guarantee that the places where Americans are most vulnerable are also those places that are better protected.

Under current spending proposals, the homes, workplaces, and outdoor spaces in which most Americans spend most of their time would not receive any additional protection from direct attacks that are intended to cause maximum civilian casualties—bomb explosions in crowded office buildings, poison gas releases in concert halls, or toxic materials dispersed through hotel air conditioning systems. As matters currently stand, the systems that undergird modern society undoubtedly would be better protected than individuals and families or other human groups. People might reap some safety benefits from the trickle down effects of infrastructure protection but those would likely come too late for the victims.

Much effort in the coming years will be devoted to assessing the risks of terrorist acts for purposes of avoidance and prevention, but greater attention to vulnerability-sensitive strategies is needed, and may prove to be more effective in the long run. For example, an exploration of links between values and vulnerability could be a prime subject in future research. The threat of terrorism is only useful as a weapon in relation to its perceived effect on what the targeted population values; terrorists know this better than most. As the disasters at the World Trade Center and the Pentagon illustrate so starkly, places and the people who construct them have different meanings and are valued differently by humans. The values-vulnerability nexus is now a neglected topic in the broader reaches of research that deserves greater attention.

The events of 9/11 raise a series of major challenges for hazards researchers. First, they challenge us to accept that the balance between safety and danger has tipped toward the latter in even the most hitherto secure parts of affluent societies, and thus we need to assist in the development of appropriate human adjustments. Second, they challenge us to accept that human-made risks are now capable of inflicting losses on a scale comparable to those of nature, and they encourage us to reorganize our intellectual domain to take account of this situation. Third, they challenge us to carefully examine changing relationships between the two main components of environmental hazard (risks and vulnerabilities), and to increase our efforts to understand the more neglected component of the two, vulnerability. Although all of these challenges are important and worthwhile to explore, the last one seems to offer particular timely advantages as a research priority.

URBAN VULNERABILITY AS A FOCUS FOR TERRORISM RESEARCH

Though vulnerability was long recognized as an essential component of environmental hazard, over the past half century it has run a poor second to risk in terms of the amount of attention that it attracted from researchers, hazard managers, policy makers, and the public. For hazards geographers, that period of neglect ended two decades ago and since then there has been a steadily rising tempo of activity (Blaikie et al. 1994, Hewitt 1997, Comfort et al. 1999, Cutter 2001, Kasperson and Kasperson 2001). Specific research on urban vulnerability first was undertaken by the IGU Study Group on the Disaster Vulnerability of Megacities (Mitchell 1999) and later by the still-continuing U.N. University-sponsored Urban Vulnerability project. Other innovative research on urban vulnerability was carried out by geographers engaged in integrated assessments of long-term climate change in metropolitan areas of the United States (Rosenzweig and Solecki 2002).

Unfortunately, the task of convincing nonacademic hazard stakeholder groups to focus on global vulnerability has proved much more difficult. However, a breakthrough initiative was undertaken by the United Nations Development Program, in the form of a proposed annual series of *World Vulnerability Reports*, and an accompanying set of vulnerability indicators—similar in structure and orientation to the highly influential *World Development Report* and development indicators. The first annual edition is scheduled for publication in early 2003. Hazards geographers are prime movers and leading contributors to this initiative.

Just as knowledge about vulnerability is now informing the domain of hazards management, the events of September 11, 2001 propelled vulnerability issues onto center stage among national leaders and the public in More Developed Countries (MDCs), including the United States. Four days after the twin towers of the World Trade Center collapsed, Frank Rich, the noted *New York Times* columnist, offered the observation that everything had changed as a result of what happened on September 11, 2001. He judged that the guiding principles of future American life would no longer be hubris and hedonism, but rather fear and sacrifice. Similar themes were echoed in newspapers and television programs throughout the country. Most agreed that vulnerability would become the new watchword, especially in cities whose occupants considered that they were protected against sudden collective catastrophes.

Unfortunately, characterizations of urban Americans as newly aware of their vulnerabilities and newly determined to act in light of this knowledge betray a lack of understanding about the nature of vulnerability and its role in the calculus of hazard. Vulnerability is an independent, active process that is shaped by the choices humans make, not—as so often understood by the public—an inherent dependent state that is revealed by an external event. Because vulnerability is such a potent driver of hazard and because it is so sensitive to human actions, much more can be done to reduce vulnerability than to affect risks, which tend to come from less accessible sources. Second, characterizations of disasters as agents of fundamental change ignore copious evidence that no great event ever wipes away everything that came before. As postmodern scholars often point out, all societies carry with them the accumulated experience of their pasts; the place of new events is always negotiated within this context. For the large cities of North America, Europe, Japan and other developed regions, the context of disaster is especially complex, contradictory, and dynamic. In the search for appropriate public policies about urban hazards, we must be prepared to fit new environmental threats carefully into these larger puzzles of city living.

Evidence about the World Trade Center disaster casts new light on debates about urban vulnerability. Some aspects of the experience were unprecedented and others were quite mundane. In particular, the risks and impacts were close to unique, but the vulnerabilities and responses were not at all unusual. Unfortunately, postevent analyses tended to focus heavily on the risks and on strategies that address them. Rather than viewing the disaster as a (probably unrepeatable) surprise, commentators regard it as a new risk archetype—the first in a series of similar events that may be yet to come. As a result, policymakers have rushed to enact new airport security measures and to worry about threats to tall buildings. Those fears might be justified if society was confronted by a natural hazard whose behavior is a function of knowable parameters, but it is inappropriate for an event that derives its power from the fact that instigators deliberately sought to make it unlike anything that had occurred before. In short, by focusing heavily on risks rather than on vulnerabilities, there is a danger of generating a lopsided public discussion that does not do justice either to the experiences of September 11, 2001 or to the vast range of knowledge that already exists about the human contexts of hazard.

Risks are difficult to assess. The range of possible future urban risks is more or less infinite. The events of 9/11 make this abundantly clear in connection with terrorist threats. Among other factors, the process of globalization ensures that some sources of future urban risks are further removed from—and invisible to—victims than ever before. Combinations of natural and technological hazards also are producing new hybrids of risk, and the very act of addressing one type of risk often produces new ones. All of these things hamper the development of stable risk-based policies for hazards management. In contrast, indices of vulnerability are recognizable among the human populations that occupy or use cities, and appropriate public policies can be crafted to readily address them. Measures of resistance or resilience are relatively independent of specific risks and usually are identified for discrete human groups and institutions. Measures of exposure are more difficult if the risks are unknown, but assumptions are often substituted for precise data, and aggregate patterns of exposure to a range of existing risks also are helpful surrogates. For all of these reasons and more, it makes increasingly good sense to address the bulk of public policies to the reduction of vulnerability rather than the control of risks.

A PROPOSED URBAN VULNERABILITY
RESEARCH STRATEGY

Bearing in mind the preceding observations, the time is ripe for a major effort to investigate the full range of vulnerabilities that affect major cities of the United States, with a view toward providing information that can be used to address issues of terrorism within broader understandings of urban governance and urban hazards. Representative examples of the kinds of questions that such investigations might address are listed in Issue Box 2.2.

Clearly, Americans are only near the beginning of a long learning curve about the meanings that the public and experts attach to terrorism, and the adjustment strategies that may be employed to reduce the threat. As people who were victims of terrorism already know, direct

ISSUE 2.2
Urban Vulnerability Research Questions

- How are vulnerabilities constructed in U.S. metropolitan areas? Among others, what roles in the creation of vulnerability are played by human values, "invisible" populations, advanced socio-technical systems, and privileged populations?

- To what extent are the perspectives of vulnerable individuals and groups incorporated into existing hazard adjustments? How do people and institutions that are subject to multiple vulnerabilities prioritize or sort among such problems or resolve related ambiguities, contradictions, and paradoxes?

- Which parts of metropolitan areas are differentially vulnerable to existing natural, technological, and biological risks, to expected risks of climate change, and to possible future risks of terrorism? What are the most effective ways of representing and mapping such metropolitan vulnerabilities?

- What types of vulnerabilities are most likely to be exploited by perpetrators of terrorist acts and what places, facilities, or groups are the most likely targets because of their vulnerabilities?

- To what extent are the residents of U.S. metropolitan areas aware of their vulnerabilities to terrorism or other risks, and fearful of the consequences?

- Are existing theories and methods adequate for framing and conveying information about vulnerability to appropriate user groups?

- What opportunities exist for collaboration among different urban interest groups (including differentially vulnerable populations and institutions) in support of vulnerability reduction measures and mitigation strategies pertaining to terrorism and similar urban threats?

- What can be learned from metropolitan areas in other countries that have greater experience with terrorism and other environmental hazards than their U.S. counterparts?

- How can experts on vulnerability and experts on risk best cooperate in support of efforts to reduce urban hazards, including the hazards of terrorism?

experience of this hazard is unusually costly not just because of the deaths and damages that occur, but because terrorism undermines the kind of trust in fellow humans that is necessary for the functioning of almost any society. Moreover, indirect knowledge of terrorism—obtained from educational institutions, the mass media, and other agents of culture—is tightly hedged with fears, anxieties, prejudices, and misrepresentations, as well as an ingrained human reluctance to make security a routine but major concern of daily living. We already are beginning to understand something about the risks of terrorism. It is time to complement that knowledge with a determined effort to understand the equally important realm of vulnerability to terrorism.

2.3

EMERGENCY PREPAREDNESS AND RESPONSE

Lessons Learned from 9/11

GERALD E. GALLOWAY[1]

EMERGENCY MANAGEMENT INVOLVES four interrelated actions: mitigation, preparedness, response, and recovery. Mitigation focuses on taking actions to reduce risk. Preparedness recognizes that while mitigation actions can reduce risk, they do not eliminate the vulnerability to hazards. Preparedness actions seek to establish authorities and responsibilities for emergency actions and to assemble the resources to support these actions. Response involves actions to reduce casualties and save lives, protect property, and restore essential government services once an event has occurred, while recovery encompasses those efforts to restore the social and economic infrastructure and clean up, to the extent possible, the environment of the affected community following the emergency (FEMA 1996). One way to depict this is through the emergency response cycle (Figure 2.3.1), which is applicable to a wide range of potential threats ranging from natural disasters to terrorist bombings.

The September 11, 2001 terrorist attacks on the Pentagon near Washington, D.C. and the World Trade Center (WTC) in New York took the nation by surprise not only in their impact but also in the very fact that this type of an event could actually occur within the United States. The Federal Emergency Management Agency's (FEMA's) current *State and Local Guide for All-Hazard Emergency Operations Planning*, published in 1996, provides attachments dealing with all types of hazards. The annex on "terrorism" was not issued until April 2001. Following the September attacks, it was restructured and released as a separate document, *Managing the Emergency Conse-*

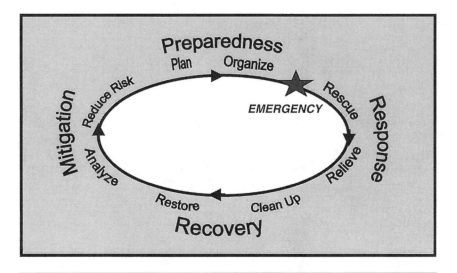

FIGURE 2.3.1 The Emergency Response Cycle (From Thomas et al. 2002)

quences of Terrorist Incidents: Interim Planning Guide for State and Local Governments. In 2002, FEMA also issued *Tool Kit for Managing the Emergency Consequences of Terrorist Incidents: Interim Planning Guide for State and Local Governments.*

The emergency responses by federal state and local governments to the attacks highlighted the impressive ability of the emergency management community to adapt to changing circumstances during the immediate disaster period. These actions also identified areas where improvements in both preparedness and in response could be made to mitigate the impacts of such events in the future. This paper discusses the geographic aspects of these lessons learned.

PLANNING FOR THE UNTHINKABLE

In the United States, local governments carry the principal responsibility for emergency management, supported as necessary by the state and federal governments. The United States has a robust and world-envied emergency management system that effectively coped with major natural disasters of the magnitude of Hurricane Camille in 1969 and the 1993 Mississippi floods, both of which involved many states, thousands of people, and millions of dollars in damages. Historically, the United States has been prepared to deal with natural events whose parameters are understood reasonably well, although the timing of the events are not always predictable. The 1993 attack on the World Trade Center and the 1995 Oklahoma City bombing gave some indication of the possible impact of terrorist activity; however, 9/11 took the nation by surprise because of its intensity and its focus. Both attacks were targeted to produce damages to critical and visible infrastructure and people, and severely tested the preparation for and the response to such attacks. They also identified preparedness and response areas in need of attention.

Preparedness planning requires the maintenance of emergency management structures at a point of "readiness" in order to prevent these capabilities from falling victim to the emergency itself, and identifies augmentation that will be required in an emergency. This pre-impact planning is referred to as continuity of operations. Preparedness plans are based on an expected emergency (hurricane, earthquake, hazardous material spill) and must "note the geographic and topographic features that may affect operations" (FEMA 1996: 2–11). A variety of hazard models are available to match the hazard to the affected landscape. Response is the test for the plan and it is normally carried out in mock exercises (FEMA 1996). In those instances where an event actually occurs, reviews of the emergency response occur in after action reports, a process that allows emergency managers to share experiences and thereby improve response capabilities based on the lessons learned. A post-event assessment of emergency response is vital for improving local, state, and federal efforts in hazard and disaster management.

LESSONS LEARNED

From a geographic perspective, the lessons learned from the preparedness for and response to the September 11, 2001 terrorist attacks highlight the importance of knowing where things are and having the ability to use this spatial information with Geographic Information Systems (GIS) and other geo-technologies under a wide variety of circumstances. While there are many important lessons learned from the management and response to 9/11, a number of them are especially relevant to the geographic community.

Current Baseline Information on Critical Infrastructure

Emergency managers and those associated with response and recovery must have access to current or near-current data and information on the location and status of critical infrastructure including transportation systems (such as roads, railroads, subways, bridges, and tunnels), communication and utility systems and nodes, sensitive facilities (hospitals, schools, and so on), and the population at risk (see chapter 5).

New York City was fortunate in having NYCMAP, a base map that was developed over the previous five years, and one that contained digital high-resolution vector and orthophoto data. The base map provided a common framework for additional data as it became available from multiple sources following the attack. The city was fortunate to have a director of Citywide GIS (Geographic Information Systems) in its Department of Information Technology and Telecommunications, who was well versed in the city's GIS capabilities (Cahan and Ball 2002).

Major infrastructure-related businesses (utility and communications) also had well-developed baseline information available. The presence of these data from the start of the response effort greatly facilitated subsequent operations, and permitted considerable predisaster training on potential nonterrorist related disasters. It also was apparent that data must cover both the macro- and the micropictures. Data on the critical nodes of New York's deep infrastructure—water, sewer, gas, electric, steam, sand, and telecommunications—buried under the city, were as important, in many cases, as data on roads and buildings (GeoCommunity 2001, New York City 2001). Most were available in one form or another prior to September 11, 2001. As noted by Cahan and Ball (2002: 27), "Geography provided the common denominator for all response and recovery efforts."

GIS is Essential

GIS and supporting geotechnologies provide an indispensable capability to assist in the pre-event preparation and postevent conduct of emergency operations (Greene 2002). Information is of little use if it cannot be displayed and manipulated and GIS offers this capability. During a review of World Trade Center (WTC) operations, former FEMA head James Lee Witt noted, "I can't stress how important it [GIS] is"(Greenman 2001:Section G, p.8). In the minutes and hours following the attack on the WTC, emergency personnel sought to identify who was harmed, where survivors could be taken, what roads and transportation systems were still available, what alternative routings could be applied. The location of critical telecommunications nodes in the WTC area, and the large number of power lines that crossed Manhattan under and near the WTC, focused attention on how these systems could be put back into service. In the days following the attack, the emergency managers were faced with handling the flow of the millions of people who traveled daily into and out of the city, and getting them to their destinations near the WTC.

In Washington, emergency managers used GIS and geotechnology-based systems to route fire and rescue equipment in response to the Pentagon's call for assistance (GeoCommunity 2001). Having a coordinated GIS enterprise in place prior to a disaster is clearly the ideal situation (Thomas et al. 2002), a factor that greatly enhanced New York City's response.

Capacity to Rapidly Update Baseline Information

Emergency managers and associated agencies must be able to update and manipulate the data and information in their base systems. Procedures must be established to permit the rapid transfer of information among agencies involved in the post-disaster operations. As new information becomes available, it must be provided to all parties engaged in the response and recovery efforts. For example, the New York City Board of Education had an elaborate emergency response plan in place prior to the attack, including the use of Stuyvesant High School as a potential shelter site. The Board of Education was forced to rapidly adjust its plans, since the high school was now in the affected area near the WTC (O'Brien 2002). Because of the breakdowns in communications systems, updates were frequently distributed by compact disk (Schutzberg 2001).

The mechanisms for obtaining and processing data from various sensors and sources should be in place prior to any event and links to technical support established, including universities, private firms, and federal, state, and local government agencies. For example, in New York, the (state) Office for Technology (OFT) coordinated requests for remotely sensed data (such as thermal, LIDAR, and aerial photography) (Thomas et al. 2002).

Multi-Jurisdictional Cooperation

The wide range of GIS that exist in most communities must be tied together in a manner that ensures that all agencies involved in disaster response are able to share and communicate the spatial information they have. Today, most emergency management agencies and other governmental agencies make extensive use of GIS, but not all of them have compatible systems. Predisaster coordination among New York City agencies and between city and state and federal agencies facilitated the sharing and exchange of existing information. Being part of a single jurisdictions greatly eased this exchange during the 9/11 response. However, the need still exists for predisaster coordination among adjacent jurisdictions and among levels of government where the links may not be as strong as they were in New York. Turf issues and data sharing can be difficult during normal periods, but the lack of coordination and cooperation during a disaster period could translate into more casualties and economic losses, simply because the data were not available to responders in a timely fashion.

Redundant Systems

To ensure continuity of operations, emergency planners must identify alternate emergency operation centers and ensure that their information base is available to the alternate center. The geographic technologies used in the alternate centers must match those in the principal centers (Thomas et al. 2002). Since New York City's emergency command center was destroyed in the attack, emergency managers had to establish alternate command centers in other locations in the city and gather the tools needed to support response and recovery. While most of the baseline geographic information needed to reestablish the center was in the city, it was scattered among many different agencies. In the hours immediately following the attack, the geography department at Hunter College became an important source of GIS products for the emergency operations (Cahan and Ball 2002).

Decision Support Systems

Decision Support Systems (DSS) and their included models provide the capability for emergency managers to quickly develop answers to critical questions: What are the alternative routes available? What hospitals are closest? However, they must be enhanced to be able to deal with the immensity of this new form of hazard. As systems are developed, they should be shared. For over a decade, the Department of Defense (DoD) has been employing sophisticated DSS on the battlefield to provide its leaders with the capability to rapidly analyze large volumes of geospatial information obtained from a variety of sources, and to identify the most important elements. DoD's experience with DSS should be brought to bear on the problem of information proliferation in postdisaster environments.

Public Communication

Geographically-based products must be available to the public as an easy to understand source of hazard and response information. Government officials need to let the public know how to respond to the events—what subways are operating, what streets are closed, where shelters are located. In both New York and Washington, maps produced by the media and the emergency operations activities enabled people to know where they could and could not go, to appreciate the true nature of the disaster, and to make plans for recovery (Weber et al. 2002). Maps and other spatial information were seen in newspapers and on television, or were accessible through the Internet. Prior to the attacks, many government agencies, particularly in the environmental and public works areas arena, were making increasing amounts of information and data about infrastructure and hazardous material sites available to the public as part of community right-to-know efforts. These policies now are being reevaluated out of concern that this same information can fall into the wrong hands (Manion et al. 2001; New York City 2001).

Private Sector Role in Emergency Management

The contributions of businesses in mitigation, preparedness, response, and recovery activities are underestimated. Emergency management requires the full cooperation of all affected parties—government, business, and the public at large—and methods must be developed to ensure that information can be shared vertically and horizontally. It is apparent that the private sector plays vital and varied roles in emergency management. Following a disaster, firms provide volunteers, donations of needed supplies, use of health and safety facilities, direct medical care, and serve as vendors for emergency management supplies. They also can play a significant role in information dissemination (Weber et al. 2002).

While this section focused on the preparedness and response efforts of government agencies, the same necessity for preparedness and response, including the concomitant need for geographic information, exists within the nongovernment community. The September 11, 2001 attacks caused severe disruption to the activities of many firms and organizations in the vicinity of the WTC and throughout the New York metropolitan area. Transportation and utility services were disrupted, buildings closed, and employees scattered. As business tried to reestablish operations, they called upon the same information and tools that were used to support government emergency response and can profit equally by the lessons learned.

FUTURE CHALLENGES

The availability of geographic information made a difference in the ability of emergency managers to prepare for and respond to the disaster of September 11, 2001. This success points to the need for further efforts aimed at better integration of geographic technologies into the entire emergency response cycle. Planning the flow of geospatial information and technologies through the organizational structure is vital to its successful use. Geographers and emergency managers must work together to address the many challenges they face in developing preimpact plans and postevent responses. A few of the most important questions include:

- What baseline data are critical to a community and in what form are they best stored and displayed?

- Where can data best be stored within a community so that the data may be shared rapidly with alternate emergency operations centers and with other agencies? How can this capability best be exercised?
- What steps should be taken to ensure the ability of alternate emergency operations centers to seamlessly accept the GIS activities of the principal center?
- What models are needed to support GIS based decision support systems to rapidly develop answers to questions such as, "what is the fastest alternate route from one location to another?"
- What forms of geoinformation are best suited for use by the media and government officials in informing the public about actions connected with emergencies? What information should be excluded from public viewing?
- How can nongovernment geoinformation resources best be linked with government resources prior to and during emergencies?

THE MESSAGE OF 9/11

Within minutes of the terrorist attacks on New York and Washington, emergency managers were putting geospatial information to use. Over the next hours and days, additional geospatial information was being collected, processed, and put into play in the vast response and recovery effort. Given the suddenness and enormity of the events, the ability of these managers to find and use this information was remarkable, and stands as a tribute to both the hard work of these professionals during a period of great stress, and the foresight of those who had earlier developed and exercised these geospatial capabilities. The lessons learned in the aftermath of September 11, 2001 will serve well those who must now prepare for such unpredictable disasters.

2.4

TRANSBORDER DISASTER MANAGEMENT

RICHARD WRIGHT, PAUL GANSTER, AND DAVID DOW

THE TERRORIST ATTACKS of September 11, 2001, and the responses in the days that followed, highlighted many of the difficulties in maintaining the efficient circulation of peoples, goods, services, and information in the United States-Mexico borderlands while still providing for adequate homeland security in the United States. Hazards pay little attention to political boundaries, so disaster management increasingly has involved coordination across jurisdictional boundaries and cooperation among local, state, and federal agencies. While progress has been made in cross-jurisdictional disaster management within the borders of the United States, much less attention has been given to coordination across the nation's international boundaries. However, 9/11 and its aftermath indicated the critical need to increase the level of attention to transborder disaster planning.

Proximity to international borders presents planners, policymakers, and emergency response agencies with many challenges. Economic, social, and political differences, variations in the perception of the nature and scope of threats, and the willingness and ability to plan for—and respond to—emergency situations are amplified by international boundaries. Issues of geographic or institutional jurisdiction, functional capabilities and requirements, and cooperative planning and response that are normally addressed as local or regional activities within a national context, become foreign policy matters where international boundaries exist. Effective disaster planning and response on each side of the border and the coordination of efforts across borders can be enhanced by the availability and use of geospatial technologies (such as geographic information systems and remote sensing) and by shared, current geographic data.

THE UNIQUENESS OF BORDERLANDS

The traditional function of borders has been to demarcate the territory of one nation from that of its neighbors, and to guarantee the security and sovereignty of a nation. Borders served as barriers and were often defended with military installations against real or perceived threats of territorial aggression from other nations. Often, border regions were spatially, politically, and economically isolated from the national capital, and border populations were discouraged from interactions with counterparts on the other side of the border. Policies regarding borders and border regions were made in the national capital, often with negative impacts for border populations. As neighboring countries developed more cooperative relations and the threat of military conflict receded, the function of borders was transformed from barrier to that of integrating interface or transition zone.

The economic forces of globalization were often a driving force behind this change in the perception and function of borders. At the same time, interaction of peoples across the international boundary often served to create a cultural transition zone or interface between one nation and another. This was especially true in the United States-Mexico border region where the settlement pattern of most of the population concentrated in twin-city pairs across the international boundary. There, daily interactions of Mexican and U.S. border residents and the long-term increase of Mexican-origin populations in U.S. border cities produced strong cultural linkages that transcended national boundaries (Martínez 1990).

Although the last armed conflict between the United States and Mexico took place in the middle of the nineteenth century, the shared border retained many barrier functions through much of the twentieth century. Mexico saw the border as protection from the overwhelming economic, political, and cultural might of its northern neighbor. The U.S. government was concerned with the northward flow of undocumented workers and drug trafficking (Ganster and Sweedler 1990). These security concerns, however, were overshadowed from the 1980s onward by the growing forces of the global economy that culminated in the creation of the North American Free Trade Agreement (NAFTA) in 1994. Increased transborder flows of goods, services, and investment stimulated significantly enhanced cross-border cooperation in the United States-Mexico border region, a shift that was fully supported by both national governments as well as local populations.

THE UNITED STATES-MEXICO BORDER REGION

The events of September 11, 2001, however, forced the reexamination of the United States-Mexico border. Terrorism brought a very real

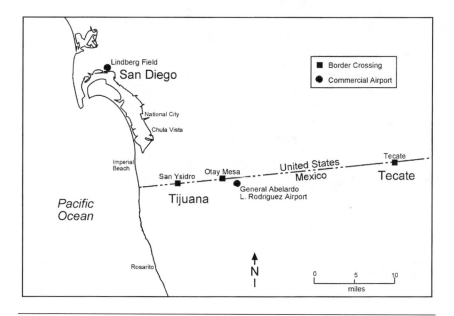

FIGURE 2.4.1 The San Diego-Tijuana Border Region

threat to national security, not through traditional means such as invasion by a foreign army, but rather through infiltration of terrorists and weapons across traditional land boundaries, and through airports and ports. September 11, 2001 brought significant changes in how the U.S. and Mexican governments viewed the common border and impacted the lives of border citizens in many ways.

The San Diego-Tijuana region is one of the most dynamic areas of the world in terms of economic growth and population expansion (Figure 2.4.1). In 1990, the combined San Diego-Tijuana population was 3.2 million; in 1995 it was 3.6 million; in 2000 it was 4.1 million; and is projected to be 5.4 million by 2010 (Peach and Williams 2000). This population growth was accompanied by significant urban growth of an extensive nature on the San Diego side and an intensive nature on the Tijuana side. Manufacturing and trade also saw rapid growth. Cross border trade between Mexico and the United States more than doubled from the implementation of NAFTA in 1994 to 2000. Manufacturing in Tijuana, largely concentrated in the *maquiladora* (assembly) industry, grew from 414 plants and 59,870 employees in 1990 to 788 plants and 187,339 employees in 2000. The growth in trade and manufacturing for export also is responsible for increased truck traffic at the border. In 1994 there were 439,654 northbound crossings of heavy-duty trucks into San Diego from Mexico; in 2000 that figure was 688,340 (U.S. Department of Transportation 2001).This impressive economic expansion, particularly in Tijuana, saw a similar growth in the use and transportation of hazardous materials, increasing the risk of occurrence and severity of spills or incidents. A recent study by the U.S. Environmental Protection Agency estimates that in 1999 approximately 80,000 tons of hazardous materials and waste were imported into San Diego through Otay Mesa and some 532,000 tons were exported to Mexico through the same port of entry (USEPA 2001b). Although our focus is on the San Diego, California-Tijuana, Baja California region, which includes the busiest crossing along the United States-Mexico border, the recommendations for future research are broadly applicable to other border areas included in NAFTA and elsewhere.

DISASTER MANAGEMENT
IN THE SAN DIEGO-TIJUANA BORDER REGION

Management of disasters in the San Diego-Tijuana metropolitan region, whether natural or human-induced, requires close cooperation between Mexican and U.S. government authorities and agencies at local, state, and federal levels. Historically, the national political systems and other factors, such as economic asymmetries, discouraged direct formal transborder interactions in the San Diego-Tijuana region among state and local authorities (Ganster 1993, 1998). Instead, the principal transborder issues and impacts were addressed by federal and international agencies. Water and sewage disposal are handled by the International Boundary and Water Commission, where American and Mexican sections report to their respective foreign relations ministries, not each other. Increased population growth in border twin cities resulted in the 1983 La Paz Agreement, an accord between the two nations to systematically address broader-based environmental issues. Other border concerns, such as criminal justice issues, trade-related problems, or public health concerns, were dealt with through specific agreements between U.S. and Mexican federal agencies, often on an ad hoc basis.

By the 1970s and 1980s, increasing interaction between Mexican and U.S. authorities was evident in the San Diego-Tijuana region. Often, this was the result of concerns about specific issues such as trade and commerce, border-crossing bottlenecks, and renegade sewage flows across the border. Both the city and county governments of San Diego established offices to handle border problems and opportunities, while regional planning agencies increasingly worked with Mexican counterparts. Only sporadically did San Diego and Tijuana cooperate on issues related to emergency response. For example, the City of San Diego would send equipment and personnel across the border to help the Tijuana Fire Department fight major fires and the two departments participated in joint training exercises. In 1993, the two cities signed a letter of agreement to establish a framework for city-to-city cooperation and subsequent local administrations have reaffirmed that agreement (Guillén and Sparrow 2000).

The federal governments of Mexico and the United States took measures in the early 1990s to better address increasing environmental problems in the border region to pave the way for NAFTA. Building on the La Paz Agreement, in 1992 the two governments created the Integrated Environmental Plan for the Mexican-U.S. Border Region (IBEP) and in 1996 a follow-up effort known as Border XXI was launched (http://www.epa.gov/usmexicoborder).

Both U.S. and Mexican authorities clearly recognized that the two federal governments alone could not address the many transborder issues that impacted regions such as San Diego and Tijuana. In 1992, the two federal governments created the Border Liaison Mechanism (BLM), first implemented in the San Diego-Tijuana region in 1993. The BLM empowered local consuls general of the two countries in border cities to convene government stakeholders of all levels in the regions for direct interactions to address critical issues. The initial committee of the BLM in the San Diego-Tijuana region worked on border crossing issues at the ports of entry, and later, committees were established for public safety and mutual aid, migration and consular protection, water, and culture and education. For the first time, local governments could legally and directly work jointly on local border issues (Guillén and Sparrow 2000).

Since NAFTA and Border XXI, a more comprehensive approach to regional bi-national issues is evident on a number of levels. In some cases, NAFTA stimulated new cooperative efforts. In others, NAFTA supported and strengthened ongoing activities, such as a regional transportation system, harmonized data sets that produced the *San Diego-Tijuana International Border Area Planning Atlas* (Ganster 2000), and cooperation on health matters (http://www.borderhealth.gov/index.html). The U.S. EPA and Mexico's Federal Environmental Protection Enforcement Agency (PROFEPA) established a protocol for mutual notification of hazardous spills and chemical emergencies, although its provisions have not yet been utilized in the San Diego-Tijuana region (Fege 2002). The U.S. EPA has assisted other border communities in the development of emergency response plans for hazardous spills under the Border XXI program (U.S. EPA 2001a), and in development of an emergency response plan for the San Diego-Tijuana region (Volpini 2002). Over the years, there have been sporadic interactions between San Diego (city and county) and Mexican counterparts regarding topics such as earthquake preparedness, public health emergencies, and hospital capacity in the region. However, these efforts were

---

ISSUE 2.4
Binational Flood Warning Systems:
A Demonstration Project

San Diego State University is now working with thirteen U.S. and Mexican government agencies at local, state, and federal levels to develop a binational flood warning system for the lower portion of the Tijuana River Watershed. This is an area that has a history of flash floods resulting in considerable loss of life and damage to property. The flood warning system consists of new stream and rain gages to capture flow and rainfall data for each sub-basin, modeling and forecasting capabilities, antennas to receive and transmit data to emergency response units, and software to allow San Diego State University and universities in northern Baja California to access real time data for modeling purposes. The warning system, in turn, builds on the Tijuana River Watershed National Community Demonstration Project. This project was one of six national projects selected by the United States Federal Geographic Data Committee (FGDC) to demonstrate the value of GIS and the National Spatial Data Infrastructure (NSDI) in addressing local problems (Conway et al. 2000). It involved a binational risk assessment to identify vulnerable human communities and natural environments in the Tijuana River Watershed associated with flood events of varying intensities. The risk assessment focused on watershed, sub-basin, and canyon scales (Wright et al. 2000).

---

generally ad hoc arrangements and have not resulted in the systematic coordination of disaster management across the border.

Although considerable progress was made toward effective cross-border cooperation in the San Diego-Tijuana region in the past five years (see Issue Box 2.4), needs clearly have outstripped the ability of the region to manage issues that spill across the border. For example, in San Diego there is a GIS-based system available to emergency responders providing location and amounts of hazardous materials in the region, yet similar information and systems are unavailable for Tijuana. Thus, in an emergency situation, Mexican authorities have little information regarding chemicals involved in fires or spills. Despite possible impacts on San Diego, U.S. authorities (local, state, and federal) have extremely limited data on the potential magnitude of chemical disasters originating in Tijuana or at the border.

BORDER EFFECTS OF THE 9/11 RESPONSE

The reaction in metropolitan San Diego to the events of September 11, 2001 illustrates how Tijuana, often ignored by authorities north of the border, is viewed. On September 11, 2001 and for days following, San Diego's international airport and numerous general aviation airfields were closed. The international border was closed for a time and all traffic and persons were subject to a rigorous inspection when the border reopened. However, on September 11 and thereafter the Tijuana international airport remained open, even accommodating several flights from Asia that were diverted from landing in the United States. The Tijuana airport is approximately fifteen miles from the center of San Diego. From a regional security sense, not adequately considering the operating airport in Tijuana was a failure in analysis and policy.

An unintended consequence of the reaction to 9/11 was a significant economic impact on the San Diego-Tijuana border zone. Some 40,000 people commute daily from Tijuana to work in San Diego. Many of these workers missed work or arrived late due to waiting times of up to four hours for pedestrians and up to three hours for vehicles at the border. Tijuana residents, who regularly cross to make retail purchases in the community of San Ysidro (adjacent to the port of entry), significantly reduced shopping trips, resulting in a severe loss of business for local U.S. merchants. U.S. tourists also cancelled trips to Tijuana, resulting in a precipitous drop in tourist-related economic activity in Mexico. There also were long delays for commercial cargo vehicles crossing into San Diego, increasing trade-related costs. The border still has not returned to normal, more than two years after the event. Long border crossing delays still inconvenience local residents and burden the regional economy. Future efforts for regional disaster response planning need to carefully consider how potential events might impact the border-related activities of the two communities, and what mitigation strategies should be included in the planning.

BINATIONAL DISASTER PREPAREDNESS: AN UNMET NEED

While there are current binational efforts to address disaster management needs along the United States-Mexico border (U.S. EPA 2001b), both the scope and geographic extent of these efforts reveal several regional challenges—the growing population density, the regional and economic integration of the San Diego-Tijuana region, and accompanying and increasing interdependencies including negative spillover effects—all of which make the case for more effective coordination, planning, and governance across the border. While there are periodic calls for development of transborder governmental mechanisms in mission areas ranging from environment to infrastructure investment, the asymmetries in the U.S. and Mexican systems, along with traditional concerns about sovereignty in both countries, make the creation of new administrative structures difficult.

More effective disaster management in the border regions could be obtained if responsible agencies and individuals were to maximize the use of geospatial technologies to improve pre-event, event monitoring, and response, as well as postevent relief, recovery, and monitoring efforts. Such activities must consider the range of possible hazards, whether they originate from natural events such as earthquakes, landslides, floods, fire, and strong winds or human-induced phenomena such as bioterrorism, conventional warfare, terrorist bombings, and toxic spills. These activities must be accomplished within a geographical context that takes into account an area's physical environment (vegetation, topography, hydrography, and climate); social, economic, political, and educational characteristics; infrastructure, including transportation, communications, government, and public safety; and technological capacity.

There is a clear trend in both San Diego and Tijuana toward greater interest in binational coordination in many areas, including emergency response. However, all of these efforts are frustrated to some extent by the lack of harmonized geospatial data and a GIS for the binational region that could serve as an effective decision support tool for decision makers. For a GIS to be useful in a transborder setting, many matters must be addressed, including broad issues of data access, data acquisition and integration, visualization of data, systems interoperability, scale and resolution, analytical and modeling protocols, education and training, and language differences (a matter of primary importance along our borders) (Wright et al. 1997, Wright and Winckell 1998).

From a research perspective, a number of questions remain unanswered. For example, what cross-border disaster management organizations exist in the border region? What institutional agreements and/or changes in policies and management practices need to be implemented to more effectively develop and employ digital geographic data in pre-disaster planning, concurrent disaster monitoring and response, and postdisaster response? What changes in spatial data standards, GIS software and hardware, and geographic training are necessary to improve the effectiveness of binational disaster management?

Many of these issues already have been identified as national priority research and education challenges by the University Consortium for Geographic Information Science (UCGIS 1996, Kemp and Wright 1997, Radke et al. 2000). Research on these and other GIScience priorities within a border context could dramatically improve the capability of the nation's border agencies to respond more effectively to disasters and to minimize social-economic and environmental impacts should a disaster occur.

CHAPTER 3

Understanding the Root
Causes of Terrorism

INTRODUCTION

Looking several decades into the future, we all share the hope that—rather than continuing to be caught up in responding to terrorism and seeking to deter terrorists—we can live in a world where fewer people choose terrorism as a way to achieve their objectives. One key to such a vision is improving our understanding of why terrorism occurs: its root causes, its driving forces, and its enabling structures.

Perspectives on this critically important long-term challenge will come from many scholarly disciplines. They will address such issues as how poverty gives root to desperation, especially when it is associated with access to information about how others live better; how religion and nationalism contribute to feelings of alienation; and why some individuals and groups feel that less violent approaches are unsatisfactory for addressing their grievances.

The sections of this chapter are a small sample of geographic perspectives on root causes of terrorism, generally associated with a tradition in geography of foreign area studies (a tradition that has suffered in recent decades because of a shortage of support for field research). Clearly, however, root causes of terrorism do not just exist in areas outside the United States. As Oklahoma City showed us so vividly, they are an issue internally as well; and we need to pay attention to causes, consequences, and avenues for reducing root causes in all parts of our world, here as well as there.

In the papers that follow, Alexander Murphy considers how the world is divided into a mosaic of spatial units, real and perceived, that often differ from what shows on a map and that are closely associated with causes and realities of conflict. Colin Flint points out how spatial units, especially when they are associated with power and control, relate to definitions of "insiders" and "outsiders" that in turn can provide fertile grounds for definitions of grievances. Marilyn Silberfein focuses on terrorism in the context of struggles for territorial control, including driving forces for conflict and conditions that sustain insurrections. Kent Mathewson and Michael Steinberg discuss how source areas and networks of terrorism can interact with other spatial patterns, using drug production as an example of a process and pattern that is, in some instances, underwriting terrorism. These short essays are only beginnings, but they illustrate how root causes of terrorism can be enlightened by attention to geographic dimensions.

3.1

THE SPACE OF TERROR

Alexander B. Murphy

THE HUMAN WORLD is most frequently viewed as a set of spaces defined by the boundaries that circumscribe the countries of the world. That set of spaces is enshrined in the map that commonly hangs on the walls of our homes, our classrooms, and even our foreign policy institutes: the map showing each of the 200-odd countries of the world in a different color. As the circumstances surrounding the events of September 11, 2001 reveal, however, the traditional world political map is of remarkably little utility when the object of concern is terrorism. Terrorist activities frequently operate outside of the logic of that map, and they often involve specific challenges to its underlying spatial order.

None of this is meant to suggest that states are irrelevant to terrorism. Yet any hope of understanding the causes of terrorist activity, or of assessing how and why terrorism flourishes in certain places, requires a much more sophisticated view of space than that suggested by a political map of the world's countries. In short, there is a clear need for the academic and policy communities to turn a critical eye towards space, using the perspectives and tools of geography to elucidate the ways in which different spatial arrangements and understandings both foster terrorist impulses and facilitate terrorist activities.

There are at least three types of spaces that deserve attention in this regard: activity spaces, policy spaces, and perceptual spaces. Geographers and others have written much on each of these (overlapping) types of spaces, but there is little published work that links them directly to terrorism. What follows is an overview of the few links that have been made, together with a consideration of the insights that could be gained from further exploration of those links.

ACTIVITY SPACES

Throughout history, insurgent movements of various sorts have sought to base their activities in areas that are difficult to access because of the strategic advantages those areas offer. This point certainly has been made in the geographic literature (McColl 1969). The challenge is to move beyond broad generalizations to a consideration of how particular spatial niches are understood and used in different parts of the world. The potential of such research is suggested by Rob Kent's (1993) analysis of the Shining Path (Sendero Luminoso) in Peru. Drawing on an intimate familiarity with local and regional sources, Kent offered telling insights into the spatial character and strategies of the Shining Path movement. He was able to show, for example, how Shining Path followers exploited their understanding of the Andean ecosystem to spread their movement along a north-south axis that followed the path of the Andes.

Those pursuing research along these lines must be careful not to view the environment in deterministic ways; indeed looking at the physical environment alone is rarely sufficient. Yet there is clearly something to be gained from a consideration of the types of physical and social spaces that groups have exploited for particular purposes, for this can lead to insights into diffusion strategies and the types of challenges groups are likely to face as they expand. It follows that there is much to be gained from research into the spatial distribution of groups, facilities, and actions, as well as from analyses of the relative location of centers of terrorist activity in relation to critical transportation networks, political nodes, symbolically important spaces, and areas of wealth and poverty.

In assessing the spaces of terrorist activity, it is also important to consider the specific advantages and disadvantages of particular spatial niches. Fuller et al. (2000) adopted this approach in an analysis of ethnic conflict potential in Southwest Asia; they were able to highlight areas with particularly high probabilities of conflict by focusing on the motivating and enabling conditions of groups in particular places. In most cases a key enabling condition is control over resources—a central issue in the work of Le Billon (2001a, 2001b). Le Billon's studies of Angola showed how the ability of the MPLA and UNITA (ruling party and rebel group, respectively) to control diamonds and oil was of critical importance to the trajectory of conflict in that country. In the context of recent events, this suggests the value of investigating, for example, how access to oil facilitated al-Qaeda activities, as well as how the issue of control over oil was used to promote support for the movement.

Geographical analysis is not just important to an understanding of specific terrorist activity spaces; it can provide insight into dominant assumptions about the spatial character of terrorist activity itself. In the aftermath of September 11, 2001, for example, some specialists on the Middle East/Southwest Asia questioned the degree to which there really is a widespread international terrorist network of the sort portrayed by government and media sources. A historically grounded effort to document the links that do and do not exist between groups in the region could facilitate efforts to assess the validity of such representations.

Finally, studies of terrorism can benefit from analyses of the activity spaces of political and economic actors, as well as those of terrorist groups. Government authorities, corporations, and others use space in ways that can feed directly into terrorist resentments and can promote or undermine their activities. Studies of the nature and character of these activity spaces—and their relationship to the territorial ideas and practices of insurgent groups—can provide critical insights into the root causes of terrorism. Since such spaces are often the product of government decision making, it is appropriate to turn next to the policy arena.

POLICY SPACES

The policies pursued by governmental authorities clearly have an impact on the development and spread of terrorist activity. Intense antipathy to policies that threaten or undermine existing territorial rights and arrangements can foster frustration among those who feel incapable of being heard through established mechanisms. At its extreme, frustration can boil over into terrorist activities aimed at bringing down the existing political-economic order. To understand these dynamics, consideration must be given to the spatial character and geographical implications of government policies.

Jordan's (1993) study of post–civil war Bosnia shows the potential of analyses of this kind. Drawing on research into social interaction patterns before the outbreak of hostilities, Jordan was able to posit the existence of micro- and macrofunctional regions in the country. He then compared those to a partition plan proposed by Cyrus Vance and Lord Owen after the war was underway. The disjunction between the Vance-Owen plan and prewar functional regions in Bosnia provided key insights into why all sides opposed the Vance-Owen plan and why its implementation could have heightened, rather than diminished, interethnic tensions.

Jordan's study shows the importance of examining the spatial relationship between patterns of terrorist support or activity and the policy spaces that go along with strategies designed to contain or marginalize terrorists. In a related vein, Murphy's (1989) comparative assessment of territorial policies in multiethnic states offered insights into the types of policies that exacerbate or mitigate ethnic conflict. Studies such as these suggest that there is much to be gained from analyses of the spatial congruities (incongruities) between terrorist activity spaces or recruiting grounds and areas where policies have fostered particular social, economic, or political conditions.

On a larger scale, there is a clear need for consideration of the ways in which different geopolitical strategies can promote or undermine terrorism by dividing the world up into ideologically distinct (sometimes opposing) regions. To what extent is the world really breaking down into competing blocs based on cultural-cum-religious differences? What kinds of spatial variability within the Islamic world or in the West undermine such dichotomizations—and what forces are tending to expand or reduce that variation? Questions such as these are of clear contemporary importance, but they should be raised in conjunction with research on the impacts of specific geopolitically motivated initiatives. To what extent did the U.S. effort to promote an oil pipeline from the Caspian Sea, which avoided Iran, prompt the United States to take initiatives that gave credence (at least in the minds of some) to the idea that the United States wanted effective political control over Southwest Asia? What is the conflict potential of the American policy decision to turn its attention to Iraq as part of its "war on terrorism?" Research along these lines is important to an assessment of the development and spread of terrorism.

Investigation of such geopolitical topics rarely leads to hard and fast conclusions, but it can highlight issues of clear policy relevance. A case in point is Wixman's (1995) analysis of geopolitical shifts that could occur if the conflict in the former Yugoslavia were to spread to other parts of the Balkans. His scenarios were necessarily speculative, but they were informed by an in-depth understanding of historical geographical arrangements and contemporary regionalization initiatives. As such, they highlighted important possibilities that could inform policy making. In extrapolating to more recent events, could a quick "revenge response" to the attacks of September 11, 2001 have resulted in "toppling Saudi Arabia and other conservative Islamic regimes into alliance with the radical movements already powerful in Iran, Sudan, Algeria, and influential in Egypt, Pakistan, the Balkans, the Caucasus, Central Asia, and sub-Saharan Africa" (Pfaff 2001), as some commentators suggested? Investigating how policies can alter existing geographical patterns and understandings is critical to policy formulation in an environment marked by terrorism.

PERCEPTUAL SPACES

One of the most amorphous, yet important, dimensions of research on terrorism concerns how different spaces are understood. What places are of signal symbolic importance to different peoples? How do peoples view their places and their relationships to one another?

Whatever may be said about the circumstances that precipitate terrorism, we cannot afford to see them in reductionist economic terms. To put it simply, if issues of ideology and space were not at play, the greatest centers of terrorism would be in places such as Burkina Faso and Haiti, which are facing even greater economic problems than the countries usually linked to terrorism (Pakistan, Malaysia, the Philippines, and so on).

There is not a strict correlation between economic well-being and terrorism because how space is perceived can be as or more important than how it functions. Statements released by al-Qaeda sympathizers after the attack on New York City and Washington D.C., highlight the significance of this point. A common theme of those statements was opposition to what was described as U.S. interventionism in the "Islamic World." The existence of a clearly defined Islamic World is debatable, of course, but its significance as a perceptual geographical construct cannot be ignored if we are to address the motivating forces behind recent terrorist activity.

Geographers have long been concerned with the symbolic dimensions of different spaces—and recent work has turned specifically to the ways in which these are implicated in conflicts (White 2000). This work highlights the importance of considering both the large-scale perceptual spaces that underlie particular conflicts and the diversity found within those spaces. No matter how defined, the Islamic World is quite heterogeneous, including areas that were never effectively colonized or "Westernized" through the efforts of an Ataturk (Afghanistan, for example) and countries such as Turkey and Jordan. Considering how such historical differences affect understandings of space and place is of obvious relevance to an assessment of where and why terrorist movements develop.

Focusing attention on the perceptual spaces of government actors can also offer important insights into terrorist activities and motivations. U.S. policy in Southwest Asia has targeted specific areas for attention based not simply on where terrorist activities have been found, but on ideas about the strategic and economic significance of particular places and arguments about the destabilizing potential of the regimes in power in specific countries. Understanding the nature of the perceptual geographies behind these policy stances—as well as their intersection with the perceptual spaces deemed to be important by insurgent movements—can shed considerable light on the nature and dynamics of terrorism.

CONCLUSION

In the interest of brevity, I have not raised the fundamental question of what constitutes terrorism, but this question cannot be ignored.

The complexity behind this issue is revealed when one considers that the United States has supported—and even encouraged—various activities in the past that some have labeled as terrorist. These include the efforts of Afghans to oppose the Soviet occupation of the 1980s, the efforts of Kurds to oppose the regime of Saddam Hussein over the past decade, and (in a more muted way) the efforts of Chechens to oppose Russian hegemony in Chechnya. We even look back with approval at those colonists who rose up violently against their British overlords in 1776.

One can and should draw distinctions between all of these movements and what happened on September 11, 2001, but to date there has been little effort to stake out where and how those distinctions might be drawn. Focusing attention on the spatial dimensions of terrorism can help in this regard, for meaningful distinctions among and between violent insurgencies cannot be made without consideration of the contexts out of which violent antisystemic movements emerge, and the circumstances under which particular violent actions are perpetrated. Taking the spaces of terrorism seriously is thus important not only for understanding the development of particular problems; it can help clarify the normative foundations on which future policies can and should be based.

3.2

GEOGRAPHIES OF INCLUSION/EXCLUSION

Colin Flint

THIS ESSAY EXPLORES one component of the root causes of terrorism, the processes that create a binary of inclusion/exclusion and the spatial manifestation of that binary—the geography of inclusion and exclusion. Inclusion and exclusion refer to control over access to political institutions (such as state citizenship), acceptance in particular identities (the American nation, for example), plus the ability to participate in the economic livelihood of the place. The geography of inclusion/exclusion refers to the way borders and the territories they define facilitate both participation and membership in identifiable groups, as well as noninvolvement and exclusion. For example, political borders and sovereign territory define insiders and outsiders (into such categories as citizens and aliens) by controlling mobility. Economic development may facilitate wealth generation by some groups (citizens), while impoverishing others by altering access to land or capital, for example.

The attacks of 9/11 were the most deadly in a series of terrorist acts that changed the relevant scale of inclusion/exclusion from the nation-state to the global geopolitical system. In other words, national separatism no longer appeared to be the main motivator of terrorism. Rather, it was reaction to the norms and geographies of the global geopolitical system that was the root causes of this terrorism.

WORLD POWER AND THE CREATION OF INCLUSION/EXCLUSION

Since World War Two, the United States has played the dominant role in identifying the norms of the global geopolitical system. On the one hand, this is seen as an act of benevolent world leadership that benefits the whole system (Modelski 1987). An alternative approach is to see the United States as a self-interested hegemony that uses its power to further its own position (Arrighi 1994). Either perspective requires us to acknowledge the role of the United States in defining not only those who are to be included and excluded, but also within what geographies inclusion and exclusion take place.

During its rise to power, the United States had a particular global geography in mind, a system of free-trading, sovereign, and self-determined nation-states. Geographies of empire were taken apart as they no longer met the norms determined by the global power. First, the existing empires of Britain, France, and other European countries were dismantled and reconfigured into newly independent countries and included in a global system of United Nations. Second, the emerging empire of the Soviet Union was challenged and its world power diminished. The result was one dominant ideal (in theory but not practice); the belief in the coherence of nation-states and the desire to maintain their territorial integrity. From these norms grew the grievances of territorial separatists and national independence movements, and their need to cultivate audiences sympathetic to their claims. For example, in 1970 Palestinian terrorists hijacked passenger airplanes and landed them at an abandoned military airport in Jordan. The terrorists renamed the base "'Revolution Airport,' hoping that the hijack would attract international attention to the plight of the Palestinians" (Bregman and El-Tahri 2000:183).

STRUCTURES OF INCLUSION/EXCLUSION

The classifications of included and excluded groups and nations have both political and geographical elements, but they also have normative features that help differentiate them (Cresswell 1996). Who should be in and out of what, and what are the proper means by which the excluded can gain inclusion are defined by a historically- specific set of understandings. For example, the term "illegal immigrant" is based on accepted understandings of territory, citizenship, and sovereign legal structures regarding visas and residency.

Three major structures of inclusion are dominant in the contemporary world. The first is the capitalist world economy. States pursuing other forms of socio-economic organization (such as the socialism of Cuba) are defined as outside this structure and therefore oppositional. Second is the geopolitical system of states. In this context, the United States (based on its superpower status) is the key definer of the norms of behavior, who is violating them, and what, if anything, should be done about it (Klare 1995). The categorization of Iraq as a rogue state or member of "the axis of evil" is derivative of the American perspective, while Pakistan, a nation with a dubious past in support of terrorist activity, but currently an ally in the war against terrorism, is not. The third structure is the nation-state, which attempts to homogenize populations and exclude those who dispute its territorial integrity, such as separatist movements (Torpey 2000).

DYNAMIC PATTERNS AND PROCESSES

The global geopolitical system is a dynamic process and the role of world leader or hegemonic power is constantly changing as well. The current moment in the processes of hegemony is defining new political geographies, new norms, and, therefore, new modes of inclusion and exclusion. The terrorist attacks of 9/11 were the latest in a series of violent responses to grievances emanating from this new geography of inclusion and exclusion. From Arrighi's (1994) perspective, the process is caused by an economic need for increased flows of global capital investment and speculation, currently experienced as globalization.

Globalization has undermined the once accepted notion of how politics should be territorially organized—the world political map of sovereign nation-states (Torpey 2000). State sovereignty has experienced various degrees of erosion in the past, and presently in its place is an increasingly dominant geography of flows and networks with their own specific geographies (O'Tuathail 2000). To be included now is to come in contact with universal economic, political, and cultural practices. It is within this changing geography that the focus of terrorism has moved from the nation-state to the global stage.

However, the global geography of flows and universal norms is still primarily driven by one nation-state, the United States (Hardt and Negri 2000). Hence, the United States becomes the prime target of this new terrorism and its public seen as one that should be made to suffer in order to become aware of the terrorists' grievances. The grievances and audiences of terrorism result in the interaction of both territorial and network geographies.

GRIEVANCES AND AUDIENCES

There are two key components of terrorist activity: the definition of grievances and the identification of an audience (Crenshaw 1981, Hoffman 1998). Grievances that foster terrorism may result from being excluded from particular political arenas (such as participation in the government). Grievances also can stem from the disorientation that is caused from being either at the center of the maelstrom of change (such as globalization) or the frustration of missing out of its perceived benefits.

Terrorists simultaneously address two different audiences. One is the general public that the terrorist wishes to reach to make them aware of the particular motivating issue and ultimately to become sympathetic to the terrorist position. The other is a more selective audience, the potential recruits—individuals who are sought by the terrorist as likely followers or members of their movement. The existence of these two audiences implies separate groups of people—a separation that is geographic as well as social. By definition then, the terrorists and their followers become excluded from civil society of the mainstream, while the sympathetic public remains included.

SPATIAL DEMENTIA

It is this changing and complex geography that has provoked confusion among policy makers about the purpose of contemporary terrorism. It was once fairly clear who were the audiences for terrorism—national or ethnic majorities and minorities within states. Those people disenfranchised by the processes of globalization are one audience for terrorism, while the audience that needs to become aware is the citizenry and policymakers of the United States. There is a new geography here that transcends our dominant world political map, the mosaic of nation-states. Now we have to make connections that are defined by networks of economic and political power, which are dynamic processes, not static territorial units. The World Trade Center and the Pentagon were perceived as the central nodes of United States economic and political power that had global manifestations. As such, they became symbolic targets for attack. We can no longer compartmentalize terrorist grievances and audiences within sovereign territorial boxes, as a Palestinian issue, for example. The geographic span of terrorist grievances is now defined by global economic flows and geopolitical reach.

Policymaking is suffering from a "spatial dementia" (Oas 2002) in which non-territorial security threats still are being addressed within a mentality of territorial sovereignty. Although the processes of globalization have eroded state sovereignty, they have not destroyed it. Looking solely at networks inspires policies that will be counterproductive in a nation of territorial states. For example, to counter networks of terrorism, it is argued that global and immediate reach by the forces of counterterrorism is required (Arquilla and Ronfeldt 2001). The recently published National Security Strategy (2002) makes it quite clear that the United States will send troops to fight across the globe, preemptively, and without the consent of allies or the United Nations. Focusing upon the geography of this strategy highlights the stated intention of the United States to enter other sovereign spaces whenever it identifies a security threat. Such a strategy of targeting nodes of terrorist networks requires the violation of national sovereignties. Countering an aterritorial network by violating national spaces is likely to be perceived in the occupied countries as an act of military bullying that injures national pride. Citizens on the receiving end of U.S. counterterrorism are likely to focus upon the incursion into a national space rather than the targeting of particular nodes. Such incursion may be seen as an expression of global hegemonic power, which created contemporary terrorist grievances in the first place.

Inclusion and exclusion, especially with reference to the flows of globalization, define the grievances of terrorists such as bin Laden and their followers, whether based on the disorientation of modernization, distress at being excluded from these processes, or some combination of the two (Armstrong 2000). At the same time, a nation-state (the United States) is the major player in the flows of globalization, so responses to networks of terrorism also must consider state versus state politics.

POLICY IMPLICATIONS

Effective responses to terrorism must consider the processes of hegemony or world leadership, and the interaction of political geographies of networks *and* territorial states. Globalization is the chief structure that defines contemporary global networks of inclusion and exclusion, but diverse social groups in dissimilar places experience it differently. To understand why globalization causes social grievances, we must transport ourselves out of the social setting of the United States and other wealthy countries and into geographic contexts experiencing rapid change and deprivation. We must lose the hubris of globalization and be sympathetic towards, and act against, the humilities that it causes in other parts of the world. This is true for the economic aspects of globalization as well as its political counterpart, democratization. The question is inherently geographical, pitting the universalizing tendencies of globalization against cultural particularities of the local.

Second, security policies must acknowledge that defense is a matter of the intersection of state sovereignty and networks of antistate politics. Resorting to established policies that assume territorial integrity are insufficient, but a sole concentration upon networks is cavalier as well. For example, defense policy against attacks in cyberspace must realize that citizens living in particular countries may be using a variety of computer servers across the globe. It is impossible, for example, to punish Denmark for an act of cyberterrorism committed by a Dane using a server housed in India. On the other hand, as discussed earlier, military counterterrorist actions must be sensitive to principles of national sovereignty.

Finally, the connections between nodes define the political realities of the contemporary world, not the maintenance of impervious borders. This requires a geographic mind-set that connects the Pentagon with Medina, in networks of political power over cultural terrains. Once we have such a global vision, we will have a better understanding of the footprints that American economic and political power are leaving across the globe, why they may cause grievances, and, hence, why United States citizens have become an unwitting public in contemporary terrorist visions.

3.3

DRUG PRODUCTION, COMMERCE, AND TERRORISM

KENT MATHEWSON AND MICHAEL STEINBERG

THE GLOBAL DRUG TRADE concerns not only the use and abuse of substances that circulate through geographic spaces, but also involves military/terrorist activities, economic development, and indigenous and ethnic minority human rights in production regions. Drug production and eradication efforts locally impact the stability of nation states as well as relations between states (McCoy 1991, Bagley and Walker III 1994). Drug production and efforts to halt it often distort national and local development efforts (Smith 1992), and provoke human rights violations (Sanabria 1992, Kent 1993). Drug profits support governments, insurgent movements, and terrorists both locally and in areas far removed from the source region.

This paper focuses on the relationship between drug production, its commerce, and terrorist activity. The complex geographical relation between drugs and terrorism, including examples of where drug production underwrites terrorist activity, is used to show how globalization is increasingly implicated as the process most centrally linked to the formation of the new geography of the war on drugs and terrorism.

GEOGRAPHICAL SITE AND SITUATION

The core element in the definition of terrorism (intimidation through violence) has not changed much since its initially coinage in 1795 (during the so-called Terror phase of the French Revolution). The social, economic, and political contexts, however, have shifted over time, and in their geographical extent. At its initial inception, terrorism referred to state violence aimed at intimidating the citizenry. Only later did the authorial direction become a two-way street, when, in the nineteenth century, citizens directed terror at autocrats and heads of state leading up to World War I. Throughout much of the twentieth century, nationalist wars of liberation unleashed new dimensions and levels of terrorist violence. Following the Cold War, new actors emerged with a bewildering array of religious, political, and economic agendas.

These newer terrorists can be grouped in three main categories: religious fundamentalists, political insurgents, and criminal entrepreneurs. Figuratively, they constitute contemporary terrorism's three estates (with interesting correspondences to the original ordination of: religious, aristocratic, and commercial interests). There is also a largely elided and collateral danger to the horrific events and searing images of 9/11—narrowing terrorism's definition to only the violent actions or agendas of groups operating outside the bounds of states and international norms. In this context, the State itself can become terrorism's fourth estate. But contrary to Carlyle's (1840) original notion of the fourth estate, terrorism's fourth estate functionally becomes one of limiting and controlling discussion and information, especially information concerning its own activities.[1]

In the two centuries since terrorism's initial naming, state monopolies have been replaced by a multiplicity of agents, while the image of the state-as-agent has been blurred beyond recognition in many places. In framing a clear and coherent big picture of the connections between drugs and terrorism, all obvious and visible evidence must be admitted. Governments of many varieties—from the most authoritarian to some of the most democratic—at various times have engaged in or sponsored actions and policies that must be judged as terrorist in intent and effect. These actions and policies include state tolerance of or support for illicit drug production and distribution, which aid both terrorist and counterterrorist objectives.

To date, there have been relatively few scholarly attempts to put either the geography or history of illicit drugs and terrorism into global perspective (Courtwright 2001, Anderson and Sloan 2002). There is a clear need to map (literally and figuratively) these geographies at the global scale (Mathewson 1991). Putting these phenomena into a global geohistorical perspective, not only illuminates antecedent conditions, but also offers possibilities for projecting future developments.

TERRORIST RELIANCE ON ILLICIT DRUG PRODUCTION

During the post–Cold War period, U.S. and Soviet military aid to third world client states dramatically decreased, thus ending many civil wars that were largely prolonged by superpower support. Hostilities, especially those based on ethnic and religious differences, arose in other regions, so that the end of the Cold War has brought little respite from violence in places such as Colombia, Afghanistan, Angola, and the Balkans (Huntington 1996). Without superpower support, governments and insurgents were forced to seek alternative funding venues and various sources, both legal and extralegal, have been developed. These include: trafficking in precious metals, materials (such as nuclear materials), and gems (ediamonds in Africa, for example); contraband and stolen goods (such as cigarettes and motor vehicles); extortions and kidnappings; counterfeiting and laundering money; armament sales and shipments; and, perhaps more than any other single source, illegal drug production and trafficking (Lintner 1999, Steinberg 2000, Goodson 2001).

Today, there are three major drug regions that support embattled and/or pariah states, insurgent movements, and terrorist activities. They are: the North Andean (Figure 3.3.1) centered on Colombia, Central Asian centered on Afghanistan (Figure 3.3.2), and Southeast Asian hearths centered on Burma (Booth 1992, Smith 1992, Clawson and Lee III 1998). All have become zones of primary production (cultivation), refining, and distribution for the world market. Each claims indigenous cultivation and use patterns over considerable time periods. Portions of neighboring nation states have become closely integrated into these zones as well. In addition, there are a number of secondary zones within countries such as Mexico and Peru, and regions such the Horn of Africa and the Levant, which function as producing and trafficking centers within local contexts of civil war, insurgency, and criminal terrorism. Given the right conditions, they also could become major drug regions supporting large-scale terrorist activities. At lesser geographical scales and articulations there are countless places and points where illicit drugs are grown, refined, transported, marketed, and consumed in ways that also contribute to terrorism in both its minor and major expressions.

Colombia provides a powerful example of how revolutionaries, paramilitary forces, criminals, and a besieged state can all become dependent upon drug production and trafficking (MacDonald 1988). Colombia has been at war off and on with itself since the late 1940s. From the 1960s through the 1980s, Marxist guerrilla groups received inspiration and some aid from Cuba and the Soviet Union. Since the Soviet collapse, groups such as the Revolutionary Armed Forces of Colombia (FARC) were largely orphaned, both ideologically and materially. They increasingly have turned to illegal drugs for revenue, at first simply taxing local drug dealers, and then later taking control over the trafficking (Dao 2002). Colombia produces 80% of the

FIGURE 3.3.1 North Andean Drug Producing Regions

world's cocaine and a growing proportion of the world's heroin. A majority of these drugs are grown and processed in rebel or paramilitary controlled territory (Booth 1996). Insurgent groups or pariah (stateless) governments can field well-equipped armies indefinitely with money generated by illicit drug production and trade. To combat such trade, central governments (such as Colombia) tap into vast resources from the United States and European Union for drug-related counterinsurgency efforts, although the likelihood of success is low, given conventional approaches and the borderless nature of the enemy.

The second example, Afghanistan, presents an interesting case because of the role played by the United States in facilitating linkages between drugs and insurgency. There are two contemporary phases of war-driven poppy production in Afghanistan. The first occurred dur-

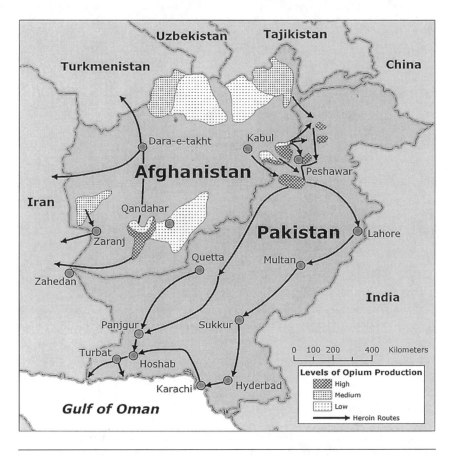

FIGURE 3.3.2 Primary Production Region for Opium Poppy and Routes of Heroin Trafficking

ing the Soviet occupation (1978–1989) and the second during the post-Soviet era civil war (1989-present). During the first phase, the massive U.S. military aid provided to the mujahadeen was augmented by poppy cultivation and opium exports. The Islamists' large-scale involvement in the opium trade was open local knowledge. Cold War logic and geopolitical goals, however, demanded a blind eye to the expanding poppy culture and heroin labs in the region (McCoy 1999). The United States refused to press their Afghan or Pakistani allies to reduce drug production or exports because these issues were considered secondary to the larger battle against the Soviets. The contours of phase two are generally well known. Part of the terror and free-for-all that followed the Soviet retreat was fueled by competition to control the drug trade (Goodson 2001). Taliban ascendancy and near hegemony simply meant that chaotic production and market conditions

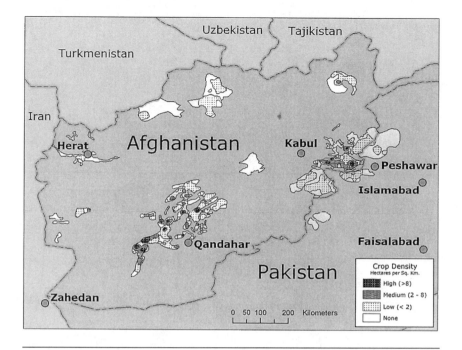

FIGURE 3.3.3 Crop Density of Opium Poppy Production, 1999 (Source: Unpublished data from the Central Intelligence Agency)

came under strict control and by 2000, Afghanistan produced over 70% of the world's supply of illicit opium (Hutchinson 2002). Save for the U.S.-purchased hiatus in the first part of 2001, opium production and exportation grew explosively under the Taliban (Figure 3.3.3). Among those who profited directly from this rationally exuberant expansion were small farmers, the Islamists, heroin refiners (especially in Pakistan), and traffickers of all scales across networks encircling the globe. Since the fall of the Taliban, Afghani opium production and commerce appears to be one sector of the economy that has rebounded and then some (*Economist* 2002).

The third major hearth, interior Southeast Asia, is somewhat different than the previous two. It is not presently the site of large-scale military conflict, only local insurgencies. Perhaps related to this, drug refiners in its famous Golden Triangle region have launched major initiatives toward diversifying their products. Observers report polydrug use and increasing trends in trafficking within the global drug culture (O. G. D. 1998). In recent years, long established heroin labs in the border areas of Burma, Laos, and Thailand began producing massive quantities of illicit amphetamines. The key precursor, ephedrine is readily accessible in the form of *Ephedra sp.*, which is imported from China's Yunnan province, where it grows wild. Most of the amphetamine production is targeted to Southeast Asian markets, where it used more for utilitarian purposes (such as allowing sweatshop workers to labor long hours), rather than recreation. There is some evidence, however, that these labs also are experimenting with the so-called boutique or designer drugs such as ecstasy (MDMA) and its analogues, which permeate the North American and European markets. These developments underscore the simultaneous convergence of global drug cultures and networks, and the spreading practices of polydrug production, trafficking, and consumption. One of globalization's key precepts—diversification amid convergence—seems to apply to both drugs and terrorism with accelerating definition and accuracy.

THE ROLE OF GEOGRAPHICAL INQUIRY

Illicit drug production and commerce and associated terrorist activities involve interconnected cultural, environmental, political, and economic variables. Geography is ideally suited to address questions regarding these convergences given its groundings in the social, environmental, and mapping sciences. There are many ways our discipline can contribute to this crucial and emerging field of study. One priority is to better understand how and why peasant farmers continue to produce most the world's illicit drug-producing plants, and also often serve as terrorism's ground troops.

Second, geographers should be educating both policy makers and the public in questions of distant lands and peoples. Geographers provide the fine-grained local analyses that are absent in many large-scale, politically driven statements and studies of drugs and terrorism.

Third, geographers' ability to analyze human impacts on biophysical environments and attendant ecological consequences is critical in this research area. Environmental stress is often a contributing factor in drug plant production. For example, the prolonged drought in Afghanistan, coupled with the destruction of many irrigation works, has driven farmers to plant the more tolerant opium poppy, rather than the less drought resistant staple food crops such as wheat (Baldauf 2001, Goodson 2001).

Fourth, remote sensing techniques and geographical information systems (GIS) provide a media with which to map spatial changes in drug production at various geographic scales ranging from local to global. To identify and locate small-scale producers, laboratories, distribution networks, and other beneficiaries of the illicit trade requires detailed geographic and economic analyses. In turn, these findings could provide templates or models for studying other networks and for identifying emerging situations wherein drugs and terrorism are closely linked.

Finally, combining and directing geography's tripartite groundings in the social, physical, and mapping sciences, and a focus on specific and tractable questions and problems, should yield more comprehensive understanding of the root causes of terrorism. Study of the cultural and environmental impacts of drug production and commerce in specific places has hardly begun and large-scale comparative work awaits us.

The composite landscapes of drug production and commerce, and terrorism in all of its varieties, are difficult and daunting topics for research. However, they offer multiple opportunities for geographers to contribute to disciplinary advances while at the same time mitigate urgent problems. The role of illicit drugs in terrorism's current trajectories represents one of the most pressing and yet underinvestigated topics within the discipline.

3.4

INSURRECTIONS

Marilyn Silberfein

SINCE **1989,** there have been 111 armed conflicts, the vast majority of them involving a central state government and oppositional forces (Bulletin of Atomic Scientists 2002). Although the rebellions that proliferated during the last decade were multifaceted and defy simple explanations, a significant factor in their emergence was the failed state syndrome. Failed states are characterized by a loss of legitimacy resulting from their inability to control sovereign territory, provide economic opportunities, or make basic services available for their citizens.

The international geopolitical system relies on a state's ability to govern its territory, so the process of state decline poses a serious threat to the global system of nation states and ultimately the world order (Rotberg 2002). Typically, state decline is marked by the emergence of alternative sites of political or economic power, including those based on a unique cultural identity or feelings of economic or political exclusion. Under these circumstances, disillusionment with existing governmental policies and actions can lead to violence, with local warlords (or oppositional groups) laying claim to national territory that is under their de facto control. There is a tendency on the part of both the state and the rebellion to use terrorism as a tactic in the confrontations that follow. In fact, insurrections might be one of the initial precursors to the formation and maintenance of regional and global terrorist organizations.

CAUSAL FACTORS

Insurrections usually begin within localized areas of the national territory. These places can be in the hinterlands, far from day-to-day observation by a central authority, or they can be at the heart of the state, as in the slums within major cities. In the latter case, neighborhoods are filled with young, unemployed men, some of whom learn about violence in street gangs or working as enforcers for corrupt government officials. Rebellions also may develop in remote areas, places that long have suffered neglect by the central government, have been isolated from any economic growth, or regions that have been discriminated against because of a minority identity. In Africa, rebellions are especially prevalent in these remote areas ostensibly due to the lack of rigid control by a central governmental authority (Herbst 2000).

Ethnic Diversity

The mere existence of ethnic diversity within a state does not always lead to violence, although diversity is highlighted as a potential threat to state stability. In reality, the evolution of the modern state (and the globalization of communication, transportation, and economic systems) may have actually produced a more cosmopolitan setting where broader feelings of community are engendered (Spencer 1998). The issue is made more complex by the theme of self-determination, a concept that was enshrined in the U.N. charter, but one that has never been fully codified to determine which groups or territories should be recognized as sovereign, and those groups that should not (Busumtwi-Sam 1998).

Although the state can be exclusionary and marginalize subgroups of citizens, for the most part, social groups within a state coexist peacefully. When conflict does erupt between a state and a distinct ethnic group within its boundaries, often it is because political leaders have used real and imagined grievances for their own ends rather than because of any ancient hatred (Issue 3.4). Ethnic identities can be easily manipulated for political purposes and take on significance in keeping with the historical reality (Ali and Matthews 1999).

Politics of Exclusion

Rebellions also occur as a result of economic exclusion or a more generalized dissatisfaction with the existing political order (see Flint in this chapter, van Creveld 1991). When grievances cannot be redressed through existing sociopolitical structures, violence (and terrorism) becomes the primary mechanism for trying to equalize imbalances such as starkly unequal land distribution. This is especially true given the proliferation of small weapons throughout the world. Although separatist movements usually begin with a strong ideological base, as they evolve they often mutate and diverge from the originating cause. There often becomes a pressing need to focus on keeping the movement intact as a source of power and generating the income to do so

ISSUE 3.4
Ethnic Conflict as a Root Cause of Terrorism

In Angola, an intractable civil war endured for over three decades until the ceasefire of April, 2002. It was funded first by Cold War allies (the United States and the Soviet Union) and then by the sale of resources, such as diamonds, that may have fed terrorist networks. The war pitted leaders against each other who represented different regions and ethnic groups, the most important of which were Augustino Neto and the MPLA party (the Mbundu people) and Jonas Savimbi and UNITA (the Ovimbundu). Savimbi used his identification with the Ovimbundu as part of a calculated strategy to further his insurrection. His ideological underpinnings were vague and inconsistent and his association with the apartheid state of South Africa was unpopular, leaving only Ovimbundu identity as a consistent source of support. Although the Ovimbundu had not shared equally in the colonial economy and had frequently been forced to migrate to earn a living, any resentment of their economic position would not have been enough to create a sustained conflict had not UNITA manipulated the situation to its advantage. Savimbi artificially emphasized differences that had not previously been significant and encouraged ethnic hatred.

(Keen 2000). Many rebellions move in the direction of organized crime, using extortion, drug sales and other illegal and quasi-legal mechanisms to fund their activities. Others support themselves through resource exploitation.

Environmental Degradation

There is another interesting source of insurrections. As valuable resources become depleted, transnational companies reach out to increasingly remote locations for new sources of raw materials, effectively linking isolated areas to the global economy (Gedicks 2001). Resource extraction by these multinational companies negatively impacts local environments and undermines established livelihood systems, and can precipitate a rebellion. There are many examples of this causal mechanism. For instance, the island of Bougainville had an open-pit copper mine that continued to be operated by Rio Tinto Zinc after Bougainville was united with Papua New Guinea (PNG) at independence (Klare 2001). The people of Bougainville eventually seized the mine and later seceded from PNG in response to economic neglect—as very little of the wealth accruing from mining remained on Bougainville—and the lack of compensation for land and water pollution. Violence ensued when the PNG army hired mercenaries and tried to invade the island to regain control of the mine. PNG finally resorted to negotiations, which are still in progress.

Sustaining Insurrections

While insurrections often start in inaccessible areas of a state, they need to be linked to the outside world if they are to be sustained. Thus, insurgencies have several specific locational requirements: 1) a home base (zone of security) where they can be relatively secure; 2) an exploitable resource ideally located within that territory; 3) a network that connects them to trading partners who will purchase the resource, and supply weapons in exchange; and 4) when possible, access to an international border or ocean port that facilitates contact with trading partners (Duffield 2000).

The ideal location for the zone of security is a remote border region, where, as previously mentioned, government capacity to effectively respond to thwart the uprising already may be compromised. Here, smugglers, thieves, army deserters, demobilized soldiers, and those simply seeking a livelihood congregate in the absence of alternative opportunities (Bayart 1999). The phenomenon is sometimes referred to as "entering the bush" and it contributes to the build-up of criminality, which is then readily transformed into the violence that challenges the existence of the state itself (Roitman 2001). In Sierra Leone, for example, diamond diggers formed their own villages deep in the forest near the Liberian border, and these villages were especially responsive when an insurrection spread into the area in 1991 (Richards 2001, Campbell 2002).

While the spatial structure of rebellions often conforms to the prototypes described above, there are interesting and important variants. For example, in Colombia the government tried to control a long-term insurrection by designating an autonomous territory that would be administered by the major rebel group, the FARC, literally creating a state within a state. This strategy was designed to encourage productive negotiations, but when it failed, the Colombian army invaded the FARC territory itself and initiated a new, more deadly phase of the war. In Burma, the government did not recognize formal zones of rebel operation, but it has allowed selected, ethnically-based rebel groups *de facto* control of their own territory. The circumstances were such that the government and the rebels profited from the opium trade (Brown 1999), so this accommodation met the needs of both.

There is a tendency for the region impacted by an insurrection to grow over time. The drug trade that financed rebel causes in Colombia already has expanded into adjacent areas in Brazil and Ecuador as part of an effort by the FARC to evade pursuers and expand cocoa cultivation (see Mathewson and Steinberg, this chapter). These spillover effects can undermine the security and economic well-being of neighboring countries (Brown 1996). Similarly, the mining of diamonds and gold and the harvesting of hardwood forests have linked together conflicts in the states of West Africa that are part of the Mano River Union: Liberia, Sierra Leone, and Guinea. A civil war that began in Liberia in 1989 contributed to an uprising in the adjacent country of Sierra Leone, which endured for more than a decade. The regional conflagration briefly reached Guinea in the late 1990s before subsequently returning to Liberia, where it is currently still simmering. Even in the absence of any military invasion or infiltration, the massive movement of refugees from zones of danger to zones of safety creates social and economic problems for neighboring host countries.

Conflicts that begin in remote corners of failing states, which are sustained by marketable natural resources (diamonds, crude oil, coca), are difficult to bring to a conclusion. All too often the perpetrators, both state actors and rebels, find the chaos of war conducive to the accumulation of personal wealth. Ongoing conflict provides opportunities for looting or the collection of protection money. This is especially true if, as is sometimes the case, the insurgents are able to cooperate with the state army to avoid pitched battles and share the spoils. While the perpetrators profit from the arrangement, civilians may suffer horrible atrocities. In insurrections where resource exploitation plays a critical role as a funding mechanism, civilians are dispensable unless they can be impressed into service as soldiers, porters, or sex slaves. Rebels often use the most efficient strategy for preparing an area for resource exploitation—intimidating the local population into abandoning their land (Renner 2002).

LANDSCAPE CHANGE

There is a specific landscape associated with insurrections. The ubiquitous feature of this landscape is the checkpoint, a location for shaking down the civilian population or traders moving merchandise along a motor road. Such barriers are usually mobile, and either established by rebel forces or government soldiers seeking to augment their income, or by paramilitary groups, well known for their intimidation tactics with documented records of past atrocities. Even more widespread in the landscape are the signs of destruction and disrepair, as deserted villages are left without any standing structures, roads are rendered impassable, and cultivated fields revert to bush. These warscapes, areas that are dangerous to enter and strewn with thousands of land mines like Bosnia (Nordstrum 1997), may become one of the most pervasive outcomes of insurgencies and terrorist activities in the future.

Landscapes of ruin and destruction stand in stark contrast to the landscape changes brought about by internal population movements. Overcrowded camps for internally displaced persons have been hastily constructed on the edges of cities as people flee their homes in search of safe havens. These camps often lack essential services such as clean water, sanitation, adequate food, and fuel for cooking, and in turn, may foster additional discontent adding more potential recruits to the insurgent or terrorist movements. Environmental degradation ensues as the occupants broaden their search for water and fuel (Goldstone 2001).

GEOGRAPHICAL INSIGHTS

There are aspects of insurrections that are particularly appropriate for geographical analysis and help us to understand some of the root causes of terrorism. For example, the spatial pattern of control changes as the state withdraws from part of its territory and areas of opposition appear. These patterns, in turn, relate to the distribution of ecological stresses, ethnic diversity, and population density as well as the structure of transportation and communication networks. It is equally important to understand the distribution of natural resources—diamond mines, hardwood forests, oil deposits—which are able to both instigate and sustain conflicts. Interestingly enough, a scarcity of natural resources is less likely than a surplus of them to become the focal point of a sustained insurrection.

Given the difficulty in bringing insurrections to a conclusion, can a geographical perspective be applied to the peaceful resolution of conflicts? For example, it would be useful to study the circumstances under which zones of peace are created in the midst of an area engaged in armed conflict. During the Mozambique civil war, some areas remained safe from attack because of geographic isolation, the political maneuverings of chiefs, or other forms of negotiation (Nordstrum 1997). This type of situation shows some promise of success, and geographers need to examine the concept of zones of security and how they can be facilitated so as to reduce the threat posed by insurrections in fomenting terrorism.

Finally, how can our geographical knowledge be used to predict which insurrections lead to, or feed into, larger interstate terrorist movements? Are the identifiable precursors to insurgency movements the same as some of the root causes of global terrorism? Can we identify similarities in circumstances that lead to the early identification of potential source areas for terrorist activities? These questions provide the basis for an active research agenda for the discipline, as well as for area specialists within the social sciences.

CHAPTER 4

Geospatial Data and Technologies in Times of Crises

INTRODUCTION

The progress of Geographic Information Systems (GIS) has continued at a rapid pace since its inception in the early 1960s (Longley et al. 2001). However, the synergistic interaction of dynamic new geographic technologies such as real-time GPS/GIS (Richardson 2001), and progress in the development of new models of geographic data representation (Fonseca et al. 2002, Mark et al. 2003) are providing the information fusion capabilities needed to make an intelligent geographical information infrastructure a reality. They already are providing the catalyst for an explosion of loosely linked Geographic Management Systems (GMS), which are relevant to a broad range of stakeholders and applications.

These transformational geographic technologies are coalescing just in time to respond to the new threats of global terrorism, and the challenges of homeland security. They offer an opportunity for geography and GIScience to contribute to the safety and security of the world, the ongoing protection of our natural and built environments, and to forge a deeper understanding of the geographic dimensions of terrorism.

The papers that follow explore some of the many interrelated ways in which geospatial data and geographic technologies can serve as an integral part of the infrastructure necessary for meeting emergency management and homeland security needs, and for understanding terrorism. Mike Tait provides an overview of current geospatial data infrastructures, and underscores the importance of data standards, intergovernmental coordination, and policy development in the effective integration of disparate geographic databases across the nation. Andrew Bruzewicz examines the critical role of satellite imagery, aerial photography, and LIDAR (light detection and ranging, a type of sensor system) in responding to the World Trade Center attacks, and assesses the opportunities and current obstacles to using georeferenced remote sensing imagery as an integral component of geographically-based disaster response and recovery systems in the future.

Key research needs in the areas of geographic data access, accuracy, and interoperability are identified by Michael Goodchild, who complements the discussion of these fundamental issues with a concise overview of geospatial data modeling for emergencies. Intriguing opportunities for using 3-D Geographic Information Systems for emergency response applications, particularly within buildings, are then proposed by Mei-Po Kwan. In conclusion, Douglas Richardson and Frederick Abler discuss the emergence of Geographic Management Systems, which rely on dynamic geographic technologies such as real-time interactive GPS/GIS for homeland security applications requiring rapid response, distributed decisionmaking, and ongoing operations management in a continuously changing space-time environment.

4.1

THE NEED FOR A NATIONAL
SPATIAL DATA INFRASTRUCTURE

MIKE TAIT

OVER THE LAST TWO DECADES, the collection of digital spatial data has grown beyond the few early adopters to virtually all resource management, facility management, and governing organizations in the United States. In 2001, for example, the combined expenditures for software in the geospatial industry exceeded a billion dollars (DaraTech, Inc. 2002). Over the last fifteen years, the industry has spent more than $3.5 billion on the collection and maintenance of digital spatial data. Data were collected both in raster imagery form as well as detailed vector databases to support general mapping, facility management, resource management, visualization, and spatial analysis. Raster data are features that are represented by pixels—a value that corresponds to a particular feature (National Research Council 1998). Most remotely-sensed data are raster data sets. Examples include surface temperatures, land use/land cover, digital elevation models, snow coverage, and nighttime illumination. Vector data represent features as points, lines, and polygons. For example, a point represents a city, a line a city street, and a polygon represents the area served by the city water supply system. The uses for these data across the nation are many and varied, as shown in Table 4.1.1.

These data exist at various scales from small scales with national-level coverage, low accuracy, and infrequent coverage to large scales with local, intermittent coverage and higher accuracy. The prime motivations for the collection and maintenance of these data sets are to provide more efficient management of facilities and resources, more effective analysis of geospatial relationships, and a simplification of the mapping of data. While a wide range of spatial data exists, how

TABLE 4.1.1 Spatial Data Themes

Theme	Example
Streets	City, suburban, rural roads
	U.S., Canada, Mexico
Administrative	Cities, counties, states
	U.S., Canada, Mexico
Demographics	Current census demographic statistics and geographies, business demographic statistics by census geographies
Business Locations	Business facilities identified by Standard Industrial Classification (SIC) Codes
Points of Interest	National, state, and local parks, shopping malls, amusement parks, financial districts, public health facilities
Lines of Communication	Highways, railway lines, subway lines, bus lines, telecommunication lines, telecommunication hubs, natural gas pipelines, electrical transmission lines, bridges, flight paths, navigation equipment
Transportation	Airports, harbors, ports, rail yards, trucking depots, bus stations.
Natural Resources	Rivers, streams, lakes, forests, swamps, marshes, geology
Environmental	Ecosystems, hazardous sites, habitats, weather
Agriculture	Soils, crops
Industry	Power plants, refineries, factories
Imagery	High resolution, current black & white/color
Digital Elevation Model	High resolution

these spatial data resources are collected and how they can be marshalled to support anti-terrorism and crisis response activities is a key concern and focus of this paper.

METHODS OF SPATIAL DATA COLLECTION

There are a variety of methods used to collect spatial data. These methods are grouped into four main categories: field collection, in-situ sensed, remotely sensed, and secondary collection. Each of these methods has inherent strengths and weaknesses which influence the accuracy and currency of the spatial data (Longley et al. 2001). These strengths and weaknesses are important to understand, as they affect the applications and those analyses that utilize them.

Field Collection

Field collection is carried out via one of two primary mechanisms—Global Positioning Systems (GPS) and traditional field surveying. Both of these methods yield the most accurate data possible because they involve on-the-ground observations and exact instrument measurements (Nusser 2001).

The use of GPS is ubiquitous throughout the United States and much of the developing world, both by professionals and amateurs. The ability to support differential GPS (the use of GPS base stations to triangulate and verify a unit's location) yields even greater levels of accuracy ranging from centimeter- to millimeter-level measurements. Data collected using these devices have the greatest levels of accuracy. One weakness of this collection method lies in the instrument's inability to accurately measure location when satellite coverage is not available, such as when the object being measured is below ground or indoors.

Traditional field surveying and the subsequent data entry of coordinate information through the use of latitude/longitude or coordinate geometry is a long standing method for collecting property ownership and facility information. Most city and county governments and utilities use these methods to collect required spatial data. A weakness of this collection method is that it is extremely time consuming, and thus it is only utilized in cases where a lack of accuracy might be costly, such as property ownership and boundary disputes, or where easement locations or the identification of below ground facilities are required.

In-Situ Sensed

This method involves the use of sensor-based collection systems where the sensor's location is known or can be derived, and the specific measurements are known and pre-established as part of the sensor's characteristics. This is a rapidly expanding area of data collection, as sensor units are becoming smaller, less expensive, and more capable of extracting a wider array of information (Estrin 1999). Examples of in-situ sensed data include weather monitoring and utility infrastructure monitoring of pipelines. Some of the emerging uses include military applications, such as troop and vehicle movement, chemical, biological, and nuclear monitoring, and non-military uses such as transportation network flows. This type of spatial data collection is especially appropriate for applications and analyses associated with antiterrorism and crisis management. Strengths of this method are locational accuracy and real-time data feeds, and the weaknesses include management of data volume and sensor maintenance (Heidemann 2001).

Remotely Sensed

Remotely sensed data are primarily collected from source imagery gathered from aircraft or satellite based sensors (see the following paper by Bruzewicz). Pixel-based data collected from these remote sensors are processed to create either raster data sets or vector data sets. The strength of this method is that a large area of the earth can be sensed relatively quickly and inexpensively, and the data can be generated through automated processes. Data also are updated easily using the same techniques. Weaknesses of this method are the limited availability of sensing platforms, the length of time it takes to process the data, and the inherent dependency on the interpretation process, as no interpretation is ever completely accurate.

Secondary Collection

Secondary collection of spatial data refers to converting information that was originally collected and stored in a non-geospatial medium. This process is less than ideal because the accuracy of the converted data is less than if it was collected through a primary means like field collection.

The two main collection methods used to produce secondary spatial data sets are raster to vector conversion, and computer assisted design (CAD) file conversion. Raster to vector conversion involves the scanning of hardcopy maps or design drawings and the application of interpretive algorithms that automatically trace the features in the drawings. Accuracy can be a problem for both the scanning and interpretation processes. CAD file conversion transfers digital data from CAD format to a geospatial format. Features converted from georeferenced CAD files are more easily integrated in the spatial database than those that were converted from non-georeferenced files. The overall value of secondary collection, however, outweighs any inherent weaknesses in accuracy, because conversion allows a large amount of pre-existing and often critical spatial information to be transferred into a digital geospatial medium.

Spatial data collection methods are part of the first step in the process of making spatial data available. The next step supports access and integration of spatial data in a way that is meaningful and effective for the antiterrorism and crisis management community.

OVERCOMING BARRIERS TO SPATIAL DATA ACCESS

In 1994 then-President Bill Clinton signed Executive Order 12906 calling for the development and implementation of a National Spatial Data Infrastructure (NSDI). The intent of the NSDI initiative was and is "coordinating geographic data acquisition and access in support of a national spatial data infrastructure" (FGDC 2002b). This executive order recognized the importance of geospatial data in supporting spatial applications that help manage and preserve key infrastructures and resources.

Since the enactment of the NSDI, the federal government has established a Federal Geographic Data Committee (FGDC), supported by all federal agencies responsible for spatial data collection and dissemination, and by state and local agencies responsible for the same. Commercial organizations working in the spatial data and technology markets are also partners in this effort. The goal of the FGDC is to support the sharing of geographic information and spatial data between all levels of government, as well as public and private entities.

In the last ten years, the FGDC succeeded in building awareness of and support for sharing spatial data throughout the industry. The FGDC defined three programs (or frameworks) that put this concept into action: 1) the definition of framework layers for a national map; 2) the establishment of spatial data metadata standards; and 3) the implementation of a network of spatial data clearinghouses. These programs addressed many barriers to accessing spatial data, however, cooperative relationships allowing full access to distributed spatial data must be realized within the U.S. geospatial community. The federal government should take a strong leadership role in working with primary data organizations to establish standards for collecting spatial data to ensure that these data are available to meet the needs of antiterrorism and crisis management organizations.

Spatial content and interoperability standards are two key elements on which these cooperative relationships can and must be built. Over the past year, the dispersal of consistent, comprehensive geospatial data across jurisdictions to support rapid response in antiterrorism and crisis management events has emerged as a critical responsibility of the geospatial community within the United States. The implementation of interoperable systems by all spatial organizations will help meet this goal.

Standards

The single most complicated issue facing the geospatial community is the definition and adoption of spatial content standards. For nearly a decade, research and standards activities (FGDC Framework Layers) worked at designing a system for a definitive set of spatial data layers that all agencies, organizations and vendors would use as a basis for GIS implementation. This ongoing work is seminal to the success of the Homeland Security initiative currently underway.

With a standardized set of spatial content and interoperability standards, the goal of a distributed network of spatial data, which is maintained at the source by the original creator, and accessible by the whole community, is possible. There is an unprecedented opportunity for the spatial science community to forge a greater partnership with the spatial policy community to design and propose a comprehensive standard for spatial content. This should focus on three issues:

1) Identification of the appropriate layers for a national digital map.
2) The logical and physical model for each of the proposed layers.
3) Content population and coordination responsibilities.

The focus of these efforts should be the implementation of a national digital map that supports anti-terrorism and crisis management as a primary mission. Clearly there will be secondary benefits from such efforts. Leadership from the federal government must be strengthened and participation in content decisions made mandatory for governmental agencies and key private organizations. While this approach may be seen as heavyhanded by some, the unavailability of timely spatial information for this critical government function is unacceptable.

Interoperability

There has been significant activity in the past several years addressing interoperability between distributed systems. The information technology industry rapidly has developed Internet based standards to support interoperability of distributed systems on the Internet. The latest iteration of interoperability standards focuses on the definition of a web services architecture. The web services architecture builds on previously adopted standards like Hypertext Transfer Protocol (HTTP) and eXtensible Markup Language (XML). Web services are independent, self-describing applications, discoverable and executable over the Internet. Web services allow organizations to share functionality and data with other users on the Internet (World Wide Consortium 2002).

Within the geospatial industry, the emergence of the Open GIS Consortium (OGC) was a direct result of the need for organizations to connect to many different geospatial technology platforms both within their own enterprises, as well as to external systems. Since its inception, OGC has supported the definition of a number of industry standards for interoperability. Most recently, these standards focused on using Internet based (HTTP/XML) protocols to implement interoperability specifications such as Web Map Server (WMS), Web Feature Server (WFS) and Geography Markup Language (GML) (Open GIS Consortium, Inc. 2002).

At this juncture, two standards efforts have merged, but an effective critical review of them has yet to occur. Research and evaluation of spatial industry standards and their integration with other standards activities such as the World Wide Web Consortiums (W3C) and the International Standards Organization (ISO TC211) help the industry to better understand where conflicts and/or lapses occurred. Standards, effectively implemented, support the integration of a vast array of distributed spatial databases and help define a spatial network marshaled to support homeland decurity requirements.

SPATIAL DATA INTEGRATION:
A NATIONAL SPATIAL DATA NETWORK

The vision for spatial data integration is to support antiterrorist and crisis management events by establishing a national spatial data network. This network would be the physical embodiment of the NSDI initiative, and would serve as a national GIS. It would extend beyond the boundaries of a single enterprise and directly link to strategic spatial information within the public and private sectors. Creation of these linkages, securely and directly, ensures that those responsible for homeland security have the most accurate and up-to-date information available. By giving the participating organizations the means to post situational and status reports based on spatial content directly into a national spatial data network, ensures the system's viability in times of crisis.

To realize this vision, cooperative relationships in every major metropolitan area between all governmental, academic, and commercial organizations responsible for maintaining the jurisdiction's spatial data will be required. These cooperative relationships would define policies on spatial data access and implement spatial data standardization and system interoperability to support cross-jurisdictional activities. Working at the local level insures that the needs for spatial data at the national level are met, creating a bottom up implementation of the vision of a national spatial data network.

Figure 4.1.1 provides a view of a national spatial data network. The network has three primary elements: spatial content providers, spatial clearinghouse and aggregator, and spatial applications.

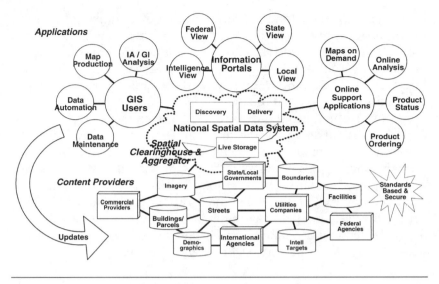

FIGURE 4.1.1 National Spatial Data Network

The spatial content providers are made up of all the key federal, state, local, and international government agencies, as well as key commercial data providers. These providers maintain and serve content to the spatial network, including all vital spatial data and analysis functions needed to support the various applications operating within the network. They maintain and publish their assets in real time, assuring that the very latest content is continuously available via secure, standards based networks and protocols.

The spatial clearinghouse and aggregator components of the spatial network provide two functions. First, they support the registration of required content so that all participating organizations can search, locate, and access the content of the network. Second, these components aggregate spatial content, literally and virtually, into a single set of seamless, standardized spatial data layers. This function allows for the continuous update of information by the providers and users of the spatial network using their own systems and proprietary schemas, while maintaining continuous access to this content in a consistent well-known form.

Specific applications are the primary purpose of this spatial network's existence. These user functions provide the required capabilities to the clients to conduct a range of applications, including simple monitoring and visualization to high-end spatial analysis and even data automation.

CONCLUSION

The next step in the evolutionary growth of the geospatial industry is significant and must result in the development of a national spatial data network. This spatial network will provide for an integrated, distributed spatial database to support consistent visualization, query, and analysis from one area of the country to another in real time or near real time. It will permit the presentation of highly accurate and common information to emergency managers, a necessity for homeland security (Greene 2002).

The basic components needed to build a national spatial data network are in place. The elements required to complete this spatial network include a comprehensive vision for the network, strong leadership to see the vision implemented, a focused research agenda as outlined in this volume, and support to help solve the remaining technical challenges. Once these missing pieces are assembled, the reality and utility of a national spatial data network will be available to support this nation with the challenges that lie ahead.

4.2

REMOTE SENSING IMAGERY
FOR EMERGENCY MANAGEMENT[1]

ANDREW J. BRUZEWICZ

AERIAL PHOTOGRAPHY AND SATELLITE IMAGERY provide emergency responders and decision makers with critical data that can be used to determine the scope of a disaster and direct response and recovery activities. When combined with locational data in geospatial databases, the value of the imagery increases greatly, especially when used to determine how many people and facilities are found in the disaster impact area. Often, remotely sensed data are not, or cannot be collected and disseminated in a timely manner, and consequently do not provide as much value to either responders or decision makers as they could. This paper examines the utility of and need for remotely sensed data in emergency management, and some of the constraints on its use. The terrorist events on September 11, 2001 are examined as they relate to the use of remote sensing as an integral part of emergency management.

ROLE OF REMOTE SENSING

There are many different applications of remote sensing in emergency management (Alexander 1991, Jensen and Hodgson 2003). The role of remote sensing in emergencies is a function of the particular phase of emergency cycle (see Galloway, chapter 2). During the planning and preparedness phase, for example, imagery provides a snapshot of baseline conditions in the affected area, including the locations of important features (such as hospitals, water and sewage treatment plans, or power generating plants), which are often part of geospatial databases.

Both the imagery and other geospatial data assist in the assessments of potential vulnerability and the development of training scenarios to assess the readiness of responders and test possible weaknesses in response plans.

During the response phase, imagery provides more accurate and detailed information and fills the critical gap between predicted damage (usually based on scenario modeling) and the more complete impact assessment provided by on-the-ground observation. This immediate postevent time is important because reports from the ground can be spotty, biased, and hampered by communications disruptions, all of which make it difficult to determine the true extent and severity of damage. The specific types of data collected often include the areal extent of the damage and the severity of damage (typically heavy, moderate and light). Other applications of the imagery help determine the types and quantities of resources required for the immediate response (Bruzewicz et al. 1998). The response phase is when imagery typically has its greatest value and when acquisition may be frequent, with acquisition rates as high as once a day.

During the recovery phase, requirements for imagery tend to lessen. One key requirement is to track the progress of missions—identifying possible sites for sorting debris, locating temporary housing, or providing basic needs such as temporary roofing. Requests that initially were made daily become weekly or less frequent than that. Imagery acquired as part of mitigation often is contemporaneous with response and/or recovery activities. Mitigation also may be undertaken in response to vulnerabilities that exist prior to an actual event, with imagery capturing the "as is" condition.

IMPEDIMENTS TO THE USE OF IMAGERY

Imagery is rapidly becoming an integral part of disaster management. For example, panchromatic aerial photographs (Section-centered at 1:9,600) were used to estimate debris volume in the Miami area following Hurricane Andrew in 1992. High resolution digital airborne imagery showed damage to roofing and collapsed houses as a result of the tornadoes (Figure 4.2.1), while radarsat imagery was used to identify flooded areas during the floods of the Red River of the North (1997) and Hurricane Floyd (1999). Despite these examples, imagery often has not been used to its full potential in emergencies.

The ability to fly a sensor, acquire and process the image, and deliver the resulting product to users presents many challenges. Airborne

FIGURE 4.2.1 Espatial Litton/WSI/TASC 1 Foot GSD Digital Image of Tornado Damage.

sensors require suitable weather (light winds, cloud and smoke-free atmospheric conditions). For systems requiring solar illumination, the sun angle must be sufficient for the system to work. The spatial resolution poses problems as well (Hodgson and Cutter 2001). For example, detailed ground information is relatively easy to obtain with airborne sensors, but is more difficult with satellite systems, as only three commercial systems (SPOT 5, IKONOS, and QuickBird) have a 2.5 meter or better ground sampling distance (gsd). Also, the orbital paths and timing of satellites is such that acquisition of the area of interest often requires several orbits. Weather conditions may prevent the acquisition of usable data over all or part of the area of interest. An experiment to determine the spatial resolution that was required to judge whether a building was sufficiently damaged (for example, rafters were intact or not) after a disaster event, such as a hurricane or tornado, found that a ground sampling distance of 8 to 12 inches was needed to make that determination (Bolus and Bruzewicz 2002). At present, only airborne systems, not commercial satellite systems, meet this spatial requirement.

Another impediment to the use of remote sensing in emergency response is lack of knowledge. This includes lack of understanding by emergency managers about the information that imagery provides, and lack of expert knowledge of sensors on the part of personnel who translate requests for imagery into acquisition missions using specific sensors. In other words, the emergency responders don't know what to ask for, and the remote sensors don't know what's useful and relevant to the emergency managers in the field.

Once acquired, the imagery must be processed within the emergency manager's time requirements, another major constraint on its use. For photography, this means time for film processing and either printing or scanning. If rectification (placing objects in their correct planimetric position) is necessary, more processing time is required. For digital images, the imagery needs to be in a format that is compatible with the display systems currently in use—such as desktop computers, not mainframe systems. If the image is rectified, the incorporated locational data (typically global positioning system [GPS] and inertial navigation system [INS]) must be processed along with digital elevation data. This occurs while data are being acquired or shortly afterward when the plane lands. The time constraints involved in all this processing often preclude the use of remote sensing in any real-time context. An evaluation of the timeliness of this was tested using imagery from the EMERGE airborne system. Images were rectified with ground spatial distances of 3, 2, 1, and 2/3 feet at rates exceeding approximately 10 images per hour (Bolus and Bruzewicz 2002), a time-frame consistent with the demands of the emergency response community.

Just as there are technical constraints on the acquisition of imagery, there also are organizational issues that must be resolved if images are to be acquired, processed, and delivered to users in a timely fashion. Some commercial satellite providers might choose to acquire disaster-related imagery before it has been ordered by anyone (especially governments), fully expecting that it will be purchased later—though not all vendors do so. The federal government does not use accounts that can be activated immediately after an event has occurred. The first opportunity to acquire a postevent image often is missed, either because the satellite operator has not programmed the acquisition or because the government has not ordered the image.

As noted above, weather conditions or orbital parameters may mean significant time delays for that first after-event image. Similar organizational constraints exist for aerial imagery. An aircraft must be mobilized with instructions about the area to be covered, along with the specific imagery requirements. Air photo companies may or may not choose to acquire imagery speculatively. Since mobilization takes time and companies may be working on other contracts, delays can be significant, and clean up operations could commence prior to any imagery being flown. To help reduce time lags, Federal Emergency Management Agency (FEMA) has been working to develop a procurement process to insure that all necessary contracting actions are in place prior to the event, so that imagery acquisition can commence at the first feasible opportunity.

A final set of constraining issues relates to experience and perception. For emergency responders who have little or no experience with imagery, the cost of acquisition may appear to be high relative to the unknown benefits that it provides. As noted above, the absence of knowledge about remote sensing can mean that the acquisition of imagery does not meet specified needs, which were not well articulated or communicated. Similarly, imagery may have been requested but not received in time to assist the response or recovery effort. This may be due to processing time, logistics involved in getting imagery to responders in the disaster area, or distribution of multiple versions of an image in one or more formats to agencies and emergency responders that require it. Emergency managers and decision makers who feel that imagery has not provided the anticipated results in the past can be particularly resistant to requesting its use in the future. Successful use of imagery is likely to lead to more requests in the future; real or perceived failures in obtaining or using imagery are likely to result in extended periods with no future requests.

THE WORLD TRADE CENTER ATTACK

Following the events on September 11, 2001, a large quantity of imagery was collected including high- and medium-resolution satellite imagery, high-resolution panchromatic digital aerial imagery, LIDAR, thermal infrared, and hyperspectral data. More than fifty missions were flown by Earth Data (the primary contractor to the state of New York) alone, a record number of missions for any previous disaster under the Federal Response Plan. An early image acquired on September 12, 2001, for example, shows significant detail on the World Trade Center site, but much of the area was obscured by smoke (Figure 4.2.2a). Imagery acquired a week later (Figure 4.2.2b) illustrates the problem with moderate spatial resolution—the smoke plume is clearly visible, but the ability to distinguish what is damaged and what has happened is limited.

Figure 4.2.2a Space Imaging-IKONOS image, September 12, 2001.

Figure 4.2.2b SPOT Image Corporation image of the World Trade Center Region (20-meter pixels), September 19, 2001.

High-resolution panchromatic imagery was also used in the response beginning on September 15, 2001 (Figure 4.2.3). These highly detailed images provide significant information about conditions on the ground when there is no smoke obscuration, with a ground spatial distance of 4–6 inches. At the same time that these images were acquired, a different sensor (LIDAR) simultaneously captured radar-based data that is used to determine elevations and processed through a Digital Elevation Model (DEM). Figure 4.2.4 represents these LIDAR-derived data as a three-dimensional map of the debris piles following the collapse and partial clearing of the two World Trade Center towers. It was possible to calculate the volume of the debris on the ground using the LIDAR data, however, uncertainties in the ground controls available at the time these calculations were made, meant the estimates were more useful for showing trends rather than for calculating the exact volume of debris removal (K. Carlock, 2001, personal communication).

Other sensors were used during the response such as thermal infrared imagery (TIR), which was used determine the relative temperatures of the hot spots in the affected area. AVIRIS, a hyperspectral sensor, was flown on September 15, 2001 in response to concerns about asbestos levels near the disaster site, but the interpretation of the data showed no dangerous ambient levels (B. Davis, 2002, personal communication).

CONCLUSIONS

Imagery can play a significant role in the management of a disaster, from the provision of mission-critical information to the documentation of actions taken as part of the response and recovery activities. The value of the information that is available or can be derived from imagery is determined, in large part, by its currency and whether the same or similar information is available from an alternative source. Value is enhanced when the imagery is combined with other geospatial data using Geographic Information Systems. Timeliness is important because: 1) clean up must begin immediately and contracts cannot be let without estimates of the volume of debris to be removed, which requires knowledge of the true extent and severity of the damage; and 2) comparable information will become available at some point from other sources, including accumulated on-the-ground observations. Finally, imagery has little or no value if it does not reach those who could use it as part of their decision making or in their operational activities.

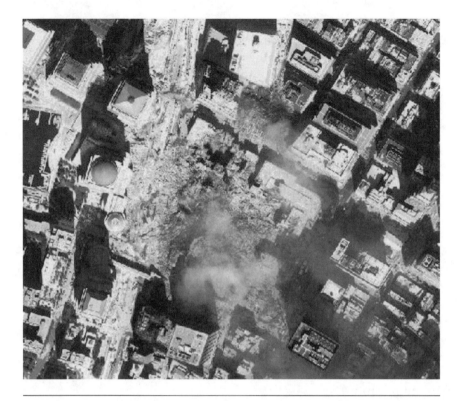

FIGURE 4.2.3. Earth Data Aviation Digital Image of the World Trade Center, September 17, 2001 (6-inch ground sampling distance).

Disasters, particularly the events of September 11, 2001, point out the need for flexibility on the part of emergency responders. Approaches that take advantage of current technology are no more robust than the technology that supports them. When telephone services and the Internet are unavailable or partially compromised, whether as the result of loss of physical capacity, high volume of use, or cyberattack and heightened computer security, alternative approaches are necessary.

The organization of events following a major disaster involves operating in a chaotic environment (Issue 4.2). The situation in New York was aggravated by the loss of the New York City emergency operations center, limits to telephone connectivity, the NIMDA attack, and possibly the relative lack of recent disaster experience, since the last U.S. mainland disasters involving large numbers of responders occurred nearly a decade ago (Hurricane Andrew in 1992 and the Midwest floods of 1993).

FIGURE 4.2.4. Earth Data Aviation LIDAR Data Displayed to Show Elevation.

Given the critical role that imagery (as well as geospatial and other data) can play in response, and to a somewhat lesser degree, recovery operations, it is important that imagery not only be requested, acquired, processed, and analyzed, but also that it be delivered to all responding groups (and responders) who might benefit. This delivery must occur within a time frame in which the data are still current and in a format that is useful to the responders. Far too often, imagery and other products that would have assisted in decision-making during response and recovery were obtained or created, but not provided to all potential users while it still had current value. Improvements are needed in the use and sharing of geospatial data by all agencies responding to disasters. The development of training modules (depending on the agency) for decision makers and emergency responders, which include specific ways in which imagery and image-derived products can help inform decisions and actions, is needed. The training should include specific examples of the kinds of products that are available, and the procedures necessary for obtaining them. Finally,

ISSUE 4.2
Communication Nightmares
in Transferring Geospatial Information

In the first several days following the attack on the WTC, the ability to communicate with federal responders in the disaster area was seriously restricted. Approximately 250,000 telephone switches in Lower Manhattan were out of commission as a result of the event. Additionally, there was an exceedingly large volume of calls in the area in the aftermath of the event, as families and others attempted to obtain information about victims and survivors. The Disaster Field Office (DFO), the center of federal response efforts, required the identification of space and the installation of equipment including the communications infrastructure, which was completed on September 15, 2001. Finally, one week into the event, the NIMDA computer virus began attacks that compromised federal agency Intranets for two days.

As a result, some of the imagery and other geospatial information acquired immediately after the event did not reach responders as quickly as it might have. Commercial telephone (and modem) connectivity with responders prior to the opening and full operation of the DFO was difficult, and large computer files were not all successfully accessed by emergency responders (M. Beaird, personal communication). Once the DFO was opened and computer systems were operational, the transfer of files was inhibited by the lack of full connectivity between the FEMA and U. S. Army Corps of Engineers Intranets. Following the attack on federal computer systems by the NIMDA virus, files with attachments from non-FEMA agencies were not allowed through the FEMA firewall and access to non-FEMA ftp sites was not available. These actions precluded Intranet transfer of computer files to the DFO in New York by non-FEMA agencies. This required movement as hard copy, floppy, CD, or DVD. These solutions can create delays, and without the ability to use the Internet it is essential that alternative approaches to data delivery be undertaken. In the immediate aftermath of the attack on the WTC, Earth Data processed its data in Albany, New York, providing copies to the State Office of Technology, and it sent the files by courier to responders in the city (J. Walker, presentation at the 2002 CADD/GIS Symposium).

improvements in the human resource base are needed, where emergency managers become more conversant with remote sensing, and those with remote sensing expertise become more knowledgeable of emergency management and the immediacy of information needs immediately following a disaster.

4.3

GEOSPATIAL DATA IN EMERGENCIES

Michael F. Goodchild

In RECENT YEARS, roughly dating from the popularizing of the Internet beginning in 1993, there has been rapid and massive growth in the use of electronic networks for sharing geospatial data. Today, it is possible to find a vast resource of geospatial data, along with such derivative products as maps, all distributed over the tens of millions of servers connected to the Internet, and accessed using simple and widely available tools. Many governments have developed digital clearinghouses and warehouses of geospatial data as part of efforts to sponsor and build spatial data infrastructures (see, for example, the National Geospatial Data Clearinghouse of the Federal Geographic Data Committee, and its proposed Geospatial Data One-Stop, http://www.fgdc. gov). This process is evident at many scales, from cities and counties to states, nations, and the globe (Masser 1998, National Research Council 1993, Rhind 1997). The totality of geospatial data resources available through some servers exceeds one terabyte (TB), and one might guess that the total global geospatial data resource available in digital form through the network is now of the order of one petabyte (10^{15} bytes).

DATA ACCESS AND VALUE

Such data resources are of enormous potential benefit in applications relating to terrorism. Many unexpected events, such as the bombing of the Murrah Building in downtown Oklahoma City and the destruction of the World Trade Center, are associated with precisely defined locations on the Earth's surface. In the immediate aftermath of a disaster event, it is necessary for those responsible for recovery to assemble and provide rapid access to information on building plans, local streets, facilities such as hospitals, the local distribution of daytime and residential population, utility corridors, and many other types of information, many of which are geospatial. The key to all of this information is the location of the specific event or impact area. Since such events are virtually impossible to anticipate and can occur in an infinite number of locations, it is essential that the means exist to search, retrieve, and assemble geospatial data based on the geographic locale (or key) as rapidly as possible, within seconds or at worst minutes. The ability to search based on geographic location defines a special type of library, or *geolibrary* (National Research Council 1999).

Unfortunately, and as a result of a number of early and fundamental design decisions in the development of geographic information systems (GIS), the Internet, and the World Wide Web (WWW), would-be users of the distributed resource of geospatial data are faced with daunting problems. There are few effective catalogs of the resources available for browsing and supporting searches for specific data. Once found, data may be very difficult to integrate because of incompatible formats and inaccuracies. Easing these problems is important for all users, but perhaps most important in an emergency, when time is of the essence. This paper explores options for improving access to geospatial data in emergency situations. The following sections expand on each of the major issues—support for search, interoperability of formats, and limitations on accuracy—and assesses the prospects for progress. The final section discusses some remaining issues and prospects for the future.

FINDING DATA

The Internet exhibits what one might term *functional* organization, rather than *spatial* organization, in the sense that its design attempts to ignore distance, and to provide equal access to information independent of location. The IP (Internet protocol) addresses used by the network resolve geographic location only coarsely, if at all, and the time required to access and retrieve information is virtually constant however great the distance between the data host and the user. The system provides no means of identifying servers that are geographically close, or of searching only over servers in a given geographic area. Instead, search capabilities are provided by a number of search engines such as Altavista or Google, using catalogs of Internet-based information resources built largely automatically through the use of *crawlers*, programs that traverse the Internet's servers following the hyperlinks of the WWW, finding and then extracting significant keywords. These keywords are then sorted into an index or catalog, which can be accessed by a user interested in a particular topic.

Unfortunately keywords are not a good way of identifying the presence of geospatial data, or of detecting those specific properties that would be of interest to a user. Although search engines provide an excellent mechanism for finding information expressed in the form of text, they are not an effective basis for searching or browsing the distributed resource of geospatial data. Other tools are more successful, but over more limited domains. For example, the MapFusion software developed by Global Geomatics Inc. (http://www.globalgeo.com) is able to scan any file system, either local to the user's system or distributed over a defined Internet domain, and detect files that use any of a wide range of standard GIS formats (Goodchild 2002). The necessary characteristics, such as scale, authorship, and date, are extracted from the file's own header information provided the GIS format contains such metadata (data about data). But, such systems are not likely to scale to the magnitude of the Internet, and would have no way of accessing or scanning most file systems (unlike WWW pages, which are more easily accessed from remote systems).

While some progress has been made in recent years in building WWW crawlers specifically designed to detect and catalog geospatial data, the problem remains a serious impediment to the successful use of distributed data resources. Instead, many agencies and companies have developed other approaches, the most common of which is the clearinghouse or portal. A clearinghouse is a WWW site containing geospatial data, together with a catalog that allows a user, having reached the site, to search for data meeting specific requirements. In some cases the clearinghouse is a warehouse, maintaining all data locally; in other cases it is a portal to a distributed resource, and several methods exist for registering each of the distributed resources with the portal (such as the ESRI Geography Network, http://www.geography network.com). None are fully automated, however, for the reasons discussed above.

Two problems limit the success of this approach. First, no single site can possibly succeed in establishing a monopoly on access to geospatial data. Different levels of government with overlapping jurisdictions frequently vie for this role, and compete with the private sector, and with individuals. Second, since it follows from the previous point that there will always be more than one clearinghouse, it is necessary for the user to possess some method of knowing where to look for a given set of data; in other words, to possess collection-level metadata that describe the general characteristics of the contents of any clearinghouse. At this point no such mechanisms exist, so users are forced to rely on personal knowledge, interpersonal networks, and guesswork based on simple heuristics (for example, that a data set is most likely to be found on a server maintained by a governmental agency whose jurisdiction most closely matches the geographic coverage of the data set) (Goodchild 1997).

INTEROPERABILITY

The technology of GIS has developed over the past four decades largely in the absence of strong overarching theory, and as a result each vendor of GIS software has tended to adopt a distinct terminology, and distinct data formats. While terms such as *topology, layer*, and *coverage* are widely used in the GIS industry, their meanings are constrained only by the comparatively vague limits of intuition, rather than by formal theory (topology, for example, has a formal mathematical meaning that has drifted substantially in GIS usage). Many standards have emerged, but usually in narrowly defined communities such as defense, or civilian government agencies, and each new effort to standardize seems merely to add to the already long list of formats. *Interoperability* is defined as the ability of systems to exchange information, based on shared understanding of meaning (*semantic* interoperability) and mutually agreed formats (*syntactic* interoperability) (Goodchild et al. 1999).

Lack of interoperability has created a very significant paradox for GIS. On the one hand GIS is a technology able to analyze vast amounts of information at close to the speed of light. On the other hand, when data are assembled from distributed sources it is almost always necessary to spend a large amount of time reformatting, interpreting different meanings, reconciling differences in classification schemes, and forcing consistency in map projections and coordinate systems. It often can take months to prepare data for just a few seconds of analysis.

In recent years the Open GIS Consortium (OGC) (http://www.opengis.org) has emerged as a powerful force in the achievement of greater interoperability. OGC's approach is not to force standardization, which itself requires enormous investment, but to use information technology and general specifications to overcome differences. For example, servers operating in compliance with OGC's WWW mapping specifications are able to supply users with data using a general format (XML or Extensible Markup Language) that is readily compatible not only with OGC's own internal formats, but with the user's client system. These new approaches have been demonstrated very successfully, in applications ranging from environmental monitoring to emergency response (for examples see the OGC Website).

INACCURACY

Perhaps the most problematic issue facing users of distributed geospatial data resources is data inaccuracy. In its most obvious form, data inaccuracies manifest themselves when an user overlays two data sets, from different servers, with different origins, and finds that they fail to fit perfectly. Since it is impossible to measure location on the Earth's surface perfectly, any two data sets will always fail to fit at some scale, but unfortunately the scale at which the problem becomes evident, and impacts applications, is often surprisingly coarse. For example, the widely used data sets of street centerlines, many of them derived from the Bureau of the Census TIGER files, have positional accuracies ranging from 10 meters to 50 meters, sufficient to confuse two ramps at a complex freeway junction, or to mix up two parcels in an urban area. The practical consequences become inescapable when such data sets are used to dispatch emergency vehicles in response to calls based on GPS locations, which themselves may be inaccurate by as much as 10 meters or more.

This problem is not likely to be resolved easily, and is only part of a much larger issue related to the certification of the accuracy of geospatial data. At best, the accuracy of geospatial data sets is described by the creators of the data sets as an important part of metadata, and distributed to users automatically. At worst, however, there is no obvious source of knowledge on data quality for many of the geospatial data sets currently obtainable via the WWW. Positional accuracy is traditionally related to map scale, or the representative fraction that proportions distance on the map to distance on the ground. On maps at 1:250,000, positional errors of as much as 100 meters are acceptable according to national map accuracy standards. But GIS and the WWW make it comparatively easy to integrate data derived from such relatively coarse and inaccurate maps with data from much more accurate sources, such as records of property ownership or engineering-grade surveys of infrastructure.

CONCLUDING COMMENTS

Geographic information technologies such as GIS, combined with the power of the Internet for rapid sharing of information, create an exciting range of possibilities for those charged with anticipating and responding to terrorist acts. Geographic location is the key attribute used to define a search for relevant information, and geospatial data clearly are extremely valuable for a host of applications related to disasters, hazard vulnerability and response.

The vast resources of geospatial data available through the Internet and WWW coupled with expertise in the use of GIS, provide a powerful basis for addressing terrorism. But this optimism must be tempered by knowledge of several critical issues related to data access and use. This paper has identified three: a lack of efficient mechanisms for searching over a distributed data resource for appropriate geospatial data; a lack of interoperability between different data sets; and inaccuracy in data. Another key issue related to use of geospatial data in emergencies, the development of common data models and procedures, was addressed elsewhere in the first essay of this chapter. The research community is actively pursuing all of these, and organizations such as the Federal Geographic Data Committee, the Open GIS Consortium, and the International Standards Organization are making substantial strides in improving interoperability through common specifications and standards. While there is progress, much more needs to be done if the current barriers to effective geospatial data access and sharing are to be overcome.

4.4

DATA MODELING FOR EMERGENCIES

Michael F. Goodchild

As a process, data modeling is often so implicit that its significance is hardly recognized. Whenever observations are made about the world and assembled in some framework, such as a table or a collection of marks on a sheet of paper, the framework constitutes a data model. A table, for example, provides a framework in the form of a collection of cells whose values can be inserted from field observations. In turn, the table provides data for analysis, which ultimately conditions and constraints the types of models and theories that can be developed as contributions to science or to practical problems. Computer databases require data models to be explicit, especially if users are to take advantage of functions related to specific data models. For example, if data are to be assembled into the framework of a table by inserting numerical values into the table's cells, then in addition to the framework itself (the basic table), functions can be provided in advance for routine table functions, such as totaling columns or printing. Microsoft's Excel represents a software environment built on this simple model of data assembled in a table, whereas Word's implicit data model is a linear stream of text. This paper describes the significance of data modeling in the context of emergencies.

GEOSPATIAL DATA MODELING

Geospatial data modeling tends to be comparatively complex relative to such applications as Excel and Word. This is due to the wide range of models in use, such as those based on rasters or vectors, and those focused on georelational or object-oriented models (for a basic introduction to GIS see Longley et al. 2001; for a review of GIS data modeling see Worboys 1995).

The earliest GIS, such as the Canada Geographic Information System constructed in the mid-1960s (Foresman 1998), developed their own unique approaches to the handling of data that were specifically adapted to the needs of geospatial applications. Two types of data models emerged during this period: vector models, in which all features on the landscape are modeled as points, lines, or areas; and raster models, in which all variation on the landscape is expressed in terms of attributes of regularly shaped rectangular cells in fixed locations. A highly specialized adaptation of the vector approach, the topological data model, became popular during the 1970s because of its high level of internal consistency and hence advantages in quality control, and its straightforward application to the representation of a wide range of geographic themes, including land ownership, political boundaries, land cover, and land use. Rather than focusing on the areas on such maps, the topological model treats each common boundary between two areas as its basic unit, and records its location as a series of coordinate pairs, together with the identities of the areas on each side of the common boundary. The properties of areas are stored in a separate data structure as a table. Thus the model has two distinct types of data elements: the properties of areas in a tabular structure, and common boundaries as a set of digitized lines, with varying numbers of coordinate pairs. In contrast, the raster model records variation as an ordered sequence of values, each corresponding to the value of a single and consistent property in a cell. Order is sufficient to establish the geographic location of each cell, and the entire raster is registered to the Earth's coordinate system at its corner points.

Neither of these early data models has much in common with the needs of other computer applications, except perhaps for the similarity between GIS rasters and digitized images, so there was little to be gained by adopting common approaches. This situation changed dramatically in the 1980s, however, with the computing industry's widespread adoption of the relational data model (Date 1975). In this framework, all information is expressed as a series of tables. Each table provides the characteristics, in its columns, of a series of similar objects, each object occupying one row. Tables are linked by *keys*, which allow information in one table (for example, characteristics of patients) to be linked to information in another table (such as characteristics of doctors; one of the properties of a patient would be the identity of a doctor).

The popularity of the relational model caught the attention of GIS designers, who recognized the advantages of using this framework to store the tables of information about areas in the topological data model. By doing so, they could link areas to tables of cartographic symbols, for example, or to tables of information about other features on the landscape. Note, however, that the relational model was suitable only for the area attribute tables; the definitions of common boundaries contain variable numbers of coordinate pairs, and could not be fitted simply into the relational structure's rectangular tables. ARC/ INFO, the GIS from Environmental Systems Research Institute that appeared in the early 1980s, adopted the relational model of the INFO software, but coupled it with specialized software for handling the common boundaries arcs) of the topological data model, in what became known as the hybrid approach (Burrough 1986). The relational model was not widely adopted as a framework for raster data. It also was not as useful for representing the hierarchical relationships that commonly exist between geographic features, such as the relationship between the runways, hangars, terminals, and other component parts of an airport and the airport itself; or between counties and their parent state. Thus, the adoption of the relational model was, at best, a partial solution to the needs of geospatial data; not all geospatial data fits easily into its tabular framework.

A more satisfactory solution became available with the object-oriented data model (Zeiler 1999). In this model all objects are instances of classes, and classes can be specializations of more general classes. For example, State Street is an instance of the class *streets*, and streets are a specialized class of transportation link. The object-oriented model also allows the coordinates defining the outline of an area to be stored as merely one additional attribute of an area, avoiding the need for the somewhat awkward hybrid model of early ARC/INFO. Object-oriented data models, implemented as special interfaces to relational database management software, are now the standard for GIS. But they still leave some problems unresolved; perhaps most importantly, there are many examples of geographic phenomena that do not naturally fit the concept of an object. Many phenomena are conceived instead as continuous *fields*, or functions of location, as is the case for elevation, or atmospheric temperature, or soil moisture content. Fields do not naturally fit a model of geographic phenomena as discrete objects littering an otherwise empty space, and are much more closely aligned with the raster model.

There are obvious advantages to being able to model geographic phenomena, and to do so within the framework of a data model developed for a wide range of computer applications. While some types of geospatial information fit the popular relational and object-oriented models well, others do not. But for those that do, the advantages are clear. Computer-assisted software engineering (CASE) tools are available to facilitate the design of data models, and to automate their implementation.

Software, in the form of database management systems such as Oracle or Access, are available cheaply and off-the-shelf, relieving the GIS programmer of the need to handle many routine data input, output, and housekeeping operations. In principle, then, GIS software development is much simpler today than it was thirty years ago.

ESRI's ArcGIS is a good example of the contemporary implementation of object-oriented data modeling in GIS. A design is first developed in a convenient graphics design package such as Microsoft's Visio. Each class of objects is represented graphically as a box, with its name, attributes, and any methods or functions closely associated with the class, using the notational standards of the Unified Modeling Language (UML). Various types of relationships between classes are represented symbolically. The graphic nature of the process makes for easy participation by users, managers, and others associated with the application. When the design is complete, a software wizard is used to build an ArcGIS Geodatabase, with all of the specified tables and links. The database is then populated from a variety of sources using data loading software.

EMERGENCY RESPONSE DATA MODELS

A comprehensive data model for a large geospatial application, such as responding to emergencies or managing the distributed facilities of a utility company, must encompass a great variety of features, capturing their characteristics and locations on the landscape. A data model for the World Trade Center (WTC) response, for example, would have to represent the locations of buildings, streets, and underground utility lines, and at a much more detailed scale, the insides of buildings and the locations of workers. In fact, this data model would need to represent any features of relevance to the response operation. The full data model for this type of complex application might contain hundreds or thousands of distinct types of information.

In the past, such data models were constructed and populated with data ad hoc in the immediate aftermath of the emergency, often without a comprehensive design. Indeed, data models tended to evolve as data sets were acquired. There are great advantages, however, to planning and constructing data models in advance. First, a data model can be largely independent of the area to which it is applied, so a data model constructed for a response at the WTC in Lower Manhattan could be equally useful in a similar situation anywhere in the nation. Thus there are strong economies of scale in data modeling. Second, an existing data model provides a framework into which data can be inserted quickly, at minimal effort, and using standardized procedures.

Such data loading procedures can be organized in advance to provide consistency checks and other quality control mechanisms. Planning in advance for emergencies by developing data models thus conveys enormous benefits in a response. Third, by organizing a data model in advance, it is possible to develop the associated functions that are needed by a geographic information system (GIS) within an emergency operations center. A GIS can be up and running much more quickly if a comprehensive data model and associated functions have been designed in advance. Finally, there is the potential for learning from past emergencies, by analyzing the data models that evolved in a specific response, and refining them for future responses in cooperation with communities of users and decision makers.

CONCLUSION

In an emergency response situation, it is crucial that GIS capabilities be available as quickly as possible. These include both the database needed to support decisions and also the procedures needed to analyze data and to present information to decision makers. I have argued in this paper that contemporary approaches to GIS database design, including visual database layout, object-oriented modeling, and semi-automated database creation and data loading, are very significant improvements over earlier approaches. They allow data models for specific purposes to be developed well in advance of applications, and to be populated rapidly.

In the past few years, much effort has gone into developing essential data model designs using these techniques for specific GIS application domains. In the case of ESRI, many of these are available on the company's web site (http://www.esri.com). Researchers at the University of California, Santa Barbara, have led the development of one of these, a data model for transportation applications of GIS known as UNE-TRANS. The development of the model involved extensive discussions over a period of two years with users in the transportation field. A similar effort conducted within the community concerned with emergency response is warranted. Making use of the experience of events such as the World Trade Center disaster, and the construction and use of a GIS database in its immediate aftermath, would ensure that emergency response employs the best of contemporary GIS database design techniques, and would do much to speed the response to similar events in the future.

4.5

INTELLIGENT EMERGENCY RESPONSE SYSTEMS

Mei-Po Kwan

HIGH RISE BUILDINGS (MULTILEVEL STRUCTURES) in urban areas pose some significant issues for emergency response largely due to their location, density of occupants, and inaccessibility for some types of emergency equipment. This paper focuses on the use of Geographic Information Systems (GIS) technologies and methods to facilitate quick emergency response to terrorist attacks on multi-level structures in urban areas, targets of choice for the recent terrorist attacks in the United States. It draws upon several research areas in geography's analytical tradition and recent developments in geographical information science that can be used in responding to disaster situations. Finally, the paper explores the development of real-time GIS-based Intelligent Emergency Response Systems (GIERS) as one contribution in reducing human vulnerability to disasters.

MULTILEVEL STRUCTURES IN URBAN AREAS

Multilevel structures such as high-rise office buildings abound in urban areas in the United States. Terrorist attacks on these structures, the World Trade Center (WTC) and the Pentagon on September 11, 2001, or the 1995 bombing of the Murrah Federal Building in Oklahoma City, result in serious structural damage or even the collapse of buildings. These attacks not only affect the multistory buildings themselves, but they impact their immediate vicinity, especially at the street level, which also can reduce the speed of rescue efforts. The complex internal structure of these buildings coupled with the restricted number of access points at the street level renders speedy escape and rescue

111

particularly difficult in any emergency situation. When disasters occur in these kinds of complex multilevel structures, a short period of time (even as short as five minutes) could mean significant changes in the disaster conditions—for example, when trapped people can escape and when rescue personnel can enter the building. Time is critically important in these circumstances and in extreme situations, may mean the difference between life and death.

One distinguishing feature of these multilevel structures is that they involve compartmentalized zones or areas connected by complex corridors (or transport routes). In addition, different levels of these structures (floors) are connected by a limited number of vertical conduits such as elevators, stairways, and utility shafts. The internal structure of the building can be represented using a three-dimensional spatial data model (Lee 2001a, b). Knowledge of this microspatial environment can be used to model potential evacuation routes out of the building, and simulate the potential responses of the building's occupants. Further, these data could be connected to the ground transportation system. This would facilitate preparedness and training by establishing a real-time (or near real-time) three-dimensional (3D) GIS that links evacuation routes to ground transportation systems to foster speedy egress from the building.

For example, nearly 80 floors of both WTC towers were initially unaffected after the planes hit them on 9/11. For at least one hour after the initial crashes, evacuations took place—until the buildings collapsed. Information derived from an operational real-time GIS-based Intelligent Emergency Response System (GIERS) that was disseminated quickly to people inside the buildings and to emergency responders might have reduced the number of casualties in the disaster.

GIS-BASED INTELLIGENT EMERGENCY RESPONSE SYSTEMS

A GIS-based Intelligent Emergency Response System (GIERS) is a spatial decision support system that is designed to facilitate the coordination and implementation of emergency response operations such as evacuation and search and rescue. A GIERS incorporates important geographic information for understanding the current emergency situation, but it also has spatial analytical and modeling capabilities to facilitate better pre-event planning and decisionmaking (Birkin et al. 1996). Emergency response personnel can use GIERS to display, identify, and analyze critical spatial patterns or relationships among event locations, shelters, transportation routes, and the population at risk. GIERS permit the interactive and dynamic visualization of the temporal progression of both the disaster situation and the evacuation of the affected population from the disaster site. More importantly, GIERS can facilitate training and exercise drills for emergency response personnel.

GIERS must have certain functionalities in order to work. These include: data collection and dissemination of data in real time; modeling and simulation of possible trajectories of change in the disaster conditions; formulation of alternative decision scenarios; and the ability to communicate decisions and desirable actions effectively among all affected persons and emergency personnel. Further, a GIERS needs to provide information and decision support to emergency operations at a suitable spatial scale and resolution. In the context of responding to terrorist attacks on multilevel structures in urban areas, these systems must contain a number of the following elements.

Navigable 3D GIS

In order to respond to emergencies that occur in 3D microspatial environments (such as high-rise buildings), it is necessary to know which rooms and floors are affected, and which routes inside the structure are feasible and safe for reaching them. In addition, multilevel structures also have several basement layers, with underground subway, gas, water, and electricity lines, all of which increase the risk considerably and complicate the tasks of emergency response (Cahan and Ball 2002).

A GIERS needs to be based on empirical data that provides the foundation of a navigable 3D GIS data model, and represents all the elements of a complex disaster. This means that data on building occupancy (number of people in what offices on which floors), architectural drawings of mechanical systems, and so forth are necessary for each building. In addition, data on the ground transportation system including a geographic database that stores and manages information about the transportation network is required. Without such basic data it is virtually impossible to construct a GIERS.

Real-Time Spatial Database

The dangers associated with a disaster site can change swiftly and unexpectedly. Decision support in real time to both emergency response personnel and the affected population is an essential function of a GIERS. This means that a GIERS needs to collect and disseminate information about the current condition of the disaster site in real time. To achieve this, the ground transportation component can be built upon or integrated with technologies developed and applied in Intelligent Transportation Systems (ITS), which use advanced communications technologies to achieve traffic efficiency and safety. A real-time traffic detection component of an ITS acquires and updates dynamic traffic information such as route condition and traffic delays in real time using various types of sensors (Kwan 1997, Choy et al. 2000). A GIERS can utilize this ITS component to provide decision support such as finding the fastest route to reach a disaster site, providing navigation guidance to emergency vehicles, and identifying the most effective evacuation routes to nearby shelters for the affected population once they are safely out of the building.

In addition, a GIERS also needs dynamic information about the microspatial environment of a disaster site such as current occupancy, locations of fires, and the structural integrity of different parts of the multilevel structure. This kind of real-time data may be obtained through an Intelligent Building System (IBS), which is an integrated digital system for implementing energy management, life safety, security, access, and lighting control as part of a building management program (Carlson and Giandomenico 1991). The data acquisition component of an IBS uses different types of sensors to collect real-time data (for example, heat sensors can tell the locations of fires and occupancy sensors can tell the locations of trapped people). Some of this data will be critical to the implementation of quick and effective emergency response operations, including rescue crews.

The WTC experience illustrated how GIS technologies and methods were useful in the emergency response. It also showed the importance of remotely sensed data to emergency response operations as Andrew Bruzewicz noted earlier in this chapter (Barnes 2001, Showstack 2001, Cahan and Ball 2002, Kant 2002). Coordination in the collection and sharing of these data among different agencies, however, is essential for their effective use in emergency response operations (Logan 2002, Thomas et al. 2002). The 3D geographic database of a GIERS needs the capability to include remotely sensed images or LIDAR data collected before and after an event.

Decision Support

Another critical element of a GIERS is its decision support capabilities, which depend on a suite of analytical, modeling and simulation functions. The GIERS also needs to provide this information to decisionmakers at a suitable spatial scale and resolution.

When a major incident occurs in one of the high rise office buildings in a densely urbanized area, for example in lower Manhattan, the emergency response center needs to make quick decisions in order to ensure a rapid and effective rescue operation. First, it needs to find the fastest route for emergency vehicles to reach the disaster site using information about the current traffic condition. Second, once the emergency response team arrives at the disaster site, the command center needs to provide detailed guidance to responders so that they can move around inside the multistory building and safely reach the rooms where trapped or injured people are waiting for help. The responders also need to identify the most effective route for evacuating the affected people from the building. As the environment within a high-rise building is very complex, making decisions like this requires specialized computational procedures. Lastly, the emergency response center also needs to identify the best rescue or evacuation plan through a careful consideration of the current condition of various areas in the vicinity of the affected high rise building (Cova and Church 1997). In order to be able to do this, a GIERS should have the capacity to help decisionmakers predict how the disaster situation will evolve and affect adjacent areas. Specialized computational procedures in the decision support system are again needed to predict how, and to what extent, risks may spread to areas adjacent to the disaster site.

Distributed Architecture and Mobile Deployment

After the WTC attacks, the critical emergency response and information infrastructure was seriously disrupted, including New York City's Emergency Operations Center at 7 WTC, the switching facility of a major phone company in the WTC, and part of the mobile phone infrastructure at the site (Cahan and Ball 2002, Kant 2002). Further, as emergency crews worked at the site, they remained mobile, and could not rely on hard-wired connections, even if they were available, for information and decision support from real-time GIERS. To remain operational during a disaster situation, a GIERS needs to be built upon a highly flexible and distributed system architecture, where the 3D GIS database and decision support functionalities remain accessible to emergency personnel through multiple channels, including wireless and mobile communications technologies. The hardware requirements are equally diverse ranging from notebook computers to various handheld and mobile devices with wireless communications capability. Through this distributed and wireless information architecture, information about the current condition of the disaster scene can be collected and disseminated in real time.

CONCLUSION

GIS technologies and methods were useful at the WTC disaster site (Barnes 2001, Cahan and Ball 2002, Kant 2002, Thomas et al. 2002). There are many insights from this experience that can be used in the development and implementation of GIS-based Intelligent Emergency Response Systems. Geographical specialists in GIS and analytical methods can contribute in a number of ways: development of 3D GIS data models, real-time and distributed geographic databases, mobile GIS technologies, and analytical and modeling methods, including simulation and interactive geovisualization (Kwan 2002). In addition to the applications to terrorist attacks, GIERS have the potential to assist emergency response in high-rise fires in urban areas, wildfires in suburban areas, earthquakes, and other rapid onset environmental threats that affect urban places.

There is tremendous potential for developing the geography of 3-D structure as a means for facilitating rapid evacuations from buildings. But there are several important issues related to real-time micro level data collection that raise serious concerns about surveillance and violation of personal privacy (Curry 1997, Armstrong 2002), an issue discussed later in this volume. There will always be the inevitable trade-off between the need for critical information for rescue operations on the one hand, and protecting personal privacy on the other. It is important to have guidelines in place before the implementation and deployment of GIERS to ensure that private information is used ethically and according to the need of a particular emergency response situation.

4.6

GEOGRAPHIC MANAGEMENT SYSTEMS FOR HOMELAND SECURITY

FREDERICK ABLER AND DOUGLAS B. RICHARDSON

CONTEMPORARY DECISIONMAKERS, such as disaster preparedness planners and first responders, face almost insurmountable challenges. They are confronted by an overwhelming collection of data obtained from such diverse sources as overhead imagery, real-time global positioning (GPS) feeds, electronic sensors, and on-site emergency services. The time frame in which decision makers, planners, and emergency managers must make critical choices has collapsed from days to minutes, and in this accelerated and noisy operating environment they are expected to manage multiple, and often conflicting, missions concurrently. To further complicate matters, traditional modes of hierarchical decision making are rapidly giving way to new models of collaboration; arenas in which decisions are necessarily made "on the ground," at several levels within organizations, and simultaneously among multiple supporting agencies and organizations.

Preparedness planners and first responders are overwhelmed by data, yet at the same time they are starved for valuable information. They are confronted with torrents of increasingly real-time geographic data, yet lack the resources needed to transform these potentially valuable data into relevant spatial information. Once vital information is created, only primitive tools exist for sharing it among disparate and geographically dispersed stakeholders. To address these seemingly intractable challenges, diffuse, multisource, and dynamic geographic data must somehow be fused into flexible streams of relevant information that enable decision makers to make better and more critical decisions within increasingly shorter time frames. This challenge is the focus of the interrelated geographic research areas of information fusion and geographic management systems.

GEOGRAPHIC MANAGEMENT SYSTEMS

Information fusion has become an increasingly important component of geographic information science research. The integration of data intensive, dynamic geographic location, and timing technologies (such as GPS) on a real time and interactive basis with the previously static worlds of traditional geographic information systems (GIS) has moved the science forward (Richardson 1991, Mauney et al. 1993). The resulting real-time, dynamic geographic modeling and management capabilities of these new interactive systems have created far-reaching opportunities for geographic researchers and have engendered broad new applications of geographic science in government and business. (Richardson 2001). Collectively, these dynamic new capabilities have been characterized as Geographic Management Systems (GMS) (Richardson 1994, 2001, 2002).

GMSs exploit the powerful real-time, real-world geospatial query, visualization, and analysis capabilities of interactive GPS/GIS environments for applications such as emergency response, live mapping, automated change detection, dynamic spatial modeling, location-based services, time-critical decision making, and increasingly, continuous operations management within large-scale organizations. GMSs enable the management of space itself as a dynamic and temporally integrated information medium, creating a real-time, geographically based operations management environment. GMSs are thus ideally suited to the challenges of threat assessment, disaster preparedness planning, first response, ongoing crisis management, and other place-based homeland security challenges.

As Geographic Management Systems become increasingly interactive, adaptive, and integrated into decision support environments (as they have evolved from map-making, to post-facto decision-making, to real-time operations management), next generation GMSs raise a number of important technical issues. Fundamentally, how do increasingly ubiquitous and real time integrated GPS/GIS and other geographic data become fused into meaningful information? Information is the rich relational context that dynamically binds data together, provides much of its operational utility, and allows people to choose among several otherwise indistinguishable courses of action. For example, because GMSs can model the rich relationships inherent in real-time geospatial data, they could inform disaster relief workers whose own locations also may be in constant flux that a particular fuel supply was recently depleted, has just been contaminated, or will soon be needed by another lifeline, and therefore should not be used for refugee evacuation transportation. The GMS would then route them to an alternate supply using updated road blockage information.

For the past four decades, computerized systems have been used for geoprocessing of data (Longley et al. 2001). However, the proliferation of real time GPS/GIS data has prompted the transformation of these systems, from single utility fixed-location batch data processors to increasingly adaptive, mobile, interactive, and real time information providers. In order for this transformation to proceed efficiently in the future, several fundamental questions must be addressed. How will the computer help us transform multisource geographic data sets and data streams into information? How will that information be meaningfully fused into existing and future models of geospatial decision support? How will relevant geographic information be automatically shared over ubiquitous computing and communication infrastructures, including mobile systems? What system architectures are needed to support the incremental development and ongoing advancement of a network of globally linked Geographic Management Systems?

MAPPING TO MANAGE

If computerized systems are to become information providers and potential collaborators in real-time information fusion, substantial amounts of geographic data must be converted to information that is available not only to human decision makers, but also to a host of distributed software agents. Agents are software modules that can "reason" symbolically, and then automatically communicate the results of their computations to other agents, including human users. For example, software agents can be used to automatically identify relevant patterns of data and relationships, and then bring those patterns to bear on human decision making at the appropriate time and place within distributed decision-support environments (Maes 1994, Bayardo Jr. et al. 1997, Kuokka and Harada 1998).

One experimental model of next generation GMSs that illustrates capabilities well suited to homeland security is the Integrated Marine Multi-Agent Command and Control System. This agent-based system provides military commanders and civilian officials with behavioral characteristics and relationships among such real-world objects as transportation assets (such as helicopters and ambulances), available personnel, infrastructure entities (like hospitals, roads, and bridges), and other real and abstract geographic features (rivers, towns, valleys, geological fault lines, service boundaries, weather events, and so on.) (Shaw et al. 1997,1999; Pohl 2001). This system, in effect, creates a virtual operations management environment that supports collaborative decision making strategies, enabling a process of interactively managing real-time geographically distributed feedback, even on a peer-to-peer basis, that can be more effective than top-down planning.

IMPROVED DECISION MAKING

Because agent-based GMSs quickly and interactively infuse information into human decisionmaking, and vice versa, the resulting decisions and actions have the potential to be more timely and better informed. Agent-assisted information fusion enables greater diversity in the types and sources of geographic data that can be considered in shorter operational time frames. GMSs effectively utilize real-time moving positioning information within a geographically data rich but also continuously changing environment. This synergistic collaboration translates into much greater situational awareness (both temporally and spatially) (Gelernter 1992), a capability vital to all GMSs but especially to homeland security applications. Because the architecture of some existing and many next generation GMSs support wireless communication, local emergency managers can immediately tap into a GMSs' information model, obtaining real-time situational awareness and updated routing instructions to an affected area, thereby arriving on-site better informed, equipped, and prepared.

Agent-based GMSs can also effectively use objects (called object-based representations) and their associated characteristics (including location) as a primary organizational concept (Mark et al. 2003), rather than, or in addition to, conventional organizational concepts centered on locations (x, y, z coordinates) with their ancillary attributes. Thus, object-oriented GMSs can enable both humans and software agents to reason on objects analogously, and human experts can invest some of their real world knowledge in agents, providing a persistent knowledge base. In this way, local emergency managers suddenly confronted with a hazardous materials release could apply embedded software agent prior expertise about a range of hazardous materials, and continuously project their behavior, within dynamic GMS flux of rapidly changing local geographical conditions, local sensor information, and related analyses.

TECHNICAL CHALLENGES FOR
WIDESPREAD IMPLEMENTATION

The technical challenges of building a global intelligent geospatial information infrastructure capable of delivering automated geographic data and information from distributed sources are formidable, but not insurmountable. One key to this undertaking is to foster additional research on several promising new ways of representing and integrating information and connecting information systems. With object-oriented GMSs, for example, several software agents can become distributed clients of a single Geographic Management System, several GMSs can become distributed clients of a single network, or several networks can become distributed clients of another GMS network. Object-based representation within GMS appears to hold substantial promise as a means for enabling meaningful information fusion at both a user and systems level, and also for enabling network-centric information fusion at multiple levels of geospatial and geopolitical organization.

Information Exchange

An important research priority for implementation of large-scale geospatial infrastructures focuses on developing more efficient methods of exchanging information, including examination of the potential of object-sharing middleware (McVittie 2001). Interest-based subscription services are one promising example of middleware, because they allow clients and GMSs to register their interests on specific objects (for example, "tell me about vehicles"). Thus, only relevant changes in the overarching object-model (such as changes in vehicle number, position, or status) are transmitted to subscribers, thereby reducing network traffic substantially. Interest-based subscription mechanisms also push relevant changes to subscribers automatically, reducing the expensive query computation associated with on-demand updates of geographic information.

Such efficiencies are important as GMS networks have the ability to utilize enormous bandwidth, particularly in terms of wireless connectivity. Although wireless bandwidth is growing, it will remain orders of magnitude less capacious than fiber backbones (Odlyzko 2001). Despite current claims of "limitless" terrestrial bandwidth, history has shown repeatedly that new transmission capacity soon creates its own demand (Falk and Abler 1980).

Access to Geographic Information

For broad based applications, GMSs will require global access to geographic information creating what some term a "GIS nervous system for the planet" (Dangermond 2002a). Within defined security constraints, access must be structured to permit the broadest possible constituency of users to take advantage of the emerging intelligent geospatial information infrastructure. New commercial service-oriented architectures offer intriguing communication models within an intelligent geospatial information infrastructure by providing a suite of geographic web services that can be used for building a broad range of globally connected and interoperable GMSs. Such web services relieve system developers from the burden of conventionally programming applications by providing ready-made value-added services. If these flexible web services are meaningfully integrated with emerging international standards and intelligent directory services (McIllraith et al. 2001), we can anticipate the development of a secure and interoperable suite of support services that will greatly facilitate the building of integrated place-based homeland security GMSs.

Interoperability of Space and Time Dimensions

A key enabler of emergent Geographic Management Systems will be the increase in both the number and the interoperability of geographically related web-based support services (for example, geocoding, gazetteering, E-911, and wireless network services). The potential exists for achieving interoperability of these services (Shepherd 1991, Gahegan et al. 2001, Schutzberg 2001b, Tsou 2001). However, much systems integration work, especially involving space and time capabilities that are embodied in GMSs, remains to be done. The underlying issue of semantics, for example, has been underestimated to date in the promotion of web services (Pollock 2002). It is clear, as well, that successful information interoperability schema will rely heavily on well-developed ontological models to make concepts explicit between systems and services (Fonseca et al. 2002).

THE NEXUS OF AND TIME AND PLACE

Many important real world and abstract geographic entities have temporally significant or even temporally dominant dimensions (Castegneri 1998, Wachowicz 1999, Khaemba and Stein 2000, Marceau et al. 2001, Wang and Wang 2002). This is especially so with homeland security concerns, such as threat detection, fire propagation, and disease vectors (see Issue 4.6). GMSs afford new insights into the geographical dimensions of terrorism by enabling dynamic time-integrated analysis, monitoring and management of the increasingly virtual and temporal political boundaries that terrorism imposes, including mapping and modeling the impacts of psychological terrorism (hostage situa-

---

ISSUE 4.6
Real Time Applications of GMS

Temporally enabled models allow GMSs to support decision making in areas that require complex dynamic spatial and temporal reasoning, analysis, and visualization. Some examples include: logistics (In what order should relief supplies be loaded into transport vehicles?); intelligence (Can emergency responders get from A to B in 15 minutes by helicopter or by vehicle?); transportation (Where should we route traffic to ensure maximal evacuation?); real-time epidemiological surveillance for bioterrorism (What is the timing and diffusion of anthrax exposure?); real-time GPS-based positioning, tracking, and deployment of assets for disaster preparedness and during crisis management (Where are the chemical burn kits and cots? What is the extent of the damaged area?), and finally the environmental monitoring of the time-based release of toxic chemicals, or radioactive waste (Where is the plume headed and what is the nature and extent of the population at risk?).

---

tions, bomb threats, and so on), modeling the regionally variable economic impacts of terrorism, and enabling ongoing investigation of and response to the multiple space-time changes occurring in the world after 9/11.

After September 11, 2001, much of the nation's expansive infrastructure now has to be regarded in a new light—as a potential liability as much as an asset. For example, many of the nation's highways and railroads are used regularly for transporting toxic chemicals, nuclear waste, and other hazards. This fact combined with the geographic knowledge that much of the nation's transportation infrastructure parallels major rivers and passes through large population centers makes such settings ideal targets for the opportunistic crimes of terrorism. However, the assessment of such vulnerability on a national scale is still in its infancy (see chapter 5). Temporally enabled GMSs are likely to find strong applications in ongoing vulnerability science and hazards research. Because of their strong simulation and dynamic modeling capabilities, time-integrated GMSs also are well equipped to become powerful training environments. Thus GMSs can further contribute to homeland security and preparedness by cross-training first responders, other civil and federal emergency response personnel, and law enforcement agencies.

CONCLUSION

Much of the science and technology for developing next generation Geographic Management Systems already exists (Richardson 2001). However, continued research and development are necessary in order to rapidly implement an intelligent geospatial information infrastructure capable of supporting the decentralized, secure, and integrated management of the geographic information for homeland security (FGDC 2002c). Interoperability standards and supporting web services will also be essential for developing new and future GMS applications in homeland security and GIScience. It is also probable that entirely new models of threat detection, preparedness, decision-support, and emergency response may arise from the crucible of continued development and implementation of Geographic Management Systems for homeland security and a broad array of other applications in the years ahead.

CHAPTER

Vulnerability of Lifelines, the Built Environment, and People

INTRODUCTION

Vulnerability is a condition that describes the ability of something or someone to resist the impacts of a threat and recover from it. It can apply to individuals (specific people, a building), to various social groups (the young, the infirmed) or systems (economic, ecosystem, infrastructure), or can be aggregated to examine societal-level vulnerability or placed-based vulnerability. Understanding societal vulnerability is important for it points out shortcomings in many of the underlying processes and systems that support our current quality of life. At the same time, social vulnerability highlights demographic and spatial inequities among populations, differences that influence capacities to respond and recover from threats. Place-based vulnerability helps us to understand those driving forces that increase vulnerability or hamper its reduction. While it is relatively easy to explain the vulnerability of a coastal community by examining the interaction between natural forces and human agency, the policy options for reducing coastal vulnerability are more complex.

The papers in this chapter underscore the urgency for understanding vulnerability, the need for new methods, models, and tools in furthering vulnerability science, and how we prepare for the unexpected. John Kelmelis and Scott Loomer identify some of the specific attributes of "critical infrastructure," noting that prioritizing critical systems is both non-hierarchical and scale dependent—what becomes a priority for the federal government may not be the same for the local municipality, and what is of major concern in urban areas may be less salient to rural regions. Tom Wilbanks describes the spatial mismatch in energy production, supply, and demand and points to the significance of location as an essential component of vulnerability assessments. Lifelines, especially communications and transportation systems, provide the focal point for Harvey Miller's paper, which describes vulnerability in terms of network reliability, access, and performance. He also emphasizes our lack of knowledge regarding the interplay between human activities and lifeline demands in both time and space. Geoff Hewings and Yashuhide Okuyama provide us with a detailed analysis of how unexpected events affect state and local regional economies (both positively and negatively), and the spatial concentration and dispersal of such impacts. Jerry Dobson reviews the current models used to estimate populations at risk including their strengths and weaknesses, and argues for the need to revitalize population geography only at finer spatial and temporal scales. Finally, Ray Dezzani and T. R. Lakshmanan explore the "network society," and argue that the need to secure interaction spaces changes over time, across space, and may or may not have a physical setting (as with cyberspace).

These papers suggest a number of important questions for further research. What is the role of security in business locational decision-making? If the goal of terrorism is to disrupt and degrade the economic system of a place, yet disasters produce an overall economic gain, then how effective are these terrorist tactics in achieving that goal? How do we explain the vulnerability of urban areas to purposeful threats such as terrorism? What steps need to be taken to improve vulnerability science as we try to explain what makes people and places where they live, work, and play, vulnerable to natural, technological, and purposeful threats like terrorism?

5.1

CRITICAL INFRASTRUCTURE

JOHN A. KELMELIS AND SCOTT A. LOOMER

THE INFRASTRUCTURE THAT IS NECESSARY for maintaining a society or conducting a war is termed *critical infrastructure*. Critical infrastructure evolves with a society. It is logically defined by sector, though there is considerable interaction and overlap. There are physical and cultural aspects of a society that make critical infrastructure both vulnerable and resilient. It is common knowledge among combatants, for example, that disabling certain of the opponent's infrastructure vastly improves the possibility of victory. Likewise, hazards professionals identify infrastructures critical to community functions when planning mitigation or response efforts. Total disruption or destruction of any one or more of these critical infrastructures, though not likely, can bring the current way of life in the developed world to a halt. Partial disruptions can have serious consequences for people and their quality of life in the short and long term.

CRITICAL INFRASTRUCTURE: DEFINITION

Many definitions of critical infrastructure have been put forward. The President's Commission on Critical Infrastructure Protection (PCCIP) stated, "Critical Infrastructures are systems whose incapacity or destruction would have a debilitating impact on the defense or economic security of the Nation" (PCCIP 1997). Presidential Decision Directive 63 (Clinton 1998) called critical infrastructures "those physical and cyber-based systems essential to the minimum operations of the economy and government." More holistically, a critical infrastructure is one that society depends on for national defense, economic security, quality of life, and/or good governance. Denial of a critical infrastructure will have a profound negative effect on one or more sectors of our society.

As the level of development in a society changes, different infrastructures become more or less important. For instance, before the invention of telecommunications systems in the nineteenth century, and their increasing expansion and adoption in the twentieth century, the transportation infrastructure provided the primary means to transmit information from place to place. The information was often slow to arrive, out of date, and thus inaccurate. A totally agrarian society was less dependent on the transportation network for information or trade because most of what was necessary for survival was produced locally. A society becomes increasingly dependent on infrastructures as its level of sophistication and specialization grows. In a developed country, like the United States, it is important to identify the interconnections among these systems in order to understand not only their vulnerability, but also their ability to withstand and recover from disruptions; in other words, their resiliency. The importance of understanding critical infrastructure interactions, vulnerability, and resilience has taken on new urgency due to the increase in terrorist activities worldwide, particularly within the United States. This makes protecting critical infrastructure a major part of homeland security.

IDENTIFICATION

Established by the President's Executive Order 13010 (Clinton 1996), PCCIP identified eight categories of critical infrastructure: telecommunications; electrical power systems; gas and oil production, storage, and transportation; banking and finance; transportation; water supply systems; emergency services; and continuity of government services (PCCIP 1997). The National Imagery and Mapping Agency (NIMA) and the U.S. Geological Survey (USGS), charged with obtaining and maintaining geospatial information on many types of infrastructure, critical and otherwise, and in conjunction with many other organizations, are developing and continually improving the collection strategies and methodologies to populate the Homeland Security Infrastructure Program (HSIP) database (NIMA and USGS 2002). Expanding on PCCIP's list, they have identified additional national infrastructures for which Minimum Essential Data Sets (MEDS) must be constructed. Table 5.1.1 lists a set of critical infrastructures that are in need of protection. Clearly, protecting even the most critical portions of these infrastructure sections will be costly and must be prioritized.

Like in the United States, identifying critical infrastructure at the national level is being done in many countries. For instance, Canada identified six sectors in its national critical infrastructure: energy and

TABLE 5.1.1 Critical and National Infrastructures in Need of Protection,
Not Prioritized

Infrastructure Category	Source
Telecommunications (information listed separately)	PCCIP 1997, PDD-63, OHS 2002
Electrical power system	PCCIP 1997, PDD-63, OHS 2002
Gas and oil production, storage and transportation	PCCIP 1997, PDD-63, OHS 2002
Banking and finance	PCCIP 1997, PDD-63, OHS 2002
Transportation	PCCIP 1997, PDD-63, OHS 2002
Water supply systems	PCCIP 1997, PDD-63, OHS 2002
Emergency systems	PCCIP 1997, PDD-63, OHS 2002
Continuity of government services	PCCIP 1997, PDD-63, OHS 2002
Public Health Services	PDD-63, OHS 2002
Agriculture and livestock	OHS*, OHS 2002
Chemical and manufacturing	OHS*, OHS 2002
Commercial, retail and public venues	OHS*
Food industry	OHS*, OHS 2002
Mail and shipping	OHS*, OHS 2002
National symbols or icons	OHS*
Defense Industrial Base	OHS 2002
Information content	None

*Proposed by Office of Homeland Security (NIMA and USGS 2002) Phase I Tiger Team.
Categories attributed to NIMA and USGS were determined by them from a variety of sources
including the Hart-Rudman Commission Report (U.S. Commission on National Security 2001),
Gilmore Commission (GC) Report (GC 2001), The Critical Infrastructure Protection Plan
(DoD 1998), and others (NIMA and USGS 2002).

utilities, communications, services (financial, food distribution, and
health), transportation, safety (nuclear, search and rescue, emergency
services), and government (facilities, information networks, and assets) (Government of Canada 2002).

State and local governments are working in conjunction with the
federal government to secure their critical infrastructures, and some
have their own initiatives. New Mexico, for example, has created the
New Mexico Critical Infrastructure Assurance Council (O'Neil 2000)
as a cooperative enterprise to exchange information between public
and private, federal and state, and local agencies. Expanding homeland
security efforts at state and local scales may be problematic owing to
budget limitations and balanced budget laws that preclude the option
of deficit spending. This can prove important because the highest priority national critical infrastructure may not be the most critical at

local scales, and those most critical in one locale may not be the most critical in another. Local, regional, and national priorities may or may not nest either spatially or hierarchically.

THREAT POTENTIAL

The threats to critical infrastructure are variable, particularly where terrorism, a hazard that can consciously adapt to a changing environment, is concerned. Adaptive hazards, like terrorism and subversion, pose an evolving threat that requires continual research and analysis to gain the information needed to keep risks at an acceptable level. These threats can use both high and low technology successfully to cause major disruption, as is evidenced in the attacks on the World Trade Center and the Pentagon on September 11, 2001.

Merely developing data to describe the type, location, and attributes of individual critical infrastructures is not sufficient. The infrastructures' relationships to one another; the vulnerability of various sectors of society to their disruption; the social, economic, and environmental costs of that disruption; the costs to society and the environment of improved protection; and many other variables must be known to correctly prioritize resource allocation for modification, protection, response, and recovery. This is complicated by the evolving nature of the threat. Therefore, we also must know the real and potential capabilities of the threat, its motivations, and its understanding of us (including our relation to our critical infrastructure). Scientific understanding of the various critical infrastructures, the hazards, and their vulnerabilities must be improved in many sectors to better combat terrorism (NRC 2002). This will ultimately help reduce the risk.

Since terrorism is an adaptive hazard, it may be possible to reduce the hazard potential by reducing the threat using such means as altering the environment that fosters terrorism. This raises questions such as: what are the changes needed to the environments fostering terrorism that would help reduce the threat, are there infrastructures critical to ensuring those changes take place and thrive, and how could those infrastructures be established and made self-sustaining? Consider for example, that there may be social, political, economic, biological, or physical conditions that make a society more prone to foster or harbor terrorists and terrorism. Would improved access to basic necessities of life, or political influence, or the ability to make decisions about their own future reduce the likelihood of that society's propensity to support terrorist activities? Is there an infrastructure or suite of infrastructures, which, if in place, would be critical to provide those necessities, ensure stability, give the population political influence, and, in general, eliminate the conditional causes of terrorism? If so, answers to the above questions could help guide foreign aid policy and military intervention. Thus, those would be critical infrastructures to reduce the threat of terrorism.

HAZARDS, VULNERABILITIES, AND RISKS

To truly understand the vulnerabilities of infrastructure, that is, the likelihood that the infrastructure will be affected by the hazard, one must understand the broader social and environmental processes that affect it. Within these processes lie the hazards. A hazard is a process or an event that can have a negative affect on an area, infrastructure, or sector. Current views hold that a hazard is a potential threat and its consequences. For example, to understand how vulnerable a community is on a floodplain, one must have information on the probability of the hazard (the risk of a flood event), the dynamics of floods, and the physiography and other characteristics of the floodplain. To understand the vulnerability, one must also understand the use or value of the infrastructure, how it connects with other infrastructures and supports society's needs for security, economics, quality of life, and governance. The probability of the hazard's occurrence (risk), the vulnerability of the infrastructure, and the value of the goods and services provided by the infrastructure combine to form the hazard potential.

In a natural hazard like a flood, the probability of an event's occurrence is independent of the vulnerability of the infrastructure or the value of the goods and services it provides. For an adaptive hazard, like terrorism, the probability of an event's occurrence is partly dependent upon the perpetrator's perception of those vulnerabilities and values. Other variables that affect the terrorist hazard are the perpetrator's motives and capabilities. These can change. Thus, when evaluating risks due to terrorism, one must continually assess several changing environments: the hazard (terrorist), including its changing motives, perceptions, and capabilities; the infrastructure and its changing vulnerabilities; and the changing values of the infrastructure including its direct values, interconnections to other sectors of society, and perceived value to society. Understanding hazards (and risk) will help in the allocation of resources for risk reduction or mitigation.

Unlike analyzing the Soviet bloc's military strength during the Cold War, which was based on well-defined indicators and data sources, "counterterrorism analysis must provide structure to information that can be highly fragmentary, lacking in well-defined links, and fraught with deception" (Isaacson and O'Connell 2002: 2). The terrorist threat is much more likely to change rapidly in response to changing defenses and security measures. Because of the complex nature of an adaptive hazard, the concepts of hazard, vulnerability, and risk should be reexamined, in order to develop a conceptual or mathematical function that would be more useful in understanding the relation of adaptive hazards, such as terrorism, to dynamic and interrelated resources such as critical infrastructure.

Motivations and goals of the terrorist can affect critical infrastructure in very different ways. For example, the September 11, 2001 attacks were largely symbolic in that they were sudden, highly visible, and had high emotional impact. They were also the result of the terrorists' adaptation to their improved understanding of the vulnerabilities. A failed attempt to bomb the World Trade Center years earlier required terrorists to find a new, more creative method to meet their objective. Given the motivation and potential patience that can last for generations, terrorists could use a more insidious approach to insure longer lasting changes in one or more of the critical infrastructures. For instance, could a number of well-trained subversives make a concerted effort over time to taint enough of the food, water, or medicine supply to significantly disrupt the quality of life of a developed nation? A more profound understanding of the critical infrastructure and the threat potential is needed in order to minimize the vulnerability of these important systems.

PROTECTION

National efforts broadly define and prioritize critical infrastructure, but that macro-view does not necessarily translate to the micro-view needed at a more local level. In addition, each critical infrastructure sector has unique characteristics and poses unique security challenges (OHS 2002). Identifying, prioritizing, and protecting critical infrastructure will vary by sector, region, level of government, timeframe, and other contextual factors. For example, the nation's water supply and delivery systems are a high-priority critical infrastructure at the macro level. However, the prioritization at the local level will vary depending on water supply vulnerability, such as whether it is from a surface catchment area with open storage reservoirs, from wells in rivers, or from wells in deep aquifers. The availability of alternative sources will play a part in the level of effort invested in security.

For the United States and the rest of the developed world, critical infrastructures are interconnected and interdependent, and often disruptions in one sector affect another. Telecommunications infrastructure, for example, plays a particularly significant role due to society's heavy reliance on rapid access to current and accurate information. Society relies on information content so much, that it may be considered an infrastructure in its own right.

The General Accounting Office found that "protecting the nation's critical infrastructure against information attack is a complicated process involving many government agencies (GAO 2002: 14)." It went on to describe the five cyber-critical infrastructure protection categories of activity in which organizations participated. These were policy development, analysis and warning, compliance, response and recovery, and research and development. While organizations must do a much better job of managing their information infrastructures (GAO 2002, OHS 2002), new technologies must be developed and existing technologies must also be upgraded to improve security (Harris 2002).

Information and the computing and telecommunications infrastructures must receive special attention due to their linkage with all other infrastructures. All other infrastructures must be protected to a greater or lesser extent as well. The wealth of geographic analysis tools can be brought to bear on critical infrastructures geographic and cyber space to help prioritize and develop operational plans and techniques for critical infrastructure protection.

SPATIAL ASPECTS OF CRITICAL INFRASTRUCTURE

The physical critical infrastructure in the United States is vast. Figure 5.1.1 shows the 133 urban areas that comprise most of the population

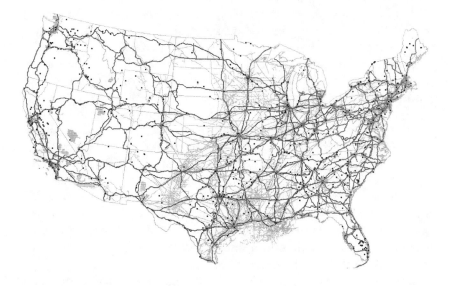

FIGURE 5.1.1 Selected Critical Infrastructure in the Conterminous United States. Note the pipelines extending into coastal and marine environments. (Illustration provided by Michael Domaratz, USGS)

of the United States and most of the political and administrative leadership; the major road and railroad networks; selected pipelines, maritime features, and federal reservations; and the major dams, airports, and power plants. Many other infrastructures that are disbursed points or are more critical at the local level are not shown. This map illustrates the vastness, complexity, and geographic distribution of our critical infrastructure and graphically demonstrates the need to prioritize our activities with relation to critical infrastructure.

Critical infrastructures can have many spatial forms such as points (wells, power plants, factories, and so on); lines (roads, power lines, pipelines, and so on); areas (such as agricultural fields and communities, etc.); volumes (aquifers feeding wells, airspace above communities); networks (road networks, power grids, land line telecommunications networks); virtual networks (such as Internet and other communications using all links, and information content); or amorphous unbounded features (information content). It is estimated that 80% of the data collected by governments are spatial, that is, having a location or being related to a place as part of the content (Dangermond 2002b). The positional information can be sufficiently ubiquitous or it can have an unstructured, undefined location so as to be considered amorphous. These different physical forms make protecting critical infrastructure highly complex and highly dependent on rapid access to accurate information.

A robust spatial data infrastructure (SDI) is needed to provide information about the critical infrastructure. Current plans such as those being driven by the HSIP (NIMA and USGS 2002) address important fundamental data requirements for an SDI to be capable of meeting most initial framework data needs of first responders, planners, and managers. The Federal Geographic Data Committee (FGDC) provides an opportunity for communication among federal agencies, states, and other organizations to develop standards and reduce costs of information exchange and use (Somers-St. Claire 1997). This is reflected in the plan for the Geospatial One-Stop (FGDC 2002b), part of the Office of Management and Budget E-Government initiative to improve the effectiveness, efficiency, and customer service throughout the Federal Government by expanding electronic government. Geospatial One-Stop is designed to provide advanced standards, indexing, coordination, and online access to digital geospatial data to advance the E-Government initiative.

Improved understanding of the evolving nature of the threat will help improve our knowledge of the type and quality of data we must collect. Improved understanding of the processes related to the critical infrastructures, as well as their relationships to each other, will help improve the application of those data to solving problems of homeland security, as well as operational problems of the day-to-day management.

An example of data collection for homeland security is the 133 urban areas project under the HSIP of NIMA and *The National Map* led by USGS. Within that project, analysis is taking place to identify the highest priority locations to collect high resolution, accurate, and extensively attributed base data. Base data sets are being prioritized and collected in compliance with continually improving standards and specifications in locations identified by analyzing a series of variables. The number of study places changes as new understanding of the critical nature of those locations is gained. The locations for which high-priority data are collected are determined as a function of population, military presence, political value, symbolic value, the location as a scientific and technological center, economic importance, frequency of disasters, importance as a transportation hub, and importance for selected energy variables. In addition, fundamental data must be collected describing selected critical infrastructure not associated with major population centers, but important individually or because of its connectivity as part of a critical network. Thus, the project will go far beyond the 133 most populated places in the United States. It will provide critical data for use in protecting critical infrastructure from terrorists or in responding to terrorist attacks. More significantly, the data will be valuable for economic development, environmental and resource management, government operations, and health and safety activities. Of course, these are only the framework or foundation data, and additional data are necessary for specific applications.

INFORMATION CONTENT AS A CRITICAL INFRASTRUCTURE

The availability of information about critical infrastructure affects its vulnerability and resilience, as well as the ability of society to function, meet its citizens' needs, and grow. The disruption of critical infrastructure by disasters or by failure of some aspect of society can change, either temporarily or permanently, the fundamental characteristics of the society, depending on society's response. The availability of information, addressed as part of the telecommunications infrastructure by the President's Decision Directive 63 (Clinton 1998) and Executive Order 13231 (Bush 2001), may be considered an independent critical infrastructure because of its importance to a democratic society. Both content and access must be protected. In a democratic society, limitation of access to data about critical infrastructure and the infrastructure itself must be balanced against the need for access required for democracy and democratic capitalism to flourish. In a free society, there will always be this tension. There are important data to be gathered, research conducted, and policies addressed to protect and enhance our critical infrastructure, including the availability of information, and to ensure that our society receives the greatest benefit from it.

An example of the critical nature of information was the decline the stock market underwent when it became apparent that Enron, MCI-WorldCom, and other corporations were not providing accurate information about their financial condition to investors. The damage to the stock market and to investor confidence, though recoverable, was greater than that caused by any terrorist event to date. It illustrates clearly that the denial of accurate information content, not merely the infrastructure that communicates the information, can have profound effects on society.

An important debate now taking place concerns how much information should be readily accessible. This debate centers around the limits that should be placed on access to information to reduce the vulnerability to terrorism while allowing sufficient access for democratic decision making and public review of those decisions. There is a larger issue as well because the balance of information access will also define the future of the United States as an open, democratic society with an economy that is built increasingly on the availability of accurate information.

RESEARCH NEEDS

The cost of protecting all the infrastructure could overwhelm the economy if wise decisions are not made concerning the allocation of resources, and if adequate steps are not taken to reduce the hazard, assess the resultant vulnerability, and develop an approach to minimize direct risk and develop sufficient resilience to mitigate the effects of residual risk. This will require a new understanding of the processes that affect or are affected by the critical infrastructure, the dynamic nature of the threat, and the data and information needed to build robust mitigation, readiness, response, and recovery capabilities to make society more resilient.

It is also important to develop an understanding of the resilience of the various infrastructures, redundancies that exist or should exist, and the losses that would be suffered if critical infrastructure was disabled. The variable nature of the loss, depending upon the physical extent of the disruption or the length of time or persistence of the disruption, is another type of fundamental understanding that does not yet exist. Are there things we do not yet consider critical infrastructures that, if a long-term subversive effort lasting one or more decades were launched against them, would compromise our way of life? If there are, how do we distinguish the negative effects of such an insidious form of terrorism from the natural evolution of our society? Fundamental advances must be made to vulnerability science. Without these it will be difficult to integrate the information we have or will gather in the most meaningful way.

Finally, developing a clear understanding of the infrastructures that exist or could be incorporated into the cultures that are sources of terrorism, which are critical to reducing the terrorist threat, might be the key to a safer world. Would such an understanding indicate needs for improvements to educational, communications, transportation, food, or other sectors of those cultures?

5.2

ENERGY SYSTEMS AND INFRASTRUCTURES

Thomas J. Wilbanks

ENERGY SERVICES ARE CRITICALLY IMPORTANT for human well-being and prosperity. They provide comfort, convenience, health and safety, mobility, and labor productivity and employment. In essential ways, energy is necessary (if not sufficient) for all these aspects of our quality of life, so much so that U.S. citizens often consider energy an entitlement, not a commodity (Aronson et al. 1984). Energy supply is expected of our national and regional institutions, and we tend to hold those institutions accountable if supplies are inadequate.

Energy services are connected with human security in other ways as well. For instance, energy supply and use systems are related to environmental emissions and health, vehicles and safety, electricity-powered control and safety systems, and information systems in an information-technology age. In addition, energy services are related to improving standards of living in developing countries so that a large majority of the population prefers avoiding instability rather than embracing it as a way to redress economic and social grievances. In other words, energy is related to the roots of global instability.

SOURCES OF THREATS

Energy services in the United States are subject to threat from two major sources. First, as we discovered in the 1970s, actions taken *outside* the United States to interrupt energy flows cause energy shortages and associated economic and social disruptions (Feldman 1995). Second, actions taken *inside* the United States also cause energy shortages and disruptions. In some cases, one cause is often blamed for the other. On several occasions in the 1970s when people were waiting in long lines at service stations for gasoline, the United States, in fact, did not have a national shortage of gasoline (an absolute scarcity). The problem was one of a relative scarcity, that is, the mechanisms for redistributing supplies from surplus to deficit regions were inadequate.

Terrorism is the emphasis of this book, but other causes of energy supply disruptions may include market manipulation (which was one contributor to the 2000 California energy crisis, according to some analyses); policy failures; institutional failures (such as the failure of a regional electric utility to assure adequate reserve capacity); physical structure limitations; or environmental variation and/or natural disasters (such as reduced hydropower production from the Pacific Northwest in 2000 due to reduced rainfall, another cause of the California energy crisis).

THE NATURE OF ENERGY INFRASTRUCTURE

Our national energy supply infrastructures can be viewed in either global or national terms. As one way of focusing the discussion, this paper considers only the U.S. national energy infrastructure within national borders—energy supply points, movement networks, storage sites, and control systems within the United States—and its vulnerability to disruptive terrorist attacks (National Research Council 2002). In this connection, energy infrastructures resemble other familiar types of national infrastructure, such as transportation and communication, on which we depend to enable spatial interaction in the United States. One difference, however, is that when compared to the other infrastructures energy systems at the national or regional scale often tend to be less complex, more dependent on a relatively small number of supply facilities or movement channels, and therefore arguably more susceptible to purposive disruption.

Energy supply infrastructures can be viewed as expressions of two types of geographic phenomena: (1) a "natural resource lottery" (Haggett 1975), which endows some regions with primary energy resources but not others, and (2) a mismatch between spatial patterns of primary energy supply and end-use energy demand, which requires structures for redistribution (Wilbanks 1982, Cutter and Renwick 2003).

Elements of an energy supply infrastructure include: site-specific energy production and conversion facilities (such as electric power plants, refineries, coal mines, and oil and gas wells), site-specific energy storage facilities, site-specific energy movement facilities (such as terminals for oil imports), and energy movement systems (electricity transmission lines, oil and gas pipelines, tanker systems for oil and oil products movement by road or water or rail, slurry pipelines, and barges for coal movement). Most citizens are aware that energy infrastructures are subject to occasional disruptions—electric power outages in the West because of storm-related damage to transmission networks, or power outages in eastern cities because of system overloads and subsequent failures. All of these can be dramatically disruptive for short periods of time, not only inconveniencing local consumers, but also producing economic impacts in the affected area and beyond.

THE SIGNIFICANCE OF LOCATION IN VULNERABILITY

Terrorism raises concerns about energy infrastructure vulnerabilities for three reasons, all of which relate to the significance of location. The more obvious reason is that targeted terrorist attacks might hurt the United States or a U.S. regional economy by causing energy shortages. Terrorists might act with the intention of causing fundamental damage to the U.S. energy system. Examples of concerns include disruptions of electricity transmission networks or control systems, disruptions of key oil or gas pipelines, or disruptions of key oil import facilities, anyone of them with the potential to cause regional, if not national, stress. Vulnerabilities to such disruptions are related to the spatial structure of energy supply movements, especially the dependence of movements on capacities at a few geographic locations such as the Gulf Coast region from Houston to Lake Charles, Louisiana.

A second reason, and perhaps the more likely, is that terrorist attacks on energy facilities could be aimed not at the energy system per se, but at the more general human and/or environmental impact of a single act. Examples include destruction of a major hydroelectric dam or a nuclear power plant, oil tanker trucks passing through cities, and nuclear waste shipments at particularly sensitive locations. Such an act might exemplify the kind of drama that 9/11 had in mind. These vulnerabilities also relate to relative location, in this case energy facility locations relative to potentially impacted populations.

A third reason, clearly of concern but probably the least likely of the three in the United States, is terrorist acts aimed at acquiring nuclear materials and/or nuclear wastes for subsequent use such as dirty bombs (Levi and Kelly 2002). Because protective systems in the United States are generally better than in some other parts of the world, terrorist organizations might be expected to target their efforts on other places, although no one dismisses this issue as a concern.

Obviously, the main strategy for increasing resiliency in the U.S. energy infrastructure is anticipating vulnerabilities and taking action to reduce them. For this purpose, dynamic spatial simulation modeling of the various U.S. energy infrastructures and their interconnections is being strengthened considerably, with many of the resulting specific insights about the current infrastructure protected by security classifications because they might suggest targets for terrorist action. It is not difficult, however, to speculate about some of the elements of current vulnerability. These might include increased attention to protecting certain key facilities, such as nuclear power plants and hydroelectric dams, and adding movement system redundancy to increase alternative pathways for moving electricity, oil, or gas in the event of a point-specific disruption. For example, it is known that energy movements to certain regions of the country are limited by transfer system bottlenecks, and those potential choke points in the system could be addressed. Another classic strategy is to increase energy storage capacities and electricity system reserve margins in order to add backup capabilities in existing systems in case of emergencies.

THE CHALLENGES AHEAD

One challenge, of course, is that most of the strategies to reduce energy systems vulnerability are expensive; and energy is only one of a number of sectors subject to terrorism, not to mention cross-cutting national concerns not specific to sectors, such as threats to urban areas. For instance, how much should be spent on energy system protection versus, say, bioterrorism protection? Another challenge is that the security sensitivity of some of the discussions limits prospects for engaging the full range of intellectual resources in coming up with innovative solutions. Still another challenge is that energy system components other than electricity are largely the responsibility of the private sector, and it is unclear how broader social concerns would be incorporated in these cases. In any event, we know that issues in selecting and implementing strategies for the near term include institutional roles (such as the federal government, state and local governments, utilities, and private firms), particular regional vulnerabilities, costs (including opportunity costs), and time frames (what is urgent now versus what can be scheduled two years or five years from now).

In some ways, the more interesting issues for the research community in general, and geography in particular, lie in looking beyond current vulnerabilities—so focused on operational strategies and security considerations—toward vulnerability reduction in the longer term. Compared with what we have now, how might a national energy infrastructure be developed ten years from now, or thirty years from now, that meets national needs at least as well, but is much less subject to impacts from terrorist acts than at present?

Most of the answers are grounded in questions of spatial pattern optimization and nature-society balance, areas where geographers have much expertise to contribute. One familiar argument, for instance, is that a distributed energy system (with energy production and storage geographically decentralized) is more resilient to supply disruptions of just about any type (Lovins and Lovins 1982), because it reduces reliance on a few location-specific capacities and reduces dependence on movement systems that are vulnerable to disruptions. Because this strategy can be related to other possible benefits of taking advantage of local resource endowments and local potentials for integrated energy systems (like combined heating and power), it has considerable appeal, although it can mean foregoing economies of scale. This argument is one that is used to call for the increased use of renewable sources of energy.

Other strategies could focus on technological changes rather than spatial pattern changes. Some types of possible technology breakthroughs, such as carbon sequestration and/or near-ambient-temperature superconductivity, could transform energy resource and technology choices. Still others could focus on consumer behavioral choices, to ask consumers to use less energy and to adopt conservation methods to reduce demand.

In general, however, energy infrastructure strategies must consider full trajectories from resource extraction to energy use, including fuel processing, conversion, transportation, waste disposal, and end-use. For instance, progress in energy efficiency improvement will reduce vulnerabilities in energy supply infrastructures by making lesser demands on them. United States national, regional, and local energy use is partly a function of how we choose to structure our activities geographically. In this sense, reducing vulnerabilities of the U.S. national energy infrastructure to possible terrorist actions in the longer term is rooted in choices that we make, and policies that we adopt throughout our economy and society, not just in the energy sector alone.

5.3

TRANSPORTATION AND COMMUNICATION LIFELINES DISRUPTION

HARVEY J. MILLER

ONE OF THE MANY LESSONS from 9/11 is that terrorism is not just about terror. Terrorism is also an attempt to disrupt the daily lives of noncombatants to achieve political objectives. Physical or virtual networks that are vital to health, safety, comfort, and economic activity are called *lifelines* (Platt 1995). The complete or partial failure of even a limited number of lifelines can have a major impact on economic productivity as well as making peoples' daily lives more difficult and in some cases nearly impossible. This is not just a matter of convenience. There are members of society with limited resources or other economic, social, and demographic constraints, whose very livelihoods depend on reliable functioning of such lifelines. The population explosion of the past two centuries combined with high rates of urbanization means that effective public transit and road networks are indispensable. Increased mobility on a daily or weekly basis, or over the course of a lifespan results in an enhanced reliance on communications networks (physical and virtual) in order to conduct daily activities and maintain relations in business, social, and family settings. The negative impacts of lifeline disruptions on economies, personal finances, and lives can be so invasive that the terrorists' political ends often are achieved as effectively as through the direct use of force.

Transportation and communication lifelines are among the critical networks required for moving material, people, and information among locations distributed in geographic space (Platt 1995). The criticality refers to their role as an essential foundation for the relatively plentiful and stable supply of food, consumer goods, and information. To disrupt them produces ripple effects not only in the region where it occurred, but extending outward to the nation and the world. The best example of this was the halting of all commercial air traffic in the United States in the few days after 9/11 and its worldwide impact in terms of travel disruptions and economic losses.

Since lifelines are so central to the functioning of modern society, yet are so fragile, it is important to understand their vulnerability to planned and unplanned disruptions. Lifeline vulnerability refers to the susceptibility of a system to incidents that cause considerable loss of service (Berdica 2000). Understanding lifeline vulnerability can lead to: 1) better protection strategies by identifying particularly vulnerable components of the network (and the benefits and costs of reinforcing those components); 2) improved strategies for recovery from disruptions (by identifying consequences and magnitudes, and effective mitigation strategies); and 3) enhanced support for long-term design and planning and related land-use systems that are less vulnerable.

INDICATORS OF LIFELINE VULNERABILITY

Many approaches have been used to measure lifeline vulnerability but most can be grouped into two major categories: performance based indicators (network reliability and network performance); and user based indicators (accessibility). These are described briefly below.

Network Reliability and Network Performance

Network vulnerability is the susceptibility to disruptions that can cause considerable reductions in network service, or the ability to use a particular network link or route at a given time (Berdica 2000). An important aspect of service is the ability to use a lifeline at a certain place and time. Another aspect of network reliability involves the consequences of disruption, that is, reductions in service. Networks that cannot quickly recover from a disruption with minimal reduction in service are deemed more vulnerable than those whose recovery is faster and with less overall disruption. For example, a transportation network that concentrates flow through a small number of links (such as the bridges and tunnels connecting Manhattan to the rest of the New York metropolitan area) is more vulnerable than a more fully connected network, since there are fewer choices for rerouting traffic if one or more of these "bottleneck" links fail.

Most analyses of network vulnerability use the related concept of reliability or adequate serviceability at a given time. Network reliability theory treats network arcs and nodes as having a random probability of failure. Network reliability also depends on flow and congestion within the network. Since urban transportation networks are increasingly saturated, localized disturbances (such as a traffic accident) can propagate widely through the network causing system-wide delays. There are several ways to estimate reliability, including the probability that an origin-destination pair remains connected by a route after component failures, or that the time required for traveling between the origin-destination pair does not exceed a maximum limit.

Network performance approaches monitor or simulate network flows and evaluate their behavior in response to real or simulated disturbances. They are being used more often now, than in the past, due to the deployment of intelligent transportation systems for monitoring flows, and the availability of dynamic methods for simulating variable time flows. Network performance measures include travel time, travel rate (travel time divided by segment length), and delay rate (actual travel rate minus desired travel rate) (Pratt and Lomax 1996).

Accessibility

Accessibility is a fundamental concept in human geography. Accessibility measures the ability of individuals to participate in activities in space and time, and the use of transportation and communication technologies to achieve this participation. Accessibility is a much broader concept than serviceability, and views vulnerability as susceptibility to substantial reductions in space-time autonomy, or the freedom to participate in events distributed in space and time. The concept recognizes that transportation and communication are derived demands and exist not for their own sake, but to help people accomplish other activities in space and time. Loss of accessibility greatly impacts abilities to earn a living, access health care, conduct parenting activities, or maintain social relations. For example, survey evidence suggests that time spent driving reduces community involvement and volunteerism (Putnam 2000). Network-centric performance-based measures do not capture these potentially widespread and devastating effects of lifeline disruption since they view the network as detached from the context of human activities.

MEASURING THE HUMAN DIMENSIONS OF LIFELINE DISRUPTIONS

Time geography is a powerful and sensitive framework for analyzing accessibility in space and time. Two fundamental concepts are the space-time path and the space-time prism (Hägerstrand 1970). The space-time path traces an individual's movement in geographic space and world time over any time scale (from hours to years). The prism demarcates possible locations for the space-time path during a travel episode, given a time "budget" for travel and the maximum travel velocity allowed by the transportation system. Figure 5.3.1 illustrates a space-time path (top half) and a simple space-time prism (bottom half) where the origin and destination are coincident and with stationary activity time not considered (time spent at a doctor's office, for example). The prism geometry is more complex with non-coincident anchoring locations and with stationary activity time. A related con-

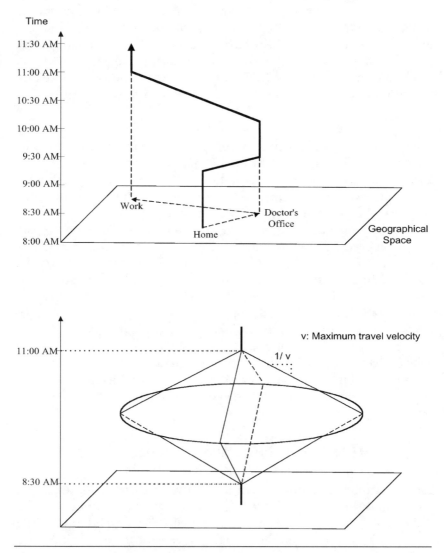

FIGURE 5.3.1 Space-Time Paths and Prisms; Top half—a space-time path (based on Wu and Miller 2001); Bottom half—space-time prism.

cept from activity theory is a space-time pattern. This is an allocation of a limited time budget (minutes of a day, hours of a week) for certain activities in space and time (such as grocery shopping, travel to work, Internet surfing). Space-time paths, prisms, and patterns can be used in two ways to assess lifeline vulnerability: direct losses of space-time autonomy and induced changes in space-time patterns.

Loss of Space-Time Autonomy

The prism can assess directly, the convergence between space and time as a function of transportation network configuration, travel velocities, scheduling constraints, and network congestion. Existing techniques are available for analyzing prisms based on travel in continuous space, or within specific transportation networks (Burns 1979, Forer 1998, Miller 1991, 1999, Wu and Miller 2001). These techniques can be extended to lifeline vulnerability analysis by examining changes in the prism before and after a simulated transportation or disruption.

Changes in Space-Time Patterns

By definition, a lifeline failure requires fundamental changes in peoples' lives. Another strategy for analyzing lifeline vulnerability is measuring changes in the spatial and temporal distribution of activities induced by network disruption. This strategy would analyze changes in space-time paths and patterns at an individual level in response to real or simulated failures. This method would require tracking and recording of the space-time paths before, during and after a planned disruption.

The disruption events that drive this type of empirical analysis could be large-scale transportation construction projects such as the "Big Dig" in Boston or the I-15 reconstruction in the Salt Lake Valley. These large-scale transportation projects produce impacts that approach the scale of major terrorist attacks (see Issue Box 5.3) Since simulation systems require individual space-time diary data as inputs to infer representative activity paths and patterns, it is important to develop location-aware technologies or intelligent transportation data collection systems to acquire them. There is a wide range of emerging dynamic flow and simulation approaches that link space-time activity paths and patterns to network performance in order to understand how people will respond and adjust to disruptions (Weiss 1999). Activity theory also provides guidance on how these adjustments occur (Golledge and Stimson 1997).

ISSUE 5.3
Network Disruption, Time, and Lives:
The I-15 Reconstruction in the Salt Lake Valley

Many cities and regions in the United States are experiencing transportation network disruptions caused by major construction projects. These construction projects can have serious impacts on people's lives and livelihoods. During 1997–2001, 16.5 miles of Interstate 15 in Salt Lake Valley, Utah was expanded from six lanes to ten. Additional congestion caused by the project generated an average of 15 minutes delay per trip. This means that a regular commuter on I-15 lost more than 500 hours during the four-year project. While commuters are expected to enjoy savings in time in the post-construction era, they will not "break even" until 2010, eight years after project completion (McCann et al. 1999). The I-15 construction corridor also experienced a substantial rise in traffic accidents and fatalities due to the shift of traffic from the highway to surface streets. Accidents on some streets increased as much as 300 to 500 percent. In unincorporated Salt Lake County alone, the number of traffic fatalities increased from 202 in 1996 to 315 in 1997 (Horiuchi 1997).

TIME GEOGRAPHY AND INFORMATION TECHNOLOGY

Accessibility is a concept that is traditionally based on movement in physical space. However, activities are increasingly disconnected from geographic space as a result of the increased use of information technologies (IT) (Couclelis and Getis 2000). Time geography can be extended to encompass IT-based virtual interaction as well as physical movement (Adams 2000). Unlike most accessibility measures, time geography is sensitive to emerging perspectives that view time as the scarce commodity of the information economy and accelerated modern lifestyles (Goldhaber 1997, Gleick 1999).

Embedding space-time vulnerability measures within a decision or policy process requires methods for supporting the exploration and comparison of vulnerability scenarios. A spatial decision support system allows analysts, decision makers, and stakeholders to develop, execute and assess vulnerability scenarios. This requires integrating a space-time prism or activity modeling system with solution exploration and comparison techniques. Geographic Information Systems (GIS) software supports such spatial database management, in addition to spatial-temporal query functions, and geographic visualization tools (Armstrong et al. 1986, Jankowski 1995).

CONCLUSION

Transportation and communication disruptions immediately following the 9/11 attacks clearly illustrate the dependence of our society on transportation and communication lifelines. Lifelines provide convenient opportunities for terrorists to seriously affect economies and lifestyles from the local to the global. In this way, they rank among the nation's most important infrastructure. Analyzing and understanding vulnerability to disruptions in lifelines leads to improved protection, mitigation, and recovery strategies. Among the techniques used for analyzing lifeline vulnerability, accessibility and time geographic approaches recognize the nature of transportation and communication as derived demands within a broader human activity context. This can allow more sensitive analyses of lifeline disruption on daily lives than methods that examine impacts only on the networks. Spatial decision support and GIS software, as well as digital geospatial and human activity data, can make this mode of analysis feasible, as well as understandable to policy analysts and decision makers.

The events of September 11, 2001 exposed not only our vulnerability to lifeline disruption, but also our lack of knowledge about the relationships between these networks and human activities. There is little fine-grained, scientific knowledge on how critical transportation and communication networks affect daily lives, and the urban dynamics that emerge from the interplay of individual activities in space and time. Gaps in scientific knowledge about the interrelationships between human activities and transportation/communication networks are disturbing since these are also at the heart of transportation science and urban theory. The relationship between individual activities and connectivity in space and time is also central to policy questions surrounding urban livability and sustainability policy (National Research Council 2002b).

There are research and development frontiers where progress will advance not only our understanding of lifeline vulnerability, but also help create more livable and sustainable communities that are responsive to peoples' daily lives. What is required are new data collection protocols and methods that exploit advances in information technologies, and position-aware technologies such as the global positioning system, intelligent transportation systems, and location-based services. Theories are needed as well as models that have detailed, individual-level linkages between transportation and communication lifelines, the organization of activities in space and time, and the interplay of these activities in creating lifeline demands and urban dynamics. Also required are enhanced versions of the space-time path, prism, and other time geographic constructs that can be disconnected from geographic space and referenced within cyberspace (the information space created by networked information technologies). Finally, researchers and developers need to create user-friendly GIS and spatial decision support tools to help emergency managers, transportation planners, and other officials to use these advanced, individual-level theories and models in real-world applications. The discipline of geography, with its established and emerging traditions of time geography and geographic information science, is well suited to make major contributions to these essential research frontiers.

5.4

ECONOMIC ASSESSMENT OF UNEXPECTED EVENTS

GEOFFREY J. D. HEWINGS AND YASUHIDE OKUYAMA

THE DAMAGES AND LOSSES FROM unscheduled events, such as earthquakes, floods, or other major natural disasters, have significant impacts on a region's economy. Demand for instantaneous damage estimates, in addition to estimates of the economic impacts of longer-term recovery and reconstruction, arise almost immediately after such events. Most analytical models of urban and regional economies, however, cannot handle these unscheduled and significant changes, since, at best, they assume incremental changes in systems over time, and the models usually are created under the assumptions of equilibrium prevailing in markets (in other words, that excess demands will be zero). The consequences associated with disaster events are multifaceted and include damages on both the demand and supply sides. The difficulties with impact analysis of unscheduled events include: 1) disentangling the consequences stemming *directly* and *indirectly* from the event; 2) deriving possibly different assessments at each spatial level—cities, region, and nation (Hewings and Mahidhara 1996); and 3) evaluating the reaction of households, which is poorly understood at this time (West and Lenze 1994).

The events of September 11, 2001 pose an additional problem, for there is little or no history upon which to draw. This is unlike other extreme events, where there is some experiential base (normally some time series) around which the event could be framed and the impact gauged. West and Lenze (1994) claimed that the sophisticated regional impact models requiring precise numerical input had to be reconciled with imperfect measurements of the damages, and they proposed a systematic way to estimate these impacts from the available data. Yet as others note, impact assessment of unscheduled events is an inexact science (Hewings and Mahidhara 1996), so that scenario simulations or sensitivity analyses often suffice given the uncertainty of available data.

PRIOR EXPERIENCE IN ESTIMATING ECONOMIC IMPACTS

The Regional Economics Applications Laboratory (REAL) has conducted a number of analyses of the economic impacts of unexpected events over the past fifteen years. Some of these studies are reviewed here to highlight analytical issues and challenges that arose in conducting such analyses.

The Chicago Flood of 1992 occurred when the old underground system of tunnels (that were constructed beneath the Chicago river and used to provide access to the early skyscrapers for moving coal in and taking garbage out) was penetrated inadvertently, resulting in the flooding of basements of the majority of buildings in the Loop. This downtown area was evacuated and several buildings were closed for days, including the stock and commodity exchanges. REAL estimated the losses at around $500 million a few days after the event; at the end of the year, a more formal assessment revealed the true damage value to be in the neighborhood of $350–400 million. To place REAL's estimation accuracy in context, another group estimated infrastructure damage at close to $1 billion right after the event, but this was lowered to $120 million at the end of the year (Crains 1992). It has to be noted that the media contributed to the inflation of the economic estimates, rounding up numbers with impunity (see Issue 5.4).

The following year, REAL assessed the damage in Iowa from the 1993 flooding of the Mississippi river. At the end of 1993, the state of Iowa GNP was *higher* than the long term forecast made from runs of an econometric-input-output model of the state's economy that we constructed in 1992! In the evaluation of unexpected events, it turned out that the infusion of state and federal relief dollars, insurance, and other payments stimulated a boom in construction activity. While the negative effects of the flooding were very real, they were concentrated spatially. This meant that many firms in diverse parts the Iowan economy benefited from this construction expansion.

The results for Iowa suggested that a more extensive analysis of unexpected weather and climate events might shed light on the degree to which these findings could be replicated elsewhere (Hewings et al. 2000). Using an econometric technique known as intervention analysis (Enders 1995), which simply uses dummy variables to test for

breaks in a time series, the methodology explored the impact of selected disaster events on the state economies where they occurred focused on the significance of changes in gross state product (GSP) (see
Table 5.4.1). With one exception—California—the results supported
the null hypothesis that the events were insignificant in altering the
growth of GSP (see Table 5.4.2). However, the listed losses were sustained and the disaster relief payments were made in a relatively concentrated time period (over several months). This suggests that annual
time scales may be too insensitive to capture the shorter-term disruptive effects from these extreme weather and climate events. If one assumed that the annual growth occurred evenly each quarter, in Illinois
for example, and the 1993 flood disrupted activity for one quarter,
then federal payments assume a much greater role—over 15% of a
quarter's GSP growth—in the economy. This finding suggests that the
time-scale of analyses should be reduced from annual to quarterly or

TABLE 5.4.1 Weather and Climate Extremes, States with Sizeable Losses, and
Federal Payments and Years of Payment

Event	Dates	States Affected	Federal Payments	Years of Payments
Flood	1982–1983	California	$120m	1983
Severe drought	1988–1989	Illinois	$870m	1988–1989
		Iowa	$921m	1988–1989
		Nebraska	$523m	1988–1989
Hurricane Hugo	1989	North Carolina	$63m	1989
		South Carolina	$389m	1989
			$9m	1990
Hurricane Andrew	1992	Florida	$1.6b	1992
			$41m	1994
			$151m	1995
		Louisiana	$148m	1992
			$2m	1993
Midwest floods	1993	Illinois	$630m	1993–1994
		Iowa	$1.7b	1993–1994
		Missouri	$1m	1993–1994
Superstorm	January 1993	New York	$55m	1993
Flood	May 1997	North Dakota	$59m	1997
Floods	1996–1997	California	$69m	1996–1997

TABLE 5.4.2 Summary of Significance Tests for Alterations in GSP Growth after Specific Disaster Events

State	Error tolerance	Significant (Yes/No)
California	7.6%	Yes
Florida	51.4%	No
Illinois	53.3%	No
Iowa	64.6%	No
Louisiana	31.3%	No
Missouri	42.0%	No
Nebraska	91.6%	No
New York	99.3%	No
North Dakota	92.6%	No
North Carolina	35.6%	No
South Carolina	98.7%	No

monthly, and that the appropriate geographic scope should likewise be directed to the county or multi-county level.

A further suggestion might be to conduct appropriate peer analysis. This approach is needed to separate out the effects of the disaster/recovery from general trends in the economy. This is accomplished by a comparison of the affected region to one or more peer regions in which no disaster occurred. Peer analysis attempts to identify "sister regions" based on their economic characteristics, growth rates, relative location, and demographic trends. Again, this analysis is most appropriate at the sub-state level.

REAL has engaged in earthquake-related analyses as well, using input-output analysis to estimate the effects of damages on the economy, the increase in economic activity associated with the reconstruction demand, and their interregional effects. In January 17, 1995, a major earthquake (the Great Hanshin Earthquake) hit the second largest population, industrial, and commercial region of Japan. More than 6,000 people were killed by this event, 300,000 people were left homeless, and the region's economy was devastated (Okuyama et al. 1999). The impacts from this event spilled over from the damaged region to other regions, and influenced the nation's economy as a whole. In constructing a model of the Japanese economy, we found that about 53% of income in the Kinki region (where the earthquake occurred) was generated by demand in the rest of Japan, while 17% of the total income in Japan was generated by demand in the Kinki region. The damage impact assessment was equivalent to 2% of Japanese GNP and

11% of the region's (Kinki) gross regional product (GRP). Further, the impact on the rest of Japan (in volume terms) was greater than in Kinki, highlighting the role and importance of interregional trade. One of the major actors in the system was the role of consumer spending; delays in spending turned out to be critical as consumers, hesitant about job recovery in an economy already in recession, delayed purchases of major items (Okuyama et al. 1999).

As Miyao (1995) suggested, the decreased value of wealth, the decrease in consumption as a result of (short term) personal depression, or the increase in layoffs and unemployment as the consequences of events may have had significant effects throughout the economy. These are certainly issues that resonate in the aftermath of the terrorist attacks in the United States.

IMPLICATIONS AND CHALLENGES AHEAD

What have we learned from these experiences and what challenges lie ahead? First, the magnitude of the initial disaster impact is not a good guide to either the short-term or long-term economic impacts. Large losses associated with climate and weather events were "lost" in the overall macro growth of state economies. On the other hand, even apparently small events can generate enormous economic impacts. In 2000 and 2001, REAL estimated the impact of gas price hikes on the Chicago regional economy and assumed there would be a redirection of $10/week/household in Chicago from the usual array of purchases (clothes, food, entertainment) to gasoline. Over the course of a year, this would create a loss of $1.2 billion in the local economy because gasoline expenditures generate a smaller ripple effect in contrast to those associated with other consumption expenditures. The loss is equivalent to almost 1.5 days of the Chicago region's gross product.

Some of the major analytical challenges ahead can be summarized into three broad areas: appropriate spatial scale, temporal disaggregation of models, and model treatment of economies as single units, not networks. No one spatial scale is preferable, instead economic impacts need to be traced at a variety of geographies to reflect different priorities. The modifiable areal unit problem and some of the proposed solutions to it would seem to be in great demand here since some impacts will be heavily concentrated spatially while others will be more diffused. Using just one set of spatial units may tend to distort the magnitude of some impacts. Within a matter of hours, the major trunk electricity lines were restored after the Kobe earthquake; restoration of other infrastructure links took much longer, and restoration of the economy even longer still. The space-time processes associated

---

ISSUE 5.4
The Media and the Disaster Loss Numbers Game

A good example of the media's role in inflating damage estimates is the economic impact of power losses during the 1999 heat wave in Chicago. Professor Hewings was called by the news media to provide veracity for the estimate of the losses amounting to $500 million. He pointed out that this figure represented 0.5 days of the Chicago metropolitan economy's Gross State Product, and thus was clearly inflated, excessively so. Nevertheless, the number was widely reported in the local news media, and on national television news that evening without any perspective or context as to what these numbers actually represent. Disasters generate expectations of significant economic loss, otherwise we wouldn't label them as disasters. But, as noted in the Iowa flood case, disaster recovery efforts often create significant (and positive) economic impacts as well. However, the former are widely reported, while the latter are rarely deemed newsworthy.

---

with the recovery pose major challenges to the economic base, for example, the impact of consumer spending (Figure 5.4.1). U.S. producers learned a valuable lesson from the Japanese earthquake experience and within days of September 11, 2001, U.S. automobile dealers were offering enticing deals and lower interest rates to encourage consumption. The result was that consumer spending on automobiles jumped over 20% in one month.

The interregional component is really critical as the 9/11 terrorist attack illustrated. The event itself was spatially isolated in three places (New York City, Washington, D.C., and in western Pennsylvania), yet it had a profound impact on other parts of the country outside these immediate areas. Decreases in transportation costs radically changed the geography of production, so much so that now the average establishment has a wider geographic market search for inputs and for its products (Parr et al. 2002). Regions continue to hollow out (Hewings et al. 1998), a process where dependence on the local markets as sources of inputs and as the location of consumption of locally produced products decreases, thereby increasing interregional interdependence. A complex interplay between changing ownership of establishments, economies of scale and scope variety of products produced resulted in greater intrastate specialization within sectors, while the macro structure of these economies became more similar. As a re-

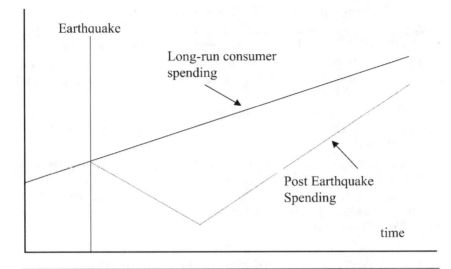

FIGURE 5.4.1 Stylized Representation of the Impact of an Unexpected Event on Consumer Spending

sult, trade is now dominated by intraindustry exchanges rather than interindustry ones, with a fragmented landscape of production across many locations. The closing of the Mexican border after September 11, 2001 seriously disrupted automobile production in the United States and Canada as assembly lines were forced to halt—one of the unanticipated consequences of just-in-time production supply chains. Many rental car companies announced that they might not buy new (2002) vehicles. These sales accounted for 12% of General Motors' production and represented 390,000 units overall. As an example of the interregional impact, the loss of just one percent of auto production in Michigan could lead to a loss of 1,500 jobs in Illinois, and 33,000 jobs in the United States as a whole even though the primary locus of the impact was initiated by events in New York and Washington, D.C.

With the exception of some recent work by Dobkins and Ioannides (2001), very little analysis is directed toward understanding how changes in one metropolitan region affect others. For example, will the losses in New York result in gains in Chicago, Los Angeles, or Detroit? Interestingly, one year after the 9/11 attack, it appeared that New Jersey was the major beneficiary, outside of the state of New York, in terms of the relocation of economic activity formerly in downtown Manhattan. To what degree are regions complements or competitors across a broad spectrum of industrial activity and to what extent is interstate trade now generated by external to the U.S. trade?

Some (admittedly crude) initial estimates for the Chicago region suggested losses approaching $1 billion in the month after September 11, 2001 (= 1.5 days GRP). The closure of the airports was the major cause, which prevented business and leisure travelers from accessing the region. Hotel occupancy rates in the single digits during this time were not unusual, however.

In the longer term, analyses need to once again explore the spatial economic impacts of reinvestment in military expenditures and how the increase in security-related spending manifests itself across regional economies of the United States. Regions that benefited significantly from the redirection of government expenditures from defense to non-defense spending in the 1990s will be the ones most affected by a return to earlier distribution patterns, which were more influenced by defense expenditures.

AN AGENDA FOR ECONOMIC SECURITY

First, there needs to be a broad-based assessment and measurement of alternative economic structures and interdependence, which centers on economic security, including issues such as renewable energy, food safety, increased inspection of international commerce, and so forth. These impacts, each of which would require a change in the way production is organized, as well as its cost, have a variety of spatial and sectoral consequences whose ultimate effects would be difficult to forecast a priori.

Second, there is likely to be a shift in priorities for some business location decision making. Consider that in the 1970s and 1980s, cheap labor and locations in right-to-work states dominated these decisions; in the 1990s quality and availability of skilled labor (a region's occupational capital) became a major issue. Will security became an important component of the location decision-making matrix in this century? How will this affect the competitive advantage of cities? Will this shift the trade-off between accessibility (central city) and quality-of-life/security concerns (suburban/rural areas)?

Finally, there is a need to rethink the role of government. In good times, small/no government is viewed positively, but in times of crisis, the complaint seems to be: "Where is the government when we need it? Can we achieve the level of security we seek while reducing taxes?" The events of September 11, 2001 created a stronger need for strategic information on the *spatial* structure and functioning of economic systems, but how can this information be assembled and used (for instance, by scholars) while protecting against the potential for misuse by terrorists? This is one of our great geographical challenges in the future.

5.5

ESTIMATING POPULATIONS AT RISK

JEROME E. DOBSON

TERRORISM AND REGIONAL CONFLICTS now have joined natural disasters and technological accidents as ubiquitous threats that can strike anywhere on earth and impact areas as large as a whole region or as small as a neighborhood, city block, or single building. For first responders and humanitarian agencies, population estimates are essential for mission planning in order to determine how many emergency personnel to send, how much temporary shelter to provide, and what types and quantities of emergency supplies are needed. Over-estimates cost time and money. Under-estimates cause unnecessary suffering and may cost lives. The first need is to estimate how many people are potentially at risk, usually before it is feasible to determine how many people actually are affected.

To meet this urgent global need, dramatic progress must be made to improve methods and techniques applicable to population geography. Geographic analysis, increasingly based on modern Geographic Information Systems (GIS) and satellite remote sensing, is essential for improving estimates of populations at risk and models of disaster scenarios employing these estimates.

POPULATION GEOGRAPHY

One of the earliest maps ever found, a silk map from the second century B.C., records the human toll of war. The war had been raging for as long as thirteen years in the Ch'ang-sha Kingdom (Hunan Province, China) when the map was drawn. Beside some cities are notes: "35 families, all moved away," "108 families, none back;" and "now nobody" (Wilford, 2000:7–9) The map is a poignant reminder that estimating people at risk and counting actual victims were vital then, as they are now.

To understand the need for spatially and temporally precise population data, simply recall how desperate New York City's first responders were to know how many people were in the World Trade Center on the morning of September 11, 2001. No reliable estimate was available, however, because the U.S. Census, like most official censuses around the world, counts people where they sleep, not where they work, shop, or play. Furthermore, the Census Bureau's number would be for the entire enumeration unit (census block or tract) and include more than just the World Trade Center. Emergency managers had no choice but to reject the (nighttime) census block count (55 people in the large block containing the World Trade Center) and make educated guesses that turned out to be two to four times greater than the actual number of people at risk and the actual number of deaths.

GLOBAL COVERAGE

Global population has been characterized in three fundamentally different databases—LandScan developed by Oak Ridge National Laboratory (ORNL); the Gridded Population of the World by the Center for International Earth Science Information Network (CIESIN) at Columbia University; and the P-95 and Rural Cell Populations by the International Programs Center (IPC) of the U.S. Census Bureau. All have been used widely but appeal to different constituencies and communities.

For nearly 30 years, P-95 and Rural Cell Populations, funded by the U.S. Department of Defense (DoD), were used for estimating populations at risk in global warfare scenarios. With a spatial resolution of 20 arc minutes of latitude by 30 arc minutes of longitude (2,400 square kilometers at the Equator), the cell size was adequate for simulating large-area threats such as nuclear fallout.

The LandScan Global Population Database (Dobson et al. 2000, 2003), also funded by DoD, has been adopted by many government agencies (the U.S. DoD, U.S. Department of State, and the U.K. Ministry of Defense) and several agencies of the United Nations (World Health Organization, Food and Agriculture Organization, High Commission on Refugees, and ReliefWeb). It has become the de facto world standard for these governmental bodies for estimating populations at risk from terrorism, technological accidents, regional conflicts, and natural disasters. Real time applications included the accidental release of radiation from a nuclear power plant in Japan on September 30, 1999 and the horrendous flooding of Mozambique in March 2000. Hypothetical scenarios used for training ranged from biological agents wafting across a few city blocks to nuclear exchanges affecting whole regions.

The spatial resolution of the global LandScan database is 30 arc seconds of latitude by 30 arc seconds of longitude. That equals about 1 square kilometer per cell at the equator and grows finer toward the poles. LandScan represents a quantum leap in precision from the previous world standard (P-95 and Rural Cells), and was made possible by a remarkable jump in the public availability of global databases in the late 1990s, and recent advances in geographic information systems (GIS) (Dobson 2001). These modern GIS technologies are powerless, however, without traditional geographic analysis techniques. The best available aggregate census counts, provided by the International Programs Center of the U.S. Bureau of the Census, were distributed to LandScan cells through dasymetric interpolation, a cartographic modeling technique invented by John K. Wright of the American Geographical Society more than 65 years ago (Wright 1936).

LandScan provides a 24-hour ambient population estimate, undistinguished by nighttime, daytime, seasonal, or other mobility factors. LandScan's suitability for emergency management and humanitarian response derives from its database structure and spatial resolution, both of which were designed specifically to suit key software programs used by the U.S. military to project air plumes associated with chemical, biological, and nuclear releases. The LandScan project at ORNL continues to provide global population data online at no cost (Land-Scan1998 is no longer disseminated; LandScan2000 is at http://sedac. ciesin.columbia.edu/plue/gpw/landscan/; LandScan2001 is at http:// www.ornl.gov/gist/).

Another estimation model is the Gridded Population of the World (GPW), now in its second version (http://sedac.ciesin.columbia.edu/ plue/gpw). This product was originally developed to help study land use and land cover in relation to population densities. Each grid cell (2.5 degrees by 2.5 degrees) is 25 times larger than a LandScan cell. GPW includes more administrative units (127,105 compared to Land-Scan 2000's 69,350), many of whose digital boundary files are precise enough for georegistering with GPW cells, but not with the finer LandScan cells. GPW cells are of a uniform size for the whole world so that population density can be calculated through simple division. LandScan cells vary in size by latitude so that density calculations require a slightly more complex but readily available equation. The principal difference between the two population models is that GPW is a cartographic interpolation of population data only, while LandScan employs population data, distance to roads, slope, land cover, and nighttime lights.

GPW has been used to study the distribution of population density by altitude (Cohen and Small 1998), and in biodiversity hotspots

(Cincotta et al. 2000). The GPW was also used to estimate global populations at risk from volcanic hazards (Small and Naumann 2001) and from coastal hazards (Small et al. 2000; Nicholls and Small 2002).

CITY BLOCK RESOLUTION

Even finer resolutions than one square kilometer are needed for many types of disasters, especially those that affect urban areas. Daytime and nighttime population estimates at 3 arc seconds by 3 arc seconds (90 meters by 90 meters at the Equator) are possible for the United States due to the nation's established collection of high-resolution spatial databases (Dobson et al. 2003). Through dasymetric interpolation block-level Census 2000 populations (by age and sex characteristics) can be disaggregated to cells equivalent to downtown city block resolution for the entire countryside. In one study area consisting of 29 counties in Texas and Louisiana, for instance, less than 0.1% of city blocks are smaller than 3 arc seconds by 3 arc seconds, and most are substantially larger. Indeed, 89% of the land area exists in blocks even larger than the global LandScan cells (30 arc seconds by 30 arc seconds). Daytime populations can be estimated by adjusting for block-to-block worker flows, placing school-age children in elementary and high schools, keeping prisoners in prison, modeling traffic flows on streets and highways, estimating the number of "shoppers" in commercial areas, and retaining the rest in their census residences.

Global threats require city block resolution not just for the United States but also for any urban area. While it is technically feasible to generate a global population database at 15 arc seconds by 15 arc seconds resolution using currently available global databases, none have been done due to lack of funding and the belief by potential sponsors that the spatial resolution needs to be roughly equivalent to a city block or even finer. Hence, no global capability currently exists to estimate populations in buildings, city blocks, or neighborhoods smaller than 30 arc seconds by 30 arc seconds, or one square kilometer. There are no immediately anticipated breakthroughs in data availability that will support such spatial resolution worldwide, and daytime versus nighttime mobility factors are out of the question in all but a few advanced nations. Yet national and international organizations, especially the United Nations, conduct humanitarian missions anywhere in the world in response to such local incidents.

Faced with overwhelming need and the impossibility of producing a suitable global database, our best hope is to develop a technique that can be employed in real time once the location and extent of any given disaster or potential disaster is known. The problem can be decomposed into two parts: 1) estimating how many people are typically in each type of building by day or night; and 2) measuring how much floor space is available for occupation. That second component— measuring floor space through field observation, map analysis, or image analysis—is labor-intensive and prohibitive in its worldwide application. It can be done for specific locations where the disaster or potential disaster is known and the need is clear and compelling. The first part, however, must be done with forethought for large world regions.

The solution requires a revival and enhancement of methods used by settlement geographers principally from 1920 to around 1970. During that era, diverse geographical studies were made of building forms, types, and styles. For example, Albert Demangeon (1872–1940) examined vernacular dwelling designs, sometimes including detailed floor plans. Fred Kniffen (1901–1993) focused on characteristic folk styles of housing, barns, fences, and outbuildings. Kirk Stone (1914–1997) focused on the spatial organization of settlements. Of these three leading experts, Demangeon's observations of building designs came closest to the type of approach needed here. His purpose was different, however, and he did not measure the area of enclosed spaces, or calculate population densities.

IN-BUILDING RESOLUTION

To illustrate the need for extremely precise, in-building population modeling and analysis, consider the anthrax investigation in Washington, D.C. In November 2001, G. B. Curtis, a GIS analyst at the Centers for Disease Control and Prevention (CDC), was assigned to investigate the Brentwood Postal Facility, a central focus of the anthrax attack (Curtis et al. 2002). Curtis faced vexing administrative and technical problems typical of any new GIS endeavor, but he had to resolve them in days rather than weeks or months. When the chips were down, he and J. Devasundaram of ESRI, Inc. had to scan hardcopy floor plans, which were ragged and stained with handwritten notes from years of use. Their objective was to follow the movements of individual employees at the level of precision of office desks, passageways, and break areas. Eventually, they produced a precise database relating such movements to positive anthrax cases and positive and negative anthrax samples.

The global need for precise in-building information cannot be met with a global database. Instead, a better working arrangement among building proprietors, engineers, and emergency managers is needed. Fire inspections, for example, should routinely address provisions for the exchange of and the digital capture of building information, including floor plans and number of workers. This type of information would then be fed into any number of spatial decision support systems including those of evacuation and emergency response.

CONCLUSION

Global population geography has advanced dramatically in the past half decade, mainly by the availability of new global databases and GIS software capable of managing and analyzing huge volumes of data. When the input data for the original LandScan arrived at ORNL, for example, it was literally a "ton of data"—two palettes amounting to 2,086 pounds of CD-ROMs. War and terrorism demand finer spatial precision in population data and better understanding of mobility factors, at least to distinguish daytime from nighttime population distributions. The capability for estimating detailed population distributions worldwide has been proven. Now the research challenge is to advance the data collection, modeling, and analysis of population geography at finer spatial and temporal scales.

Of course, population distribution is only part of the answer; the other part is predicting threat distributions. Preparing for terrorism and its unavoidable consequences will require better tools for estimating direct impacts (such as explosions or poisonings) on people and the subsequent contamination of air, water, and food supplies. GIS already has proven its worth in environmental risk modeling, often considering "worst case" scenarios that pale by comparison to what happened on September 11, 2001. Now, those same tools must be applied to purposeful contamination of streams, reservoirs, wells, and public utilities, and purposeful disruption or contamination of the food chain from farmer to consumer.

For the geographic community as a whole, our greatest contribution will be to keep on doing what we have been doing all along, especially in regard to infrastructure. We will need to map and analyze communications networks, settlement forms, utility networks, and transportation networks to determine their vulnerabilities and to recommend changes. Ultimately, we will need to predict troubling scenarios of disruptions and consequences and to propose solutions. We will need to consider whole new geographies of scarcity covering natural resources (water, food, energy), industrial goods, and personal goods and services. We will need to collaborate with economists and others to anticipate the economic stress caused by changes in resources, policies, and behaviors. In the end, social change is inevitable, and we will need to collaborate with social scientists to help ease the transition. Already, concerns are being expressed for the loss of privacy and the personal freedoms that may follow, with the GPS tracking of individual humans as a prime example. It is imperative for geographers and the GIS community to weigh in on those issues that involve our technology.

5.6

RECREATING SECURE SPACES

RAY J. DEZZANI AND T. R. LAKSHMANAN

A PERSISTENT TREND IN THE MODERN ERA has been the increasing level and pace of economic, social, and cultural interactions within countries, and over time, between them. These interactions and exchanges have been made possible in recent times by the territorial state's provision (within their geography and across borders) of key public goods: law, order, "secure" interaction spaces, and physical and non-physical infrastructure networks, all of which facilitate interactions among social and economic actors (Braudel 1984, Lakshmanan 1993).

There are many recent innovations in physical infrastructure technologies (transport and communications), and in non-physical infrastructures (such as freer markets, new financial and professional management practices and international institutions) that facilitate interactions. These have helped reduce the frictions of time and distance in the control of resources across vast spaces and assisted in economic development. The level and variety of interactions make economic activities more efficient and productive and create *new* activities never before possible. This transformation appears in the form of globalization of markets and inputs, in the decentralization and networking of firms internally, and in their relationship to other firms. The resulting local networks—supplier, producer, financial, customer, technology—are leading to international networks of competition, exchange, and association, and can be viewed as the emerging dynamic "network society" (Castells 1996, 1997).

The resultant growth and development of the world economy are evident in the explosion of global trade, globally organized production systems, widespread economic growth, extensive exchange of ideas and practices, and a "borderless world". This cycle of increasing secure interaction spaces, complex and varied infrastructure networks, and the surge of technical and social innovations have indeed led to this dynamic network society with its long-term material improvements in economy and society.

Another aspect of the evolution of the dynamic global economy is that it is subject to periodic setbacks and backslidings, which occur when the quality of the key public goods noted earlier (security of interaction spaces and functionality of the transport, information, and financial networks across national and international territories) was threatened and eroded. These threats arrived in several forms: wars with territorial enemies, often deriving from security alliances and balance of power politics; and increasingly from "deterritorialized threats," ranging from transnational terrorism and proliferating weapons of mass destruction to environmental degradation and ethnic nationalism (O'Tuathail 1999).

Since contemporary transnational terrorism attempts to alter the functioning of the social fabric and bring about political change (Laqueur 1996), its actions serve to convert the basic supportive networks of our society into high risk spaces, rather than secure interactive ones. This paper examines the vulnerabilities of societal networks to terrorism and the necessary approaches to recreate secure interaction spaces.

NETWORK VULNERABILITIES FROM TERRORISM

The political events of the last decade since the dissolution of the former Soviet Union have altered the perceptions of state security to the degree that terrorism now appears to be the leading threat to national security in the early twenty-first century. The contemporary era is not unique. Terrorist threats historically have been directed at individuals, groups of individuals, or economic and military infrastructure such as the attacks upon politically elevated personages perpetrated by anarchists and budding nationalists between the late nineteenth century and the onset of the First World War. However, the nature of terrorism has changed significantly over the course of the twentieth century from anarchists and nationalists in the early part of the century; to leftist guerrillas in the middle; to right wing fundamentalist religious groups, conservative national and ethnic organizations, and anti-systematic/globalization movements in the later portion of the century (Laqueur 1996).

By definition, terrorism is purposeful only if it alters the functioning of the social fabric (Laqueur 1996). For terrorists desirous of reducing the functionality of a society, the multiplicity of physical and non-physical networks—which govern the efficient operation of national and global economies—offer crucial targets. Table 5.6.1 illustrates

TABLE 5.6.1 Illustrative Network Types and Vulnerabilities

Type (stocks)	Vulnerabilities
Road	Spatially extensive, less hierarchical network with distributed links and nodes where many alternate paths are available for rerouting. Links are less vulnerable than key intersections. Risk can vary spatially with inconsistencies in the road network complexity.
Air transport	Spatially hierarchical, concentrated hub-and-spoke link and node arrangements. As a result of resource concentration spawned by the hierarchical structure limited node alternatives ensure that the nodes/airports are less secure.
Pipelines	Spatially constrained networks resulting from large capital costs produce a lack of link route alternatives. As a result, the pipelines are extremely vulnerable. However, as flows in the pipeline are dependent on the pump stations for mobility, the node structures are also vulnerable. Geographic isolation from population centers may also contribute to elevated risk.
Rail	Spatially hierarchical and constrained networks with some redundancy where link concentration and complexity is great. Links are highly vulnerable in low-density areas. Conduits from the exterior to the interior of sovereign territorial States.
Sea Lanes	Networks with spatially distributed but hierarchical nodes or, port facilities. The links are nonphysical, flexible, and determined by ships course and destination. As such, links exhibit low vulnerabilities, though ships may be vulnerable, (especially cruise ships carrying passengers). However, ships may be effectively policed and secured. Port facilities are most vulnerable. However, it is also more cost effective to secure port facilities. Effective port policing may reduce several different infrastructure network vulnerabilities.
Fiber Optic/ Telecommunications	Spatially complex distributed networks with high levels of link and node (e.g., router/switchers) redundancies. Nodes are least secure.
Cellular/ Microwave	Spatially distributed nodes only. The nodes correspond to cell towers, which are vulnerable, but if destroyed do not threaten the loss of the network. Much redundancy.
Internet	Spatially distributed links (cable, fiber optic), and nodes routers/servers). Much network link redundancy ensures that the routers/servers/nodes are the least secure structures.
Financial	Spatially hierarchical networks consisting of telecommunications links and markets. The physical market places are most vulnerable as the linkages provide routing alternatives.
Logistical	Spatially distributed organizations of multi-modal transport structures which minimize the total cost of transportation.

many of these networks and their vulnerabilities to terrorism in the form of the elevated risk to flows of goods and people, of information, and of finance.

In general, the more hierarchical the network the greater the vulnerability it sustains from terrorist threats. The hub and spoke airport system in which air traffic is heavily routed through specific hub airports, provides an example of such heightened vulnerability. In contrast, less hierarchical and more spatially distributed networks (with considerable redundancies), such as roads and the Internet experience less vulnerability (Table 5.6.1).

The continued functionality and growing productivity of these physical and non-physical networks depends upon the low and steadily declining costs of economic and social interactions within countries and among countries. Terrorist attacks, or even the threat of an attack directed against either the population or a component of infrastructure, will invoke a defensive response from the state in the form of short-term layers of infrastructure protection, which increase the costs of interaction. If territorial space and infrastructure networks are subject to penetration and destructive attack by hostile non-territorial terrorist actors, the costs of protecting the networks and providing secure spaces will have adverse affects on social interaction costs and consequently on economic and social development. Further, the increasing perceptions of personal risk impose new costs to social and economic interactions.

As the geometry of networks exhibits both links and nodes, one way of accomplishing the creation of secure spaces is by protecting nodes, which is always more economically feasible than protecting links. Depending on the network node (such as airports for passenger travel or ports for shipping), protection is an initial and necessary condition for reducing vulnerability.

RECREATING SECURE NETWORK SPACES: THE STATE'S ROLE

A primary function of the territorial state is to secure internal regions for purposes of encouraging economic and social interaction among residents. A prerequisite for this is the state's provision of law, order, and secure social interaction spaces. Such public goods provide predictability in social and economic interactions and lower private social and economic interaction costs, facilitate flows of goods and information, and enhance socioeconomic interactions. Recent efforts to deregulate and privatize economic activities from government sponsorship also have promoted the social perspective that state territories and cross-border spaces were becoming more "secure" from outside threats. The increasing security in territorial and cross-border space has meant that infrastructures—financial, logistical, and institutional networks— can develop more readily in the globally-interconnected world to promote the efficient functioning of the national and global economies.

TERRORIST THREATS TO NETWORKS

The majority of threats during the past twenty years that affected the stability of the international nation state system or the security of component networks have come from sub-state, nonterritorial entities such as ethnic or national groups seeking political autonomy or antisystematic movements seeking greater economic representation in the increasingly global economy (see chapter 3). The current threats to state security are no different. The secure spaces created by the territorial states over the past twenty years were enhanced by the collapse of the former Soviet Union and led to a decade of international economic growth and prosperity.

The majority of external threats in the past 50 years had been derived from the Cold War geopolitical order, which polarized ideologies as well as the location and direction of any threat potential. However, the risk associated with the Cold War threats were known, were "ordered" according to the existing state structure of potential conflict (nuclear or conventional), and reflected the enlightened self-interest of the state vis-à-vis their respective populations, territories, and infrastructures and reflected the goal of national survival (Brams 1975, Stein 1990, O'Tuathail 1999, Powell 1999).

Today, global dangers are viewed, in practice, as a parade of nonterritorial enemies like terrorists, rogue states, nuclear-armed agents, and the like. When nonterritorial entities are arrayed against the power of a sovereign state, a wider range of strategies might be employed directly against the population, territory, or infrastructure of the state because of the desire to equalize the great power differential that exists between the territorial state and the nonterritorial players (such as terrorists). In general, this situation creates greater uncertainty regarding the actions/strategies of nonterritorial and terrorist groups, which in turn leads to amorphous and pervasive dangers, and a greater range of risks associated with security maintenance.

The following example provides a useful case in point. A major network target of terrorism has been the transport system. The first phase of airline hijackings in the 1960s led to public disillusionment and enhanced danger associated with airline travel. However, through the institutional establishment of air marshals, terminal security checks, and other risk-mitigating strategies, air travel security was reestablished by the early 1970s. Improved security, airline deregulation, and associated technological improvements led to a dramatic expansion of air passenger traffic starting in the 1980s. Airports and transport aircraft cabins once again were perceived as secure spaces. September 11, 2001 significantly changed the secure "spaces" of air travel (airport terminals, aircraft cabins, ancillary transport system spaces), into high risk "spaces" associated with the public's perception of an enduring threat. The threat and consequently the risk, are amplified by the uncertain nature of terrorist activities directed at these likely spaces.

While airline travel is the most noticeable example, other transportation vulnerabilities include port facilities and rail infrastructure. Both of these operate under low to moderate security levels. This is especially true at the ports, where seamless intermodal freight moves (with minimal, if any inspection) to support "just-in-time" and "lean production systems." Ports also can serve as conduits for the potential movement of weapons of mass destruction.

Virtual spaces, produced by Internet linkages, are much harder to threaten (but not impossible) owing to infrastructure redundancy, in addition to high levels of security and "hardening" of certain portions of the physical network (Table 5.6.1). As such, the servers and routing apparatus are most vulnerable, and are usually associated with institutions such as government agencies, national laboratories, and colleges and universities. The Internet presents a major risk avenue into territorial states by non-territorial and terrorist actors.

Power projection by nonterritorial actors does not occur through normal diplomatic or territorial state pathways, as no traditional or established structure exists to conduct negotiations. Many territorial states, such as Israel and the United Kingdom, exercise policies that actively prohibit negotiation with nonterritorial terrorist actors. Infrastructures such as media and the Internet may become increasingly useful to both territorial states and the nonterritorial terrorist actors as a means of information signaling among the parties involved.

RECREATING SECURE NETWORKS FROM TERRORISM

The threat to states from non-state violent actors (terrorists) is not a new phenomenon and dates back to the fifteenth century with the extensive and creative use of nonstate violent actors gainfully acting in the interests of territorial states competing for prestige, territory and hegemony. From a geographical perspective, nonstate actors performed tasks and exercised political options that were unavailable to the forces of traditional state actors, such as the regular armed forces. The ability to routinely violate territorial boundaries was not an option for the formal state actors. As such, non-state actors represented a minimal cost solution to territorial state governments because regular armed forces could not be employed and thus, reprisals would not be forthcoming. Similarly, nonstate actors also provided a minimum risk alternative to the forces of the states because if the goal was not achieved, the state simply denied knowledge of the action. In this way, no territorial state legally violated the territory and the sovereignty of another territorial state.

The Case of Piracy

Non-state actors could be engaged for either land or naval actions. Mercenary armies roamed Europe from 1400 to 1800, and privateers scoured the seas during the same period. In many cases, when the services of these nonstate forces were no longer required, they were disbanded and scattered. However, it is not surprising that piracy greatly increased during this time period. Indeed, piracy often served the needs of weaker states against stronger states, as was the case of England in its conflict with Spain in the sixteenth and seventeenth centuries. While the names of Drake, Frobisher and Grenville were hailed with honor in England, they were decried as pirates and terrorists by the Spanish King Phillip II.

Acts of piracy involved elements of the hijacking of ships and terror enacted through the murder, rape, and torture of civilians and the poor treatment of prisoners. These activities were considered to be legal privateering raids executed by state-sanctioned, but nonstate, forces. The English privateers exploited their advantage of nonterritoriality to the benefit of the English crown. Acts such as these can be described as officially sanctioned piracy (Ritchie 1986), analogous to contemporary state-sponsored terrorism. Within a short time, owing to a changing political climate between England and Spain, these same privateers had been renamed "pirates" and became an embarrassment to the English authorities who had previously exploited their services.

When it suited the interests of states to halt piracy, the patrol of the sea lanes by the navies of various cooperating states was organized. The elimination of pirates was achieved through a combination of reforms instigated by the territorial states taking action: 1) to create mechanisms that strengthened the central state; 2) against the nonterritorial means of conducting violent activities; 3); to destroy the markets where pirated goods could be traded; and 4) to improve and secure the major trade infrastructure of the day—the international sea lanes (Katele 1988, Thompson 1994).

Contemporary De-territoralized Threats

As contemporary technology—mechanical and informational—moves fast across borders accompanied by complex money flows and the availability of skilled and unskilled labor, a "borderless world" is emerging. While this borderless world is generally positive, it also holds many risks. Our vulnerability increases from terrorists and other violent actors who use our technology and informational capabilities to build black markets for weapons and launder money to support violence against our networks. Such social enemies as terrorists, nuclear outlaws, and violent fundamentalists need to be isolated, contained, and defeated.

Fundamentalism is a contemporary phenomenon, one that actively attempts to reorder society, reassert the validity of a tradition, and use traditional values in new ways in today's world with the aid of global technical and institutional means. While fundamentalism as a movement needs to be contained, it is important to recognize that it has its origins in real discontentment with the exiting world order experienced by ordinary people. Such discontentment arises from the tensions inherent in the globalization process, in the deeply disjunctive relationships among technological flows, vast money flows, and human movement across countries (Appadurai 2001), which differ significantly in levels of their physical, human, and institutional capital. While the tensions inherent in globalization process cannot be resolved completely, efforts to ameliorate them will likely address some root causes of the fundamentalist movement.

CONCLUDING COMMENTS

Our recent history is characterized by large-scale socioeconomic interactions of ever increasing variety and intensity. The explosion of these interactions within and among countries is possible by the progressive increase of secure interaction spaces and the infrastructure networks that facilitate them. The outcome is the emerging "network society," a surge in technical and social innovations, and a cycle of long-term material economic growth and social development.

Periodic threats to the security of the socioeconomic networks in a society arrive in many forms, most recently from terrorism. The resulting vulnerabilities vary among network types—the more hierarchically-organized (such as a hub airport) are more vulnerable than a distributed system with redundancies (such as the internet or a road system). These vulnerabilities reduce the security of social and economic interaction spaces, raise interaction costs, and brake the economic growth and social development of the affected nation. Given its mission of providing secure interaction spaces and lowering threats to its functional network systems, the state attempts to isolate, contain, and defeat terrorist threats—sometimes using a supplementary strategy of addressing some root causes of terrorism which originated in the tensions inherent in the globalization process.

CHAPTER 6

Bioterrorism

INTRODUCTION

Bioterrorism is a concern that is intrinsically geographic because its expressions are locationally specific. It happens because agents are released at particular locations, spread by particular spatial systems, and have their effect in particular regions. Research traditions in geography such as medical geography, and those related to such cross-disciplinary fields such as epidemiology, ecology, and agriculture have been valuable in analyzing public health issues (such as HIV/AIDS) (Gould 1993) and ecological health issues (such as foot and mouth disease) that are in some ways analogues for the effects of terrorism.

The papers in this chapter illustrate some of the potentials for elucidating dimensions of terrorism through geographic research and assessment. Two of the three papers, by Art Getis and Marilyn Ruiz, describe applications of geographic information science (GIScience) to decision support systems for mitigating impacts of bioterrorism attacks. The third, by Lisa Harrington, discusses particular vulnerabilities of agriculture and other food-related sectors to bioterrorism, in part because of the spatial concentration of many of those sectors in rural parts of the nation. Other geographical dimensions could have been illustrated as well, including the modeling of spatial diffusion processes both forward toward areas at risk, and backward to identify source areas of initial exposure. Because bioterrorism rarely has been the subject of geographic research, there are significant potentials for contribution now that the challenge has become so salient.

6.1

UNDERSTANDING BIOLOGICAL WARFARE

ARTHUR GETIS

IN THE BEST OF ALL WORLDS, differences among peoples would be negotiated and conflict would be settled peacefully. Although there have been some periods of well-intentioned international reconciliation of differences during the last 100 years, on the whole the record is abysmally poor. Currently, a number of countries, spurred by national or ethnic aspirations on the one hand and intransigence and control on the other, are stimulating explosive situations that could have devastating results. One of the threats to the human and environmental well being of the planet is biological warfare (BW), the use of biological agents as weapons that could cause disease and deaths in sufficient numbers to greatly impact a city or region. These include agents that have high potential for person-to-person transmission, are highly infectious, are generally available, can be produced in large quantities, and do not have a vaccine or have a vaccine available in limited supply (Borio and others 2002).

In terms of its potential for mass destruction, BW is generally deemed less of a threat than nuclear or chemical warfare. Nonetheless, it is important to survey every potential type of warfare to prepare for any eventuality in our quest for survival. Most of the academic disciplines have something to offer in this regard. It is easy to see that chemistry, for example, can tell us a great deal about chemical weapons and their possible effects on humans. The transportation sciences can inform us about the delivery of weapons, either for weapon supply centers or for direct attack. Epidemiologists and entomologists can explain the potential of using virus-laden insects as weapons of war. Geographers bring perspective, the use of mapping technologies, and spatial analytical techniques to the table of understanding of BW. Much, but not all, of this geographic knowledge is embodied in what is called the geographic information science (GIScience or GISc).

GEOGRAPHY AND BIOLOGICAL
WARFARE UNDERSTANDING

The geographers' perspective must be considered in conjunction with knowledge gained from the social sciences in general. This includes the understanding of culture, human activities for economic survival, and the growth and movements of populations. This type of knowledge allows for the fundamental assessment of political unrest, its roots, and directions. For example, to what extent does population pressure on resources affect the foreign policies of governments that desire to expand their borders or promote the emigration of their population? Which societies or terrorist groups are in a resource situation, both human and physical, to engage in or abet BW? Just as geographers understand the economics and environmental conditions that lead to poppy farming for the drug trade, so, too, are they able to study the environmental conditions conducive to the spread of malaria or smallpox.

Geographic information science is in a strong position to take up the battle against BW. No threat to human survival can be studied without the use of maps. In recent years, geographers have contributed in basic science and application to mapping technologies and innovative map use. Ordinary flat paper maps, while still important, cannot be easily manipulated for analysis; sent from control centers to front lines; viewed in multiple layers, sequentially, or by critical variables; adjusted for scale and distortions; updated in the field; used to immediately identify small objects on the earth's surface and locate them by coordinates; used as a substitute for radar imagery, which is able to cut through atmospheric and other environmental barriers (night, tree cover, shadows, smoke and haze, and so on); and formed in such a way that spatial analyses can be carried out. All of these shortcomings are mitigated by the use of computer-based technology, either created by geographic information scientists or used to advantage by them.

The analytical capabilities of the geographer have much to do with the analysis of patterns on maps. For example, to determine whether the West Nile Virus or anthrax was introduced into the eastern United States as a biological weapon, it is critical to assess the relationship between origin sites and people who have become infected. In addition, the path of biological weapon diffusion must be recorded on appropriate maps in order to thwart its spread. Techniques of analysis that include spatial cluster identification, diffusion simulation, and exploratory statistical visualization and description can be used to trace the progress of the threat agent and to assist in control (Getis and Ord 1996, Kitron 1998, Morrison et al. 1998).

THE GEOGRAPHIC NATURE OF BIOLOGICAL WARFARE

The potential BW threat agents include a wide variety of bacteria, toxins, and viruses (McGovern et al. 1999). Some bacteria are anthrax, cholera, and plague. The toxins include botulinum, various mycotoxins (molds), and staphylococcus (contaminated food). Viral agents include Ebola, hantaviruses, dengue, smallpox, malaria, and Rift Valley and yellow fevers. The reservoirs or vectors for these agents range over such things as contaminated water or soil, rodents, and mosquitoes. The viruses tend not to be lethal unless they are at their most virulent, causing hemorrhagic fever. Vaccines and successful treatments are available for the bacterial agents, but many of the viruses and toxins have no vaccine or successful treatment associated with them. Research on the natural habitats of the threat agents is continuing apace, but knowing where one can find, say, the fleas that cause plague in no way reduces the chances of the agent being spread by artificial means such as a weapon of war.

One of the characteristics of BW is that the perpetrators can escape long before the threat agent incubates and results in incapacitation and death. In most instances, the attacker need not seek natural habitats in order to gather bacteria, toxins, or viruses. Most of these are available from medical suppliers, germ banks, and university laboratories. Some agents can be grown in laboratories. The critical issue for the geographic information scientist is to attempt to understand how the agent could be disseminated and, once released, what paths it will follow and what is the potential damage from the attack.

A frivolous example may make the point: viremic mosquitoes would not be released nor would their release be BW effective unless opportunities for oviposition (egg laying) were available. A serious example is the use of aerosol generating devices mounted on planes or trucks that spray particles that can lodge in internal body cavities such as the lungs. Given the length of incubation period, which, except for the toxins, generally ranges from a few days to a few weeks, the populace may not know that it has been infected until days after the attack. The post–September 11, 2001 spate of anthrax infections helps to make the point.

The effectiveness of the release of any biological threat agent will be conditioned by the nature of the local environment. The elements of weather and climate play a huge role in this. Clearly, an ice cap environment is not conducive to the spread of these agents, while a windy, hot, and humid environment presents ideal conditions for the diffusion of most threat agents. Each agent has a symbiotic relationship with the environment. For example, the *sin nombre* hantavirus is carried by deer mice that are often found in the dry mid-latitudes at high elevations, but the mouse is far more numerous after particularly wet periods. The *Aedes aegypti* mosquito that transports the dengue viruses is only found in warm, moist areas where humans reside, since it nearly always feeds on humans (as opposed to animals or vegetation). If hundreds of infected mosquitoes were released, within a week a city could suffer thousands of cases of dengue and dengue hemorrhagic fever.

A rather dated study conducted by the World Health Organization (WHO 1970) estimated the number of casualties emanating from a hypothetical biological warfare attack on a city of 500,000. The simulation had 50 kilograms of each of seven threat agents deployed from an aircraft along a 2-kilometer line upwind of the city. The number of dead varied from 20% of the people in the case of anthrax to just a few hundred for Rift Valley fever. In the case of anthrax, the downwind reach of the agent was greater than 20 kilometers, while Rift Valley fever was localized to only the immediate vicinity of the attack. Fortunately, any attack on a city's water supply would be of limited effectiveness because of modern water purification methods, but this would not be the case in many developing countries.

GISCIENCE FOR BIOLOGICAL WARFARE MITIGATION

There are opportunities for GIScience mitigation at three stages in the spread of a biological weapon:

- The monitoring stage for gathering information on the likely locations for the preparation of an attack and the likely targets of such an attack.
- Forecasting the spatial and temporal extent of an attack.
- Developing transportation and supply strategies for bringing the attack under control and treating those affected. Basic activities include; 1) casualty treatment and evacuation, 2) the quarantine of affected areas and people, and 3) the restoration of infrastructure and service.

In the first stage, aerial photographs, remotely sensed imagery, and geospatial technologies are used to monitor the environment to produce the fundamental information needed to create maps that highlight risk zones. This basic information must be coupled with reliable information about the nature of the area in question, such as the land cover, population, and population density characteristics of areas at risk. Much of the value of GIScience in all stages involves quick response.

In stage two, high-speed simulations show the likely paths for disease spread. These would be based on information gathered not only from the remote sensors but also from detailed knowledge about the area. Data must be updated constantly. Clearly, technologists, including GIScientists, and disease experts must work together to monitor, track, and then treat the affected areas.

In stage three, during an emergency, there is a great demand for maps of all types. Maps of transportation systems would be basic to any effort to intervene in the disease diffusion process. Creating models of clustering and spread that take into account time lags between stages in disease diffusion would be critical to any attempt to control. All of these efforts must be transportable in the sense of relaying information quickly from one computer system to another. The question of interoperability and standardization between and among systems (see chapter 4) becomes a significant issue when one realizes that mapped information is much more technically complex than, say, a table, chart, or verbal document.

PUBLIC POLICY IMPLICATIONS
OF BIOLOGICAL WARFARE

To protect people from a terrorist plot to spread smallpox or anthrax, our society must be ready to act. Preparation is fundamental to any strategy of mitigation. We must develop centers that are in a position to gather and map data in an emergency mode. We must greatly supplement such institutions as the Centers for Disease Control and Prevention. Data gathering and mapping centers conveniently and safely located around the country (and the world) must be in direct contact with the disease control and transportation agencies. Experts on the environmental conditions extant in the various vulnerable parts of the country must be in direct contact with these mapping and disease control centers. Governmental agencies must be integrated into all such systems. There is a need for the integration of water, sewer, health, and other relevant data sets. Data sharing systems must be devised. We must be developing the most flexible and sophisticated analytical systems to create models of disease spread. It is imperative that governmental agencies support all of these efforts. Software must be developed and made available to all of those engaged in the control process.

At an early stage in the development of public policy initiatives, a bevy of conferences must be held so that the specialists in the fields mentioned begin the arduous task of learning how to communicate with each other. These conferences should result in the development of initiatives that bring together the expertise of specialists into centers whose main purpose is to prepare for and respond to emergencies.

6.2

BIOWEAPONRY AND AGROTERRORISM

LISA M. BUTLER HARRINGTON

USE OF BIOLOGICAL WEAPONRY dates back at least to Roman times, when attempts were made to pollute enemy water sources with rotting animal carcasses. During the last century, a variety of state defense agencies and terrorist organizations have conducted a wide array of research into potential bioweapons (Alibek 1999, Rogers et al. 1999, Whitby 2002). Bioweapons are an option not only for nations and large organizations, but also for small groups and individuals. Though the identity of the attacker(s) is unknown at present, the post-9/11 anthrax letter attacks could have been carried out by only one person.

Direct attacks against human populations present the greatest concern and fear, but there are other important targets for biological or chemical attack. Potential terrorist attacks against agricultural and food-related sectors are a major concern to those involved in these activities, to policymakers representing rural regions, and potentially to the nation's food supply. In rural agricultural areas there is a growing unease regarding the potential for attacks on livestock and crops. For example, a Dodge City, Kansas, newspaper ran an October 2001 headline reading "Local feedlots address possible bioterrorist threat," and agroterrorism was discussed at the November 2001 Kansas Livestock Association Convention.

GEOGRAPHY OF AGRICULTURAL SYSTEMS AND PRODUCTION IN RURAL AMERICA

Agricultural products, particularly food products, are important for both basic physical support of the general population and for regional economies. Diverse soils, climatic conditions, and population centers result in agricultural production that varies across the country (Hart

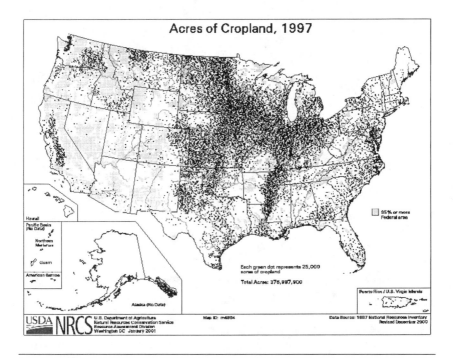

FIGURE 6.2.1 Cropland Density, 1997. Source: (NCRS 2001).

1991). As indicated in Figure 6.2.1, cropland is especially concentrated in the Midwest, Great Plains states, and Mississippi River valley. Different types of crops are clustered in different regions: there are broad areas of wheat in the Plains states and eastern Washington; corn and soybeans dominate in the Midwest; and fruit and vegetable crops are especially important in California, Florida, and the Pacific Northwest. Nationwide, intensive vegetable and fruit production often are located near cities in order to serve their larger populations.

Animal agriculture, as illustrated by cattle (Figure 6.2.2), also shows spatial variation, with particular concentrations in the Great Plains and upper Midwest. Plains cattle (Texas to North Dakota) are mostly for beef production; Wisconsin and adjoining areas produce more dairy cattle. Hogs and pigs have a different distribution, with notable production areas in Iowa and southern Minnesota, eastern North Carolina, and in the panhandle of Oklahoma (Figure 6.2.3). Other parts of the Midwest have many hogs, especially in Illinois and Indiana. A significant proportion of livestock production has moved to concentrated animal feeding operations (CAFOs), such as cattle feedlots. In contrast, much of the agricultural production in the intermountain

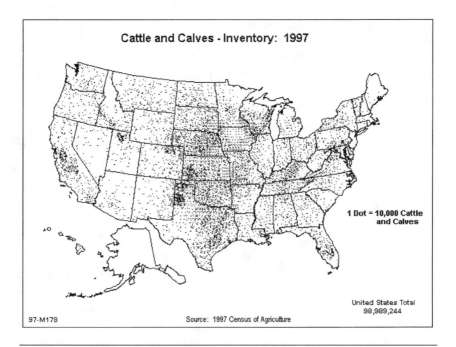

FIGURE 6.2.2 U.S. Cattle Distribution, 1997. Source: (NASS 1999).

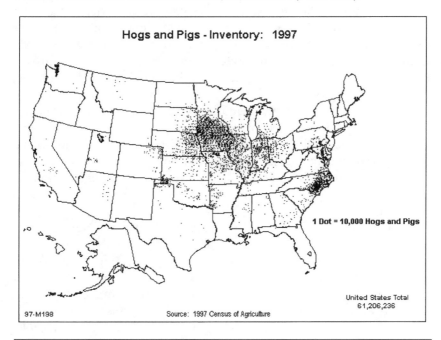

FIGURE 6.2.3 U.S. Hog and Pig Distribution, 1997. Source: (NASS 1999).

West is geographically expansive, with cattle and sheep grazing on public rangelands and private ranches, with scattered irrigated crop agriculture where conditions permit.

Not all of the nation's agricultural production is for food resources. For example, there are concentrations of cotton production in irrigated areas of California, Arizona, and Texas, the Mississippi River Valley, and the traditional areas of the Piedmont South; concentrations of tobacco production in Kentucky and the Carolinas; and Angora goats in Texas. Although attacks on non-food agriculture could be quite disruptive, attacks on food production is the greater security concern.

DIMENSIONS OF THE THREAT

Several "advantages" to biological agricultural attacks over direct assaults on humans are described in the literature (Rogers et al. 1999, Ban 2000, Chalk 2000). First, access to disease and pest organisms is relatively easy, and those that infect crops and livestock often are simple to disperse to large numbers of target organisms than human pathogens. Second, indirect attacks on agriculture are likely to be more "politically acceptable" (to either those perpetrating them or to their potential supporters) than numerous human casualties caused in a direct attack. Some researchers have suggested that attacks on crops may be possible even by organizations whose members might be morally constrained from direct human attacks (Rogers et al. 1999, Cameron et al. 2001). Although attacks on agriculture may be equally (or more) socially and economically debilitating compared to a direct human attack (Rogers et al. 1999, Chalk 2000, Pate and Cameron 2001), such a target is likely to reduce the possibility of rapid retaliatory actions by the affected nation, especially compared to attacks that produce immediate human casualties. Additionally, if destabilization is the goal of the attack, agriculture-focused aggression could be carried out with minimal detection. The source may be unidentifiable, and the event may be considered an accident at first, rather than an overt act.

There are numerous examples of regionally devastating outbreaks of disease among livestock or crops, although to the best of our knowledge these have been either naturally occurring outbreaks or caused by accidental introductions (Chalk 2000, Kohnen 2000, Miller et al. 2001). The Irish potato famine in 1845–1849, caused by potato blight, resulted in at least one million deaths and caused another million people to emigrate from Ireland (Fowler and Mooney 1990; Rogers et al. 1999). A more recent example, though not as devastating in human lives lost, is the 2001 foot-and-mouth disease (FMD) outbreak in British livestock, leading to the slaughter of over 5 million animals and international restrictions on livestock trade (Cameron et al. 2001, Countryside Agency 2001). Estimates place the total impact at £2.4–4.1 billion for 2001, with acute effects in some locales (Countryside Agency 2001). Major economic effects were felt not only through the agricultural and food industry sectors, but also in local tourism.

Chemical attacks also constitute a potential threat to agricultural systems, although the target area is likely to be smaller, more contained, and locally specific. Nerve gases used against livestock and herbicide attacks on crops could be considered potential threats. Herbicides have been used as agents of warfare, most noticeably the "Agent Orange" campaign in Vietnam. At present, chemical agents generate a lower concern than biologically based ones for agricultural systems.

Bioterrorism is the dominant concern for production agriculture because of the potential for disease-causing organisms to reproduce and propagate themselves through a large geographic area and to larger crop or livestock populations prior to detection. Among livestock, anthrax, FMD, and brucellosis are some of the most widely recognized agents that can be weaponized. Numerous diseases and other anti-agriculture agents (Table 6.2.1) have been studied by biological weapons and defense programs in the United States, United Kingdom, Germany, France, Japan, and Soviet Union, among others, although much of the research was conducted during World War II (Rogers et al. 1999, Ban 2000, Kohnen 2000, CNS 2002). Iraq's program is a recent addition (CNS 2002, Whitby 2002). Many nations, as signatories to the Biological and Toxin Weapons Convention (BTWC), agreed not pursue biological weapons development. Defensive work is still permissible, but it is often difficult to distinguish it from offensive work (Rogers et al. 1999). Although the United States was one of the original signatories of the BTWC, it has refused to sign a protocol developed to ensure its enforcement (Biliouri and Makarenko 2001) and there have been recent calls for a new Biosecurity Convention (Barletta et al. 2002).

While work has been done to weaponize a variety of preexisting disease strains, increasing technological ability to modify the genetic structure of organisms may lead to additional efforts to create genetically modified organism (GMO) weapons. Thus far, all the GMO work, at least that we are aware of, is meant to be beneficial in some way. Malicious genetic engineering may move in dangerous directions, including increased disease virulence or faster reproduction of problem organisms, for example.

TABLE 6.2.1 Examples of Biological Anti-agricultural Agents with Warfare and/or Terrorism Research History*

Anti-crop agents	
Agent (Pathogen)	Target
wheat smut (fungi)	wheat
wheat rusts (fungi)	wheat
late blight (fungus)	potato
Sclerotium rot/Southern blight (fungus)	soybeans, sugar beets, sweet potatoes, cotton; fruit and vegetable crops
Rice blast (fungus)	rice
Brown spot (fungus)	rice
Agent (Pest)	Target
Colorado beetle	potato
Corn beetle	corn
Nematodes	wheat

Anti-livestock Agents	
Agent (Pathogen)	Target
Foot-and-mouth (FMD) (hoof-and-mouth) (virus)	cloven-hooved animals (cattle, sheep, goats, pigs)
Rinderpest (RPV) (virus)	cattle
Anthrax (bacterium)	herbivores
Fowl plague/avian influenza (virus)	poultry
Brucellosis (bacteria)	cloven-hooved animals
Glanders (bacterium)	horses, donkeys, mules
Newcastle disease (virus)	poultry

*Agents listed here may affect more than the listed target species, including humans; those listed are the most likely agricultural targets. A number of other pathogens involved in past and current weapons programs are listed in CNS (2000). The international Office of Zoonotics lists additional transmissible diseases of concern (Kohnen 2000).

In the case of crops, wind-disseminated fungal diseases are the largest concern, but attacks by viral and bacterial pathogens, as well as insects could cause widespread disruption. Fungal diseases are among the most common developments of anti-crop biological weapons programs. Wind dispersal of spores would be more likely to infect large areas of crops, when compared to other potential anticrop weapons (Brown and Hovmøller 2002). Bacterial diseases, like corn blight, can be serious, but do not spread easily over such large areas as fungi (Kohnen 2000).

Viral diseases likely would be the weapons of choice for attacks on livestock (Kohnen 2000). They have various means of transmission including airborne, by direct contact, and by disease vector (mosquito-borne disease, for example). Among viral diseases, FMD is of particular concern. Bacterial diseases like anthrax also can be devastating. Either FMD or anthrax could lead to heavy losses through both the disease itself and efforts to contain it.

Assaults on the food supply as livestock and crops are processed and foodstuffs are distributed also could take the form of either biological or chemical toxins. Biological toxins, some of which are extremely potent in low doses, include foodborne pathogens *Escherichia coli, Salmonella,* and *cryptosporidium.* Instances of past, presumably accidental, contamination of public food supplies have proven highly disruptive, as well as deadly. In 1992–1993, over 500 confirmed cases of *E. coli* occurred in four states, and four deaths were associated with tainted hamburger (CDC 1993). An *E. coli* outbreak in 1996, spread by unpasteurized juice, infected at least 70 individuals in the western United States, killing one person. In an actual food-based attack in the United States, members of the Rajneeshee religious cult in eastern Oregon contaminated restaurant foods with salmonella in the fall of 1984. Over 750 cases of salmonella food poisoning were confirmed; though illnesses from the bacterium were severe, this attack resulted in no deaths (Miller et al. 2001).

FOOD AND AGRICULTURAL VULNERABILITY

The geographic distribution of key crops is essential in understanding the potential for, and impacts of, a biological (or other) agricultural attack. Once the geography is known, it is clear that vulnerabilities exist within U.S. agricultural and food production sectors. Some of these are described below.

Intensive Nature of Livestock Production

Animal concentrations and the movement of animals lead to increased opportunities for rapid disease spread among thousands of individuals. Feedlots in some regions have capacities of 50,000 to over 120,000 head; animals are brought together from wide areas to auctions, and then redistributed to CAFOs. In an infectious disease exercise in 2001, the Georgia Emergency Management Agency discovered that FMD infected cattle from one farm in Florida could cause a regional outbreak "overnight," simply through movement to a livestock market and then resale to other farms (Zwerdling 2001). Large dairy operations similarly could be targeted (BAMN 2001). Hog "factory farms" raise concerns about disease susceptibility and exposure because swine undergo increased stress associated with modern production conditions, are susceptible to some diseases carried by humans, and have more genetic uniformity under modern production. Poultry, likewise, have become concentrated in chicken and turkey production units.

Since most foreign animal diseases of concern were eradicated from U.S. livestock years ago, domestic livestock populations are vulnerable, especially animals without pre-existing immunity, as vaccines are not routinely administered (Ashford et al. 2000). This situation could affect predominantly rural areas with livestock concentrations, and the Southeast (with concentrated poultry and hog production) and the Midwest/Great Plains (cattle feedlots and hog production) are especially vulnerable to biological agroterrorism against livestock (Figures 6.2.2 and 6.2.3).

Monocultural Cropping Systems

Cropping systems in the United States are primarily monocultural, with single varieties of particular crops grown over relatively large areas. Natural disease outbreaks have decimated food production in other countries in the past when favorable environmental conditions for pathogenic spread converged with monocultural agriculture (the Irish potato blight and famine was such an instance). The unintentional spread of additional diseases to the United States such as the Karnal bunt wheat fungus, and controversial reports of the spread of genetically modified corn to a relatively isolated area of Mexico, contribute to concerns about the ease of distribution of potentially catastrophic biomaterials. In order to control introduced diseases and pests, their movements must be monitored, and often quarantined. Such procedures are already in place upon entry into the United States, as well as across certain state boundaries and within states (in Hawaii and California, for example). It has been noted, however, that crop fungal diseases can disperse themselves over very long distances. When coupled with the limited genetic diversity of modern crops, this makes agriculture even more susceptible (Brown and Hovmøller 2002).

The spatial clustering of crop types, such as vegetables in central California, contributes to agrosystem vulnerability. This spatial concentration, while helpful from an economic and agronomic perspective, creates a potential vulnerability to the rapid spread of a pathogen or chemical agent. Another form of vulnerability is seen in areas of extensively planted crops (measured by large acreages), including vital cereal crops like wheat. These crops include large acreages of land over vast areas, thus security is likely to be especially "soft," with a lack of vigorous monitoring over the entire area planted (NRC 2002a).

Role in International Trade and Domestic Economy

Agricultural production plays a key role in U.S. domestic economic and international trade. Farms contributed $79 billion, and food-related products another $137 billion, of U.S. GDP in 2000 (Lum and Moyer 2001). Although agriculture accounts for less than 2% of total U.S. GDP, in many counties, farm income accounts for over 30% of total income (Census Bureau 2000). The Department of Agriculture's Economic Research Service estimated that the value added to the U.S. economy by the agricultural sector through the production of goods and services in 2000 was $218.8 billion. In the agricultural sector, the United States exports a higher value commodity than it imports, in contrast to other important trade sectors. For fiscal year 2001, for example, total U.S. farm exports were valued at $53 billion (ERS 2001). So-called high value products (fruit, poultry, dairy products) accounted for $35.3 billion, and wheat, corn, and soybean exports were valued at $12.8 billion. Infection of livestock or crop plants can trigger international restrictions on trade, as occurred with FMD in the United Kingdom and with Karnal bunt infection of wheat in a portion of the United States. The balance of trade thus could be adversely affected by a bioterrorist attack.

The U.S. population is accustomed to low commodity prices and generally safe foodstuffs. Agricultural disruption or destruction caused by a terrorist attack on livestock or crops could increase domestic food costs and lead to questions about food safety, which in turn would affect consumer perceptions and food-buying behavior, potentially creating shortages or scarcities and hoarding behavior. Even the 9/11 attacks, with no direct relationship to agriculture, resulted in a short-term reduction in beef consumption in the United States related to changes in personal behaviors (Hegeman 2001). In addition to the direct impact on food availability, prices, and the balance of trade, employment for those even indirectly involved in agriculture could be affected.

Soft Targets

Agricultural facilities normally are considered "soft targets" that lack in security. Although many CAFOs may be monitored for unauthorized traffic, this is very unlikely on farms with many acres of planted crops. Disease outbreaks and dispersal mechanisms might not be traceable to an intentional attack. "Ingenious devices" for delivery of anticrop agents had been developed prior to United States cessation of the biological weapons program in 1969 (Rogers et al. 1999) but consideration should be given to older, more conventional means of dispersal, like crop dusters, as well as to more modern weapons and delivery systems. Historic agricultural bioweapons development and use can provide information regarding potential attacks, and historic reactions to agricultural disease outbreaks can assist in the development of potential responses to agroterrorism threats.

Ecoterrorism

There is some concern that domestic groups objecting to certain forms of modern agricultural technology could resort to attacks against agriculture even though they would not purposefully attack other humans (Kohnen 2000). Strikes against genetically-modified organism (GMO) research facilities already have occurred in the Pacific Coast states; strikes against agricultural operations using GMOs also are possible. Two groups considered likely sources of ecoterrorist attacks are the Earth Liberation Front (ELF) and the Animal Liberation Front (ALF) (FBI 2002).

Economies of Scale

Food processing, like livestock production, has increasingly shifted to very large facilities. Although they are considered a separate issue from agroterrorism, potential attacks on food products are related, given the close economic and geographic relationship between production, processing, and distribution. Thousands of cattle or hogs are processed each day in the very large meatpacking facilities. Product contamination with a pathogen like *E. coli* or *Salmonella* at one of these facilities might affect not only large quantity of food, but significant numbers of people over large geographic regions. Recalls can impact consumer confidence in related products.

CONCLUSION

In contrast to most concerns about terrorism potentials, agroterrorism largely affects rural places at least as the initial focus of an attack. It is critically important, therefore, to have a geographic understanding of the agricultural and food supply systems, including their spatial extent and linkages. Agricultural attacks could cause widespread economic loss, both directly (to producers), and indirectly (to consumers and to employees in related agricultural and food production or distribution industries). These losses will have differential impacts—in some re-

gions there may be little economic loss, while in others, the entire regional economy could be affected—although a biological attack is not
likely "to threaten the loss of an entire segment of the agricultural
sector" (Pate and Cameron 2001). Even where an attack has a fairly
limited spatial extent, there could be a panic reaction in consumer
confidence, market prices, and commodities futures markets. Understanding the spatial variability in food systems and agricultural production, tracking and monitoring the diffusion of disease outbreaks,
and monitoring the geographic extent of food contamination are areas
where geography can assist and provide support for more informed
decision making to reduce the impacts of agroterrorism.

Monitoring for any agricultural threat, whether naturally-occurring
or a result of a conscious attack, serves the same purpose. The United
States already has systems in place for monitoring agricultural diseases
and responding to food contamination, and funding in this area is increasing. The variations in plant and animal distributions, concentration of much of the meat and dairy production in CAFOs, uneven
distribution of human populations, the need to move animals and
produce along transportation networks, the spread of pests and disease, and responses to disease outbreaks all have very strong spatial
characteristics. These systems and their interdependencies need to be
understood in geographic terms in order to both minimize vulnerabilities and to plan responses to potential attack. The new National Agricultural Biosecurity Center Consortium (NABCC), which is considering
potential responses to disease outbreaks in livestock and issues related
to diffusion, does have a GIS component. Development of methods to
monitor, assess, and contain disease, is paramount to this effort.

The well-established expertise of geographers in areas related to
hazards, natural resources, and human responses to them (Burton et
al. 1993, Cutter 1994, 2001, Tobin and Montz 1997) and GIScientists
can be linked together with the expertise of livestock and crop specialists who are already involved in trying to understand and control organisms that could serve as bioweapons. Bioterrorism can strike at the
nation emotionally, economically, and environmentally. All have spatial components, and all aspects of terrorism studies can benefit from
a geographic perspective and from interdisciplinary cooperation.

6.3

SPATIAL SURVEILLANCE OF AND RESPONSE TO BIOLOGICAL THREATS

MARILYN O. RUIZ

GEOGRAPHY IS AN INTEGRAL PART of any disease surveillance system, including systems designed to detect and respond to a bioterrorist attack. Diseases occur at some location and affect a given population over some period of time. An integrated database with information on individual cases and the built and natural environment—which is then linked to spatial analysis tools—opens up new opportunities to respond to the outbreak and prevent the problem in the future. The development of digital disease surveillance systems has been an increasing priority in recent years, and new biodefense funding for public health affords more development of these systems (Fraser and Brown 2000).

This paper considers how Geographic Information Science (GIScience) contributes to efforts aimed at improving local, state, and national preparedness for a bioterrorism attack. Specifically, the paper emphasizes the role of spatial decision support systems (SDSS) as a framework for integrating spatial analysis, mapping, and database technology in a common delivery system for improved decision making (Densham 1991).

BACKGROUND

Bioterrorism is "the threat or intentional release of biological agents (viruses, bacteria, or their toxins) for the purpose of influencing the conduct of government, or intimidating or coercing a civilian population" (GAO 2001a :1). The five agents of most concern in bioterrorism are: anthrax; botulism; smallpox; plague; tularemia; and viral hemorrhagic fevers, including Marburg and Ebola. Agents in this group cause serious illness and death, have the potential to be delivered to large groups, and are the agents for which preparation is most critical (Rotz et al. 2002). The Office International des Epizooities (OIE) identifies fifteen of the most dangerous animal diseases on OIE's Group A list. Many among these could be considered biological threats against animal health, including foot and mouth disease, rinderpest, and sheep pox.

Since September 11, 2001, disease surveillance has become much more focused in public health and veterinary health agencies at all levels, with the development of national systems for human and animal disease surveillance underway. The National Electronic Disease Surveillance System (NEDSS), for example, is a CDC-led initiative to integrate and automate disease reports from local health departments (CDC 2002). The ability to map diseases has a long tradition in epidemiology (see Thomas paper) and the NEDSS system design will include both mapping and spatial analysis functions, however, these capabilities are not yet in place. This gap represents an area for potential contributions from GIScience, with the need for innovative digital mapping techniques and intuitive mapping interfaces for relatively naïve users (MacEachren et al. 1998, Springer 1999). The National Animal Health Laboratory Network (NAHLN), also under development, includes a strategy to combine laboratory data from state and federal animal disease testing facilities in an effort to improve the United States' ability to respond to disease outbreaks (AAVLD 2001).

While NEDSS and NAHLN improve or will ultimately replace the current methods for reporting disease, a new approach to disease surveillance is being developed as well. These are termed "syndromic" systems and they are based on the need for quick identification of disease outbreaks even before a full diagnosis is made. They focus on the flu-like symptoms which are common among many of the likely and identified bioterrorism agents, and do this by monitoring data from over the counter drug sales, emergency room visits, school or work absences, and routine doctors visits in order to find patterns that indicate an outbreak (Garrison et al. 1994, Barthell et al. 2002, Bunk 2002, Lazurus et al. 2002).

FRAGMENTED HEALTH RESPONSES

One of the primary concerns that emerged from the General Accounting Office Report on Combating Terrorism (GAO 2001b) was the fragmented nature of the response system. Many local health districts are taxing bodies, operate relatively autonomously, and have seen funding levels drop from local, state, and national revenue sources, which undermines the public health system. Fragmentation also occurs between and human and veterinary medicine (Tucker and Kadlec 2001, Brown 2002). Many potential bioweapons are zoonotic, meaning that the disease ecology includes an animal component. For example, 75% of emerging infectious diseases are zoonotic, and of the 1415 pathogens known to infect humans, 61% infect species other than humans (Brown 2002). Thus, any comprehensive disease surveillance and response system must account for both human and animal diseases. The integration of data from both human and animal surveillance systems in a robust standards-based SDSS holds promise for better integration of public health functions at multiple jurisdictional levels.

Ideally, a SDSS will draw spatial data from a data base in a standards-based GIS to ensure up-to-date, well-documented data. It is essential that local, state, and federal public health agencies have access to geospatial information networks so that they contribute to the content of the data, make recommendations on how their specific needs can be served, and have full access to all relevant local data. In general, health departments were not the major players in data sharing and coordination efforts, and often lack the technical expertise in this area, especially at the local level (Rushton et al. 2000).

Animal disease surveillance and response is especially difficult because of the lack of animal location data, the denominator used in disease analysis. With humans, the population at risk is usually based on census data, but comparable animal population data are not as readily available. West Nile virus (WNV) illustrates the problem. The WNV is carried by a mosquito vector, but the behavior and locations of mosquito species are not well understood across large geographic areas. WNV infects many species of birds and is frequently fatal in crows and blue jays. A survey of dead birds helps to indicate the existence of the disease in an area. Rates of dead birds, however, cannot be determined without knowledge of the number of birds of a particular species in a place. WNV is also a serious disease of horses, but even the number of horses in a county is not always available for all states, once again making it difficult to assess the risk of WNV to humans or horses. Another example is plague, which is spread by infected fleas. Rodents, such as prairie dogs and rats, contract the disease from fleas and then serve as a host reservoir to infect more fleas. Humans contract plague from flea bites, but the disease is also transmitted by direct contact with the bacterium. Many of the recent human cases of plague in the United States resulted from contact with cats infected with the disease.

Geographers are well suited to help fill the existing gap in knowledge of animal locations. Some of this work would make use of existing information, only in a more innovative way. Dog registration records, for example, could help determine the location and number of dogs in a community. Information on horse stables could determine locations and numbers of horses. Geospatial technologies, such as global positioning systems and mapping from satellite or fixed aircraft could be employed to record farm and animal locations and contribute to a comprehensive mapping of farms. In addition, geographers can help to justify the need for animal location data to various agencies and provide the knowledge of mapping technologies and methods to help structure the collection of new information, and its subsequent analysis.

IMPROVING PUBLIC HEALTH RESPONSE THROUGH SPATIAL ANALYSIS

New spatial methods should be brought to bear on understanding, modeling, and predicting disease outbreaks. Three general areas of research are discussed here: detection of clusters and other analytical methods, spatially explicit simulation models, and visualization and analysis of temporal variables.

Detection of disease clusters and models of disease diffusion are a standard part of epidemiology and should be incorporated into a SDSS (Jacquez 1997). Response to an outbreak of a contagious disease, such as smallpox or plague, may require that certain areas be quarantined. In this context, an important task for a SDSS would be to help to determine which part of an urban area should be closed off to 1) minimize the number of people affected and 2) reduce the size of the impact area. Another familiar problem for medical and economic geographers is the issue of facility location. In the event of an outbreak, a SDSS could be utilized to determine the best location for vaccine distribution and treatment centers given the spatial and environmental context of the outbreak.

Simulation models play an important role in response decisions to outbreaks. For example, the use of spatial modeling in the 2001 Great Britain FMD outbreak clearly illustrated both the power and difficulties of using modeling for a costly and controversial outbreak. Widely criticized in the popular press for being responsible for justifying higher rates of culling than necessary, modeling of FMD spread was hampered by incomplete data and lack of spatial specificity. At the same time, modeling was helpful in making the options and possible consequences clearer (Morris et al. 2001).

As a final note, GIScience needs to build on existing work in incorporating the time dimension of an event into its analysis. GIS has not been well suited to include the temporal dimension into analyses without considerable effort in processing. Yet this dimension is critical in understanding the spread of a disease (Langran 1992, Kemp and Kowalczyk 1994). In particular, research efforts should focus on visualization of events that change over time, automation of data processing with a temporal dimension, and new methods to analyze changes that occur across time.

CONCLUSIONS

Geographers involved with GIScience and public health can help detect, understand, prepare for, and respond to bioterrorism. Experience in the use of geospatial technology and in understanding spatial data will be valuable in both human and animal health efforts. The potential for biological welfare (BW) agents to be used against both civilian and military targets exist, however logistical, moral, and technical difficulties prevent most terrorist groups from carrying out a BW attack (Tucker 2000). Despite the 22 cases and 5 deaths from the anthrax incident in 2001 and early 2002, this event, while terrifying, was fairly small and contained (Hughes and Gerberding 2002). State-sponsored biowarfare is of more concern to pubic health and animal health professionals. Improved disease surveillance will enhance responses to emerging infectious diseases and food-borne illnesses, and these benefits will accrue regardless of the nature and degree of threat of BW (Geiger 2001, NRC 2002a). While the technology and methods of GIScience can make a valuable contribution to the immediate needs, advances in our ability to monitor and spatially analyze all infectious diseases, in addition to bioterrorist threats, is perhaps where the lasting contributions to improved public health will be found.

CHAPTER 7

Building a Safer but Open Society

INTRODUCTION

Balancing security with openness within a society is an issue of paramount concern to all people, but particularly to Americans, who have enjoyed freedom of movement, privacy, and access to governmental information unparalleled elsewhere in the world. It is important that we develop the means to defend against terrorism, but also that we ensure that our societies retain those qualities of openness and freedom that make them so worthy of defending. Terrorism has the chilling effect of challenging openness, and has generated considerable debate about the trade-offs between security and potential limits to individual rights we have traditionally enjoyed. Harlan Onsrud explores some of these issues within the context of public access to geographic information. These questions will likely remain with us and linger unresolved for quite some time, as we grope forward tentatively, seeking an uneasy balance between hope and fear.

A related geographical issue concerns the question of locational privacy. In a time of threats of violence, how much privacy regarding our individual movements are we willing to relinquish? How can we safely develop and implement the powerful capabilities of the advanced new geographic technologies we are creating—which hold so much promise for individual and scientific benefit—when, as with so many other advanced technologies, they have inherent within them a risk for potential abuse? As part of this policy equation, we must examine the social responsibilities of those employing spatial technologies. How can we ensure that individual rights and locational privacy are protected from inadvertent or willful misuse of such technology? What is appropriate in terms of legal or regulatory safeguards regarding their use?

205

In his insightful essay on GeoSecurity, William Wood addresses these and many related questions, such as data sharing, intergovernmental and interagency coordination, and opportunities to leverage our new geographic technologies to improve living conditions and foster sustainable development around the world. As Wood explores the opportunities, needs, and challenges facing the establishment of a federal Department of Homeland Security, it is clear that an effective struggle against terrorism involves complex technical as well as policy issues of a geographical nature. It is equally clear from the contents of this chapter, that geography and geographers will have much to contribute to meet this grand challenge.

7.1

OPENNESS VERSUS SECURITY OF GEOGRAPHIC INFORMATION

HARLAN ONSRUD

ONE MONTH AFTER THE SEPTEMBER 11, 2001 ATTACKS, government depository libraries across the United States received a request from the U.S. Geological Survey, through the Library Programs Service of the U.S. Government Printing Office, to destroy copies of a compact disk titled *Source-Area Characteristics of Large Public Surface-Water Supplies in the Coterminous United States: An Information Resource for Source-Water Assessment, 1999.* Similar instructions to hold back or destroy wide-ranging materials previously accessible to the general public were issued within and among local, state, and federal government agencies and presumably are continuing today. The requests and directive are being made with the reasoning that certain information in openly-published or accessible documents might provide knowledge of value to terrorists. Questions arise as to whether some of the withholdings, even if legal, rationally support the goal of increasing the security of communities and the nation. This raises the question of whether a general climate of restricting public access to geographic and related data actually may jeopardize rather than increase homeland security.

SOME LEGAL ISSUES REGARDING ACCESS

The purpose of the U.S. Freedom of Information Act (FOIA) (United States Code Title 5 § 552) is to require federal agencies to make their information generally available for public inspection and copying for any public or private purpose. The act has resulted, over time, in a valuable means by which any person can learn how the government works. The FOIA has led to the disclosure of waste, fraud, abuse and wrongdoing in the Federal Government, and to the identification of unsafe consumer products, harmful drugs, and serious health hazards (see HR 3802, Electronic Freedom of Information Act Amendments of 1996, http://www.epic.org/open-gov/efoia.html). Other assessments indicated that the current deference towards open access to government records in the United States contributes substantially to the economic well-being of the nation (Pluijmers and Weiss 2002).

The FOIA of the federal government as well as the open access laws of individual states, generally supports a policy of broad disclosure by government. For example, if a data set held by a federal agency is determined to be an agency record, it must be disclosed to any person requesting it unless the record falls within one of nine narrowly drawn exemptions contained in the FOIA. These exemptions are construed so narrowly by the courts that disclosure is typically favored over nondisclosure. Federal agencies also bear affirmative obligations to actively disseminate their information as defined by the provisions of the Office of Management and Budget (OMB) Circular A-130 of June 1993, and the Government Paperwork Reduction Act of 1996 (GPRA). As a result, federal agencies have placed their digital geographic information openly on the World Wide Web to make their data sets more accessible to other government agencies, for-profit businesses, nonprofit organizations, and citizens generally (for example, see http://www.fgdc.gov/clearinghouse.html).

Exemption 1 under the U.S. Freedom of Information Act states that mandates to release public records do not apply to matters that are "(1) (A) specifically authorized under criteria established by an Executive Order to be kept secret in the interest of national defense or foreign policy and (B) are in fact properly classified pursuant to such Executive Order" (United States Code Title 5 § 552 (b) (1)). Other FOIA exemptions that may justify the withholding by government agencies of geographic information in certain instances include data or records that are specifically exempted from disclosure by federal statute (United States Code Title 5 § 552 ([b] [3]), or records or information compiled by law enforcement agencies (United States Code Title 5 § 552 ([b] [7]).

The extent and conditions under which material may be withheld by the government under the FOIA exemptions and in the context of other regulations such as OMB Circular A-130 and GPRA, has been litigated extensively. Thus the case law and administrative rulings provide at least some guidance as to whether a specific information withholding by a federal agency is allowable or not.

In withholding or withdrawing geographic data and related records, federal agency personnel should be able to cite the explicit statutory and administrative provisions authorizing them to do so. In the vast majority of instances, we assume that the withholdings are made in conformance with the law. However, even if specific withholdings are adjudged legal, questions are now being raised as to whether a general climate of increased government withholding of geographic data will increase or decrease homeland security and personal information privacy.

EFFECTS OF ACCESS POLICIES ON SECURITY

The extent to which libraries and government agencies at federal, state, and local levels removed and continue to remove material in the interest of homeland security is difficult to determine. These actions typically are pursued internally with little fanfare. Much of the decision making at various governmental levels to remove specific materials appears to be rather ad hoc, without serious consideration of the harms to other social objectives that such removals may cause. The question to be addressed here is not whether some or all of the removals are legal, but whether such actions actually support the goals intended by the suppression of the information.

An example is the electronic document that depository libraries were requested to destroy mentioned in the introduction. Even the title of this document suggests that it would supply a ready-made hit list for terrorists intent on infecting or otherwise disrupting the nation's water supply. While we no longer have access to the contents of this document, the information indeed may have been of great interest to potential terrorists. However, questions remain regarding whether the information in the document would be of even greater value to those responding to terrorist acts and to the general public. It would take little investigation for a motivated terrorist to identify one or more urban water supply systems in the United States. If a terrorist incident were to occur, does the suppressed document provide valuable information that would help local emergency response teams and policy makers? Does it provide valuable information for local citizens and the news media, both of whom might want to verify that their specific water supply has or has not been affected by the incident? Would it be better that thousands of local citizens are aware of and watching the physical status and circumstances surrounding their own water supplies? Does the document provide valuable information for other important day-to-day beneficial decisions that will now be hampered?

In the World Trade Center case, locating this physical and political target took little effort on the part of terrorists. The target was obvious and no removal of mapping data would have altered the outcome. However, detailed maps and data were very much needed and relied upon by rescue and emergency personnel, as well as by government officials and the news media. As noted elsewhere in this book, the collapse of the Emergency Operations Center for New York City necessitated the reconstruction of emergency response and infrastructure information. This effort was greatly facilitated by access to copy data sets held at Hunter College (among others) as well as additional data sets held by other private and public entities (Cahan and Ball 2002). If only one or a few copies had existed, then gaining access to the data sets at the moment they were needed would have been far more problematic and could have hindered rescue and relief operations.

HOMELAND SECURITY IN THE INFORMATION AGE

The reasons for providing access to data for homeland security are many and varied. First, the basic policy assumption under U.S. law should continue to be one of open access to public records because of the large social and economic benefits this policy supports.

Second, it doesn't take detailed data or a sophisticated GIS for terrorists to locate prime targets. Such locations are readily identifiable from innumerable sources. Legislatures and the public also should recognize that anyone can go to the web and within a couple of minutes type in a house address, produce a road map with detailed instructions on how to drive to the house, and print out an overhead satellite image that includes the house. These capabilities are used daily by large numbers of people in the nation, and have many beneficial uses in society. The goal at the federal, state, and local government level should be to expand the use of spatial technologies and methods like GIS to achieve even greater benefits for communities.

Third, improved information infrastructures and ready access to data bases gives us the ability to track criminals more effectively. It is nearly impossible to operate in modern open societies without leaving digital tracks.

Fourth, if information is power, then we need to place it in the hands of all citizens so they can work together to solve societal problems and improve the quality of life. Many repressive societies control their populations by allowing only a few elite members to have access to maps and geographic information. Only a few nations in the world, for example, have FOIA laws, and none are as strong as those in the

United States. Open access to government information (at all levels) has been both the tradition and the genius of our nation. Open access supports the functioning of democracy and provides a huge economic multiplier effect. We need to expand that tradition in the information age, not retrench from it.

Fifth, the best way to preserve the strongest national defense in the world is to maintain the strongest economy in the world. In an information age, the proven way to accomplish this is to provide citizens and businesses with access to the raw materials (such as data and knowledge) they need to provide better information services and products to the nation and the world. Open societies always have a distinct competitive advantage over nations that do not provide their citizens access to these raw materials. Historically, the United States let information systems (and technologies in general) rapidly evolve with few prospective controls in order to maximize economic development. As a result, the United States has greater leeway to build on the works of others, to experiment, and to play with data in order to provide new and better products and services to consumers. This has resulted in the strongest information industry in the world. The framework for success was to provide flexibility and information exchange that allowed technologies to grow while passing laws that permitted the punishment of abusers of these emergent technologies. The presence of those who might abuse online systems should not deter us from making data available and useful to citizens in our communities. The benefits from having more readily available governmental data far outweigh the drawbacks.

Finally, democracy with strong civil liberties is the logical end-state of maximizing security (Dansby 2002). Although different from many other nations, citizens in the United States generally agree that suppression of free speech results in more damage than the effects of speech, no matter how offensive the content of that speech may be. Similarly, broad suppression of information of likely use to potential terrorists often will result in more damage to the nation than allowing the information to be accessible to all. With strong civil liberties and transparent government we are far better able to weather political, social, and economic disruptions over time.

There are obvious limits and caveats to the arguments provided above. However, these points should at least be considered along with counter arguments when considering whether or not to restrict access to a specific data set in the name of national security. These points should also be debated in formulating governmental access policies. In summary as Torvalds and Diamond put it: "People don't quibble with the need for free speech. It is a liberty that people have defended with their lives. Freedom is always something you have to defend with your life. But it's also not an easy choice to make initially. And the same is true of openness. You just have to make the choice to be open. It's a difficult stance to take at first, but it actually creates more stability in the end" (Torvalds and Diamond 2001: 229).

7.2

GEOSECURITY

WILLIAM B. WOOD

ESTABLISHMENT OF A DEPARTMENT OF HOMELAND SECURITY that improves interagency coordination and capabilities to protect U.S. citizens will be a great legislative, bureaucratic, and geographic challenge. Homeland security as an urgent national and international strategic interest has shifted from headlines about Ground Zero in New York and combat in Afghanistan to government reorganization plans aimed at implementing national security differently. While considerable attention is focused on the legislative and organizational elements of a new cabinet level department, a geographic perspective is required as well to better understand what data are needed to improve homeland security and how geographic information system (GIS) tools can help get the job done (National Research Council 1997). Such critical geographic information-based security efforts might be termed *GeoSecurity.* GeoSecurity can assess and visualize societal vulnerabilities against different types of threats and likely responses using a suite of geographic methodologies, organization and analysis of georeferenced data, and the application of GIS tools to achieve security objectives within, around, and well beyond the homeland.

GROUND ZERO GEOSECURITY

Ground Zero, the site of the collapsed World Trade Center buildings, embodies both the threat to the homeland, and the American determination to recover, rebuild, and fight back. As William Langewiesche recently observed, Ground Zero serves as "the powerful new iconography that was associated with the disaster—these New York fireman as tragic heroes, these skeletal walls, these smoking ruins as America's hallowed ground" (Langewiesche 2002: 48). The rapidly changing geography of "the pile" and its environs both above and deep below ground, and the dangerous task of un-building the collapsed structures underscored to many observers that no place in the world is safe from attack. It starkly illustrated as well that large armies and fortified borders are no longer sufficient for homeland defense.

President Bush's June 6, 2002 announcement of the plan to establish a new Department of Homeland Security out of the disjointed pieces of existing departments and agencies was an unprecedented acknowledgement that the United States needed better protection. The department was charged with four main tasks: secure the country's borders to prevent terrorists from entering the country; coordinate and communicate with state and local officials to respond faster and better to emergencies; focus science and technology capabilities to protect citizens; and synthesize intelligence and law enforcement reporting from all agencies to create a single daily picture of threats against our homeland (Bush 2002). As initially envisioned, the new department will create a unified security structure with four divisions: Border and Transportation Security; Emergency Preparedness and Response; Chemical, Biological, Radiological, and Nuclear Countermeasures; and Information Analysis and Infrastructure Protection (White House 2002). GIS applications could contribute to all four divisions, but geographical information science needs to be integrated as a core function within the new department's information management requirements.

Making homeland protection a cabinet-level institution recognizes that effective security requires cutting through the usual military, intelligence, and law enforcement stovepipes, especially when faced against a disciplined and innovative enemy. While enterprise-wide antiterrorism collaboration must supplement other congressionally mandated missions of all agencies involved, the new department will require vigorous and informed participation among many state and local officials who now will have a "need to know" about foreign or homegrown terrorist threats. This, in turn, requires an interoperable information network that can be used to assess infrastructure vulnerability, track suspected terrorist activities, and link up as many as 170,000 homeland security officers (Blair 2002).

THE RELEVANCE OF SCALE

The challenge facing the Department of Homeland Security is best appreciated by understanding the multiple scales at which GeoSecurity must function. Fundamentally, what are the parameters of the insecurity problem and how will that affect terrorism prevention? As Ground Zero epitomizes, terrorism is both a global intergovernmental concern as well as a brutally localized crisis. All threats occur someplace—a building, a city block, a small town, key hubs along an electricity grid, or even a foreign country—and thus can be mapped and assessed. At the global level, a coalition against terrorism requires working with governments that face a variety of other pressing issues, ranging from economic growth to local insurgencies, and international organizations, such as the United Nations, with many other critical missions. As the international community is demonstrating in Afghanistan, a military campaign to root out al Qaeda terrorists requires extensive humanitarian assistance, peacekeeping, economic development, and even nation building to ensure such threats do not arise again.

At the regional and national levels, terrorism prevention and response requires governments and regional organizations to cooperate in bold, new ways to cripple crossborder terrorism networks that fuel instability and violence—whether in South Asia, sub-Saharan Africa, the Balkans, or North America. Intergovernmental cooperation in such insecure regions is essential for better protection of homeland outposts ranging from U.S. embassies to military installations and vessels. Cross border cooperation against terrorists requires a capability to work in different languages and cultures, among different types of governments, and with different approaches to managing and sharing relevant data (Fulton 2002). Within the United States, federal, state, and local agencies must also work together in ways they never have been able to accomplish before; the public's demand for results will force changes in behavior to all of the offices that make up the department's evolving organizational chart. At a minimum, those contributing to the war against terrorism must share georeferenced data to see the whole puzzle, not just their piece of it.

At the subnational and local levels, states, counties, urban neighborhoods, and rural communities must assume new security responsibilities. Pioneering examples of data collection and sharing among local, county, state, and federal partners—from environmental protection to social services—underscore that the vertical and horizontal integration of information needed for GeoSecurity is doable. However, it will require political commitments at all levels of government to be realized (Greene 2000). Local officials may demand access to large-scale digital street maps and high-resolution imagery they can use as part of community based information services. This geographically enhanced information needs to be available on line, linked to other socioeconomic, health, and infrastructure data, and accessible to mobile police, fire, and health units that form the last line of defense and the first line of response. Regional homeland security offices need to coordinate efforts among several states that share security concerns and operational requirements. From a geographic perspective, multiscalar security means different types of GeoSecurity data, different types of maps and remote sensing imagery, and, most importantly, different communities of interest.

GEOSECURITY TOOLS

GIS is a computer-assisted means to manage spatially organized, security relevant data, and is a powerful tool that the Department of Homeland Security needs in order to create GeoSecurity data layers. A GIS-enabled integrative approach allows security analysts to better organize an excess of fragmented data, determine linkages among layers that are built and maintained by separate agencies, and assess threat patterns within a spatial domain. Since most government-collected data are spatial in some form already or can be linked to some place or defined area (from census records to property values to electoral districts) (NAPA 1998), the challenge is to bring this all together and to provide it quickly to those who can use it.

As noted in chapter 2.1 of this book, GIS tools are now widely used in crime mapping, in which criminal acts can be plotted against a backdrop of a city map to look for trends, patterns, and associations between the crimes and other potential factors, such as income, land use, and transportation routes (ESRI 2000). It is being used in the military for all types of terrain analysis, targeting, and battlespace awareness exercises where enemy positions and movements are monitored and relayed to the twenty-first-century warrior on the ground. GIS is used in other interagency efforts to prevent or interdict illegal activities from catching undocumented migrants attempting to cross our international boundaries to busting narco-traffickers attempting to smuggle in cocaine. All of these GIS-supported efforts generate ongoing data management challenges because they attempt to integrate or fuse data that are not traditionally correlated; in one sense it allows apples to be compared with oranges, as long as they come from the same orchard. A comprehensive homeland security GIS is a much more complicated task than that faced by any one agency because it must build on the experiences of all participating agencies.

The agencies slated to become part of the new department bring a wealth of GIS experience, but in the new administrative structure they will have to organize and apply GIS as part of an integrated command structure. Furthermore, agencies need to be ready, willing, and able to share their value-added data to prevent, or at least lessen the threat of terrorism. Should another catastrophic attack occur, agencies will be expected to respond promptly, not squabble over who should be doing what, where, and when. There are many contemporary examples of how data sharing can work based on common data standards, efficient data sharing mechanisms, seamless software interoperability, and practical metadata requirements. The Federal Emergency Management Agency, for example, uses GIS to assess floods and other natural disasters, but much of its baseline data on hydrological systems comes from the US Geological Survey. The Department of Transportation uses GIS for its extensive highway planning and data-intensive traffic modeling, but it probably works with state and municipal agencies for current road maps. The Coast Guard likely uses National Oceanic and Atmospheric Agency charts to navigate in and around our coastal waterways and territorial seas. The Immigration and Naturalization Service and Customs Service likely use GIS as part of their border security operations relying on geospatial intelligence from the National Imagery and Mapping Agency. Many of these organizations use GIS for mandated programs that have nothing to do with counterterrorism, but are still critical to U.S. national interests.

The task that agencies in and out of the new department face is how to share their GIS-enabled data as part of a corporate enterprise with a shared strategic mission: stop the next attack or, failing that, save lives. How might they work in concert to respond to a hypothetical intelligence report of a terrorist plan to dump a toxic substance or detonate a dirty bomb on a busy street corner? Where might deadly components come from internationally and how might they be smuggled into the United States? Which interstate routes are used to move hazardous materials and how might populations along those routes be made safer? Should another major attack occur, how might homeland security agencies respond effectively to secure the area, treat victims, evacuate those able to leave, and apprehend the perpetrators?

Under any homeland threat scenario, a broad range of geo-referenced information will be needed urgently. Specific data layers—terrorist movements, potential targets and vulnerable populations, infrastructure weak links and chokepoints, and site access and emergency response proximity—can provide the requisite information for an integrated decision support system. But first, significant information management obstacles must be overcome. Relevant data collected by local, county, state, or federal agencies, by semi-private agencies such as utilities, and by the private sector are often proprietary, potentially outdated, in varying formats and standards, and poorly maintained. While interesting maps, images, and charts are the most apparent GIS products, the backroom headache of data management usually determines whether geographic analysis yields value-added knowledge or just another map of our insecurity.

THE PHASES OF GEOSECURITY

Security is a never-ending cycle in which applied geographic information serves different functions during each phase (Figure 7.2.1), and
mirrors the emergency response cycle mentioned earlier in this volume.
For government agencies, the early part of the cycle entails collecting
baseline data about potential terrorist groups and targets. In the war on
terrorism, terrorists groups choose the location and timing of their next
strike while homeland defenders have the burden of being expected to
respond anywhere at any time. Theoretically, all terrorist movements, financial links, and clandestine activities should be mapped whether they
are in a foreign land or in the homeland. The reality is more difficult as
the mismatching of various types of data from sources of variable reliability often results in a threat map with many gaps.

A second phase of institutionalized security involves contingency
planning. GIS-enabled crisis simulations allow various stakeholders to

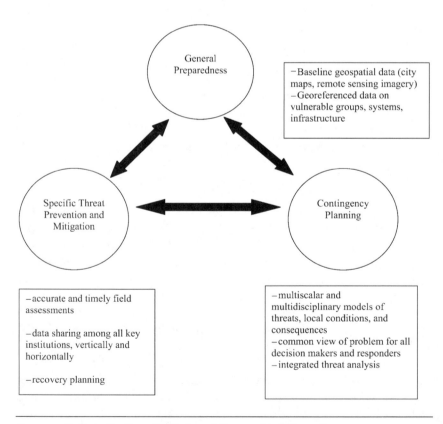

FIGURE 7.2.1 GeoSecurity Cycle and Geographic Information

work together by giving them a shared realistic view of the problem they are attempting to resolve, whether it is estimating the potential contamination zone from a bioterrorist attack or determining likely transportation bottlenecks following a hazardous materials spill. No simulation or model perfectly predicts the consequences of future terrorist attacks, but advances in computer game-based dynamic scenarios, GIS-based modeling, and artificial intelligence-based decision-making can help bridge the gap between theoretical knowledge and practical application.

A third phase of GeoSecurity involves stopping an attack before or even during its implementation, but this requires rethinking the problem of who needs to know what (see the previous paper by Onsrud). With some notable exceptions (such as the sources and methods behind intelligence-based terrorist threat reports), much of the data needed to help communities build safeguards against terrorism must be public and transparent. Those within the new Department of Homeland Security will face the never-ending obstacle course of getting the right information to the right enforcement agency in a way that can be used to get the job done in the shortest time possible.

GEOSECURITY INFORMATION INFRASTRUCTURE

In its recent report on the role of science and technology in homeland security, the National Research Council (2002a) focused on existing vulnerabilities to potential terrorist use of nuclear materials, deadly pathogens, and toxic substances. The committee addressed information and telecommunication systems as potential targets, such as cyberattacks against Internet domains or the computer systems that control electric power grids. But it also underscores the need for homeland C3I—command, control, communication, and information—to improve response and decision support, while ensuring network security. Toward that goal, it recommends an active private sector role and aggressive research and development (R&D). Unfortunately, the report limits GIS to a support role—a tool used primarily for locating victims and responders. Yet, the report recognizes the information management problem of integrating a large volume of disparate data. The broader application of GIS as a spatial decision-support tool, not just one used for search and rescue, can efficiently tackle this major challenge for the new department.

A new information infrastructure that improves security must connect homeland personnel more effectively within agencies and to counterparts in other agencies. A GIS-enabled homeland information network, though, requires common standards for geographic information sharing among country, state, and federal agencies—topics covered in previous chapters of this book.

INTER-HOMELAND GEOSECURITY

Homeland itself is a political geographic concept usually applied to regions other than the United States because it suggests a cultural region where members of a far-flung émigré community can trace their roots, often through rose-colored glasses. But the United States is largely a country of immigrants and their descendants, many of whom may still view their homeland as somewhere else. A Department of Homeland—not National—Security demands a change in that thinking. Since 9/11, national political leaders have driven home the point that the United States—despite its remarkably heterogeneous population—is the primary homeland of all Americans and its security is the government's paramount national concern. After the devastatingly direct attack on that homeland, the response by Americans has been an outpouring of patriotism, often centered on the most emotional symbol of the United States as a homeland, its flag. The creation of a consolidated Department of Homeland Security, though, should not diminish the GeoSecurity interconnectedness of the United States with other countries.

For much of the 1990s, the United States and the international community had little influence in a politically isolated and economically devastated Afghanistan, where the ruling Taliban's support for Osama bin Ladin enabled his international al-Qaeda terrorist group to flourish. al-Qaeda's remote training camps, obscure financial networks, and widely deployed terrorist cells became not just another geopolitical problem on 9/11, but the most significant attack on American territory since World War II. Suddenly, terrorism threats that routinely plague other regions hit home. Citizens from over 80 countries were killed in the attacks, underscoring the global dimension of homeland security. An important lesson from the worldwide coalition against terrorism and Operation Enduring Freedom in Afghanistan is the recognition that U.S. military prowess—though impressive on its own with sophisticated weaponry and GIS/GPS-enabled targeting and real-time data networking—works best if it can depend on the support of other governments, such as for base rights and over flights, but also for humanitarian operations and peacekeeping (O'Hanlon 2002). As of June 2002, 60,000 American troops had been deployed around the world in the war against terrorism, 90 countries had arrested or detained 2,400 terrorist suspects, and 180 countries had offered or provided assistance to U.S. efforts (Bush 2002). Though the new department will have a largely domestic focus, it will still need to coordinate closely with more traditional U.S. national security agencies that are working internationally to monitor terrorist networks, cooperate with foreign law enforcement agencies, and when needed, take forceful military action.

America's homeland defense thus depends on improved security in other homelands, which are less focused on the next catastrophic terrorist attack and more on ethno-political violence and declining socioeconomic conditions—two of the underlying root causes of terrorism (Wood 1999a, b). A strategy to tighten security in the American homeland requires sustained U.S. commitments to diplomatic cooperation, such as the Inter-American Committee Against Terrorism; military collaboration, such as the International Security Assistance Force in Afghanistan; and foreign assistance, such as to countries in Africa facing chronic malnutrition and an AIDS epidemic. Security against disease threats (natural and human-induced) in the United States, for example, requires international measures to improve surveillance and response to infectious diseases that can rapidly spread across international boundaries (Chyba 2002). GIS-based tracking of such transnational diseases as West Nile virus are critical to improved interhomeland health and security.

As in the past, the U.S. government will be called again and again to assist other countries dealing with their particular terrorism crises. While perhaps less dramatic than Ground Zero, other countries have their symbolic places to remind visitors that most victims of terrorism, civil warfare, and interethnic violence are innocent civilians. As Afghanistan demonstrates, terrorists are fully capable of exploiting chronic homeland insecurity to foment international instability. While such entrenched problems resist quick fixes, a Department of Homeland Security is more likely to achieve its ambitious goals if it can benefit from improved security and living conditions in other homelands. International GIS efforts are already supporting interhomeland cooperation by developing and sharing security-relevant data across borders such as those in the U.S.–led Geographic Information for Sustainable Development project (National Research Council 2002c).

GEOSECURITY STRATEGY

If homeland security as a crucial government responsibility is to be realized, it will require new GIS-based mechanisms for interagency and intergovernmental cooperation, new ways of visualizing problems, and new systems for collecting, organizing, analyzing, and disseminating geographic information (Issue 7.2). Such a plan will take considerable time and much effort by all involved, if it is to be done well and provide a lasting foundation for GeoSecurity. While significant breakthroughs in the utilization of geotechnologies were achieved over the past few years, especially in accessing georeferenced data and imagery

---

ISSUE 7.2
Strategies for the Effective Use of Geographic Information for Homeland Security

- Develop an interagency information strategy that identifies who needs what types of georeferenced data and how that will be accomplished.

- Establish a GeoSecurity Information Office to oversee a GIS-based data sharing network at international, national, state, and local levels.

- Ensure that all security-relevant data are organized within the NSDI framework for consistent georeferencing and metadata, and as part of a clearinghouse network linking geospatial products and services.

- Encourage the construction of a comprehensive, digital, large-scale *Atlas of the United States* that is seamless and Internet-linked to a broad range of public data—it will serve not just homeland security but all government agencies, businesses, and schools.

- Collaborate with local communities through data sharing, technical support, pilot projects, and outreach—they can provide the ground truthing to ensure security- and infrastructure-related data are updated, accurate, and useful.

- Create a small, highly mobile GeoSecurity Response Unit that can deploy quickly to anywhere in the United States with maps, imagery, and GIS tools to assist with emergency response and recovery.

- Launch an aggressive public-private GeoSecurity partnership with the GIS, data management, Internet, and remote sensing industries to take advantage of state-of-the-art R&D.

- Expand GIS-enhanced efforts to improve security in other homelands, particularly those with life-threatening emergencies.

---

over the Internet, a tougher issue is the institutional barriers that inhibit the widespread availability of relevant security information. Strong department leadership, clear legislative mandates, and most of all, pioneering federal-local and public-private partnerships are required in order to create a more secure American homeland. Wisely applied geographic information can help get us there.

CHAPTER

A Research and Action Agenda[1]

SUSAN L. CUTTER, DOUGLAS B. RICHARDSON,
AND THOMAS J. WILBANKS

Our ongoing research on the geographical dimensions of terrorism has produced an initial set of recommended Action Items and Research Priorities (Cutter et al. 2002). This is an ongoing process and we invite the participation of the international geographic research community as we collectively continue to evolve this agenda in the months ahead.

BACKGROUND

The Geographical Dimensions of Terrorism (GDOT) research project undertook a twofold investigation that: 1) addressed the immediate disaster situation in a pilot study of the role and utility of geographic information and technologies in emergency management and response to the September 11, 2001 terrorist attacks; and 2) initiated a process to help develop a focused national research agenda on the geographical dimensions of terrorism. The research agenda and recommendations will be widely disseminated to national and international governmental agencies, the geographic research community, and to related disciplines. Other proposed outcomes of this ongoing process include the establishment of multi-institutional research collaborations focused on implementing some of the study's recommendations, and the long-term enhancement of the nation's research infrastructure to address important public policy needs and issues.

KEY RESEARCH THEMES

In our discussions with national policy officials and geographic researchers, three themes or broad areas of critical national research priority have emerged repeatedly. These key areas are: 1) Regional and International Research related to the Root Causes of Terrorism; 2) Vulnerability Science and Hazards Research; and 3) Geospatial Data and Technologies Infrastructure Research. Although these three research themes are interrelated and are all based on or integrated by questions of "Where," they in turn include a thread of "Why" (the root causes), "What" (the hazards and vulnerability), and "How" (the geospatial data and technology). We address each of these research areas and related questions in turn below, along with a set of proposed Action Items that were recommended in the workshop, meetings, and discussions we have held to date.

REGIONAL/INTERNATIONAL RESEARCH AND THE ROOT CAUSES OF TERRORISM

One of geography's great strengths is its ability to synthesize information about places in order to understand the linkages between regions and the manifestation of global processes at very local levels. There is rich set of contexts advanced by regional specialists that can assist in understanding the root causes of terrorism. These should be pursued in a systematic and analytically robust manner.

Priority Action Items:

1. *Develop and implement a major multiinstitutional, interdisciplinary research program on the root causes of terrorism.*

2. *Develop systematic efforts to foster stronger linkages within the international community of geographic scholars to enhance regionally specific research and training.*

3. *Conduct a regional studies needs assessment to determine the status of training and teaching in area studies, international studies, and global studies, as a basis for identifying the priorities for strengthening these programs in our universities and schools.*

Priority Research Issues

1. How has the political control of space (or lack thereof) fostered terrorism? In stateless regions, what spaces (functional,

policy, administrative) facilitate terrorism? What is the relevant regional space of terrorism and how do territorial ideologies change it? How do stateless zones shift their patterns through time, through changing environmental conditions, and population migrations?

2. What are the spatial networks and flows of information and capital that support terrorism and terrorist acts? Can we understand and ultimately model these nodes and networks?

3. Can we improve our understanding of how borders function, especially flows of goods and people, and how borders constrain or enhance transjurisdictional responses to issues such as immigration, disaster response, refugee movements, weapons proliferation, narco-terrorism, or environmental degradation?

4. What are the differential impacts of globalization and how are these manifested spatially?

5. How might a greater emphasis on geography education in the schools and increased understanding of the world and its diversity foster better cooperation among peoples and societies? How might improved knowledge of geographical differences in culture, ideology, religion, gender status, and social and physical conditions increase our understanding of the needs and perspectives of others, and they of us?

Additional Related Research Questions

6. What is the geography of inclusion and exclusion and how might these spheres be influential in reducing or heightening spaces of reaction and/or conflict?

7. How do we reinvigorate regional studies and foster foreign area experience among our students and other practitioners of geography?

8. What are the underlying circumstances that facilitate state-sponsored terrorism? Can we identify similarities in circumstances that can lead to early identification of potential source areas for terrorist activities?

9. What is the geographic variation, internationally, of perception of the United States and its role in the world? How do these perceptions affect, positively or negatively, the vulnerability of the United States to terrorism?

10. How might the patterns of urbanization change domestically and internationally in response to terrorist acts? If businesses and workers potentially become more at risk in major cities, how will this affect future locational decisions by businesses and residents, and the processes of urban development and

suburban sprawl? What constitutes a future urban environment that is less vulnerable to terrorism?

VULNERABILITY SCIENCE AND HAZARDS RESEARCH

The meaning of vulnerability has taken on new interpretations since September 11, 2001. We need to broaden our understanding of vulnerability beyond an exposure-response framework to a more holistic view that includes exposure, susceptibility, resistance, resilience, and adaptation. We need a major effort to develop the basic data, models, and methods for conducting vulnerability assessments at all spatial scales.

Priority Action Items

1. *Establish a national center devoted to vulnerability science (improvements in data, models, methods) and the implementation of longer-term monitoring and modeling of disaster response and recovery efforts.*

2. *Compile a national tool box for local communities consisting of a set of information, data and procedures that are required for conducting pre-impact vulnerability assessments, immediate disaster response actions, and post-event activities, to insure continuity of operations in times of crisis across all jurisdictions.*

3. *Establish a Quick Response program (funded by NSF or some other agency and administered by the AAG) that enables researchers to get into the field quickly after a major world event in order to secure critical geographical data and information that would otherwise be lost.*

Priority Research Issues

1. How do we incorporate concepts such as susceptibility, resistance, resilience, and adaptation into our understanding of vulnerability to environmental threats, including terrorism?
2. How do we incorporate the notion of surprise and uncertainty in our explanations of vulnerability and how do we prepare for surprise events?
3. Can we spatially delineate the vulnerability of people and places and develop a comparative indicator to assess where

vulnerabilities are greatest and why? In other words, what makes people and places vulnerable to environmental threats?

4. Vulnerability includes not only tangible items such as infrastructure, but also many intangible ones such as quality of life. How do we identify non-structural things of value and how should these be incorporated into our analyses of vulnerability? How do we determine our vulnerability to the unknown? How do we understand the fear associated with terrorist spaces, and how do we cope with it?

5. How do we insure the continuity of operations during an emergency and thus prepare for mutual support in terms of surprise? What types of data and information are required to insure an adequate response?

Additional Related Research Questions

6. How do we delineate high probability/low consequence events from low probability/high consequence events? Which should public policies focus on? Is there such as thing as "affordable" risk?

7. How do we link the vulnerability of people and places to terrorism to other sources of environmental threats? With regard to bioterrorism, for example, what are the geographic conditions and factors that affect the diffusion of purposely introduced diseases among populations of humans, animals and plants?

8. What lessons can be learned from the events of 9/11, and how might these be useful in improving emergency preparedness and response?

9. How do we include values, symbols, and landscapes of fear in vulnerability assessments? How important is the perception of risk rather than a quantitative estimate of it in determining societal or individual response?

10. Can we construct plausible models of mega-disasters to aid in our understanding of emergency preparedness and response?

GEOSPATIAL DATA AND TECHNOLOGIES RESEARCH

The use of geospatial data and technologies was critical during the rescue, relief, and longer-term recovery from the September 11, 2001 events. This prominence is now being reflected in planning for homeland security, and in international efforts to address terrorism. There are many pressing research needs, both short term and longer term, in the area of geographic information science and technology.

Priority Action Items:

1. *Establish a distributed national geospatial infrastructure as a foundation for homeland security. This infrastructure should be designed to serve multiple other needs, such as local government, planning, environmental protection, and economic development, as well.*

2. *Establish a Geography Division in the Office for Homeland Security to advise on issues such as geospatial data sharing, integration of geospatial data, data security, back up systems and operations, and overall needs assessment for homeland security.*

3. *Develop a network of national research centers designed to better understand and anticipate the geographically variable regional impacts, including economic impacts, of terrorist acts.*

Priority Research Issues

1. What are some of the underlying research, technical, and policy challenges in the development of functionally integrated national (or international) geospatial infrastructures for homeland security? What are the specific constraints and requirements in established GIScience research areas such as information fusion and visualization, spatial information conflation, mobile feature modeling, feature-attribute level security, spatial scaling, feature representation and categorization, distributed spatial data interoperability, and so on? What data are necessary, and in what format?

2. How do we develop better understanding of spatial-temporal models in three-dimensional space and time, and can we make these models work in real-time applications such as evacuations, or emergency response?

3. What are the critical lifelines and infrastructure vulnerabilities, and how do we identify their spatial linkages and interdependencies?

4. What were the variable geographic and economic impacts of the 9/11 events and how can these be more effectively modeled using geospatial technologies? How can we develop better spatial/economic models to predict variable short and long-term geographic impacts of other potential terrorist threats or hazards?

5. How can we more effectively link GIScience to regional studies to improve data collection and understanding of our world and its regional complexity?

Additional Related Research Questions

6. How do we model mobility and flows both statically and dynamically?

7. Can we develop remote geomonitoring systems for immediate data collection, particularly ones that put machines in harm's way rather than people?

8. What are the research challenges for continued integration of transformational geographic technologies (such as GIS, GPS, remote sensing, LIDAR, wireless mobile computing) to enhance disaster response, national security, and infrastructure vulnerability assessment? What is the potential for using these integrated Geographic Management Systems to address complex processes related to terrorism, such as disaster response, meaningful reduction of world poverty, sustainable development, and a host of other needs?

9. In an era of heightened security and precautions, how can individual human rights and privacy be protected, when the powerful capabilities of advanced geographic technologies, as with so many other advances in technology, have inherent within them a risk for potential abuse? What social responsibilities will those employing spatial technologies in the future have for human rights and privacy, and how have the events of September 11, 2001 changed the terms of that discussion and debate?

10. How can we link scale and resolution more effectively in public policy decisions regarding preparedness and readiness activities (small scale maps with limited detail) and real-time response (building floorplans)?

IT TAKES A COMMUNITY . . .

It is important to bring all of our geographical assets to bear on this important national and international priority. Collaborative efforts between organizations such as the Association of American Geographers, the International Geographical Union, the American Geographical Society, the National Geographic Society, the American Society for Photogrammetry and Remote Sensing, the University Consortium for Geographic Information Science, and many others—as well as interdisciplinary linkages and partnerships with federal agencies, private firms and international NGO's—will be required as we all work toward refining and achieving this ambitious agenda.

EPILOGUE

JACK DANGERMOND

ON SEPTEMBER 11, 2001, I worried about the safety of my friends and colleagues in New York City. ESRI's office in the Woolworth Building was a couple of blocks from the World Trade Center—what seemed like a good location, close to city government and business centers— suddenly became dangerously close to the epicenter of terror. Would they get out of there in time? How far would they have to walk to safety? Would there be another attack? Thankfully, no one was hurt. But the hours of waiting to account for them all stretched out like a surreal movie. As I reflect on that day and the days that followed, I am reminded that when people pass through horrors like this, their relationship to space and time changes. I am therefore particularly gratified to see that this book has outlined a strong research and policy agenda addressing the Geographical Dimensions of Terrorism. It examines fundamental questions that are critical to our exploration and understanding of this reign of terror and in overcoming its challenges.

I look to my colleagues in New York for inspiration when addressing some of these challenges. Following 9/11 the same people who lived through so much helped our friends in the Office of Emergency Management rebuild their geographic infrastructure. I am proud to say that our geography and GIS tools were up to the task and that they helped stitch together data from many sources to build thousands of maps during the next few weeks. Our GIS professionals did something very important—they aided the relief efforts by rebuilding a virtual city from LIDAR maps of the rubble, maps of the rerouted subway system, and maps showing the status of buildings surrounding Ground Zero.

Because this information was shared with the traumatized residents, primarily through the *New York Times*, many people felt more informed and worried a little less. In the recreated space of maps, there

231

was order and reason. The maps represented a solid foundation, quite apart from the trauma residents had just experienced or witnessed on television, and I believe they had a calming and reassuring effect.

Both as a country and as geographic professionals, we are confronting new challenges on a daily basis. As this book so richly demonstrates, we must find new ways to protect critical infrastructure from terrorism, understand the spaces terrorists inhabit, and build systems that can be implemented quickly to share spatial data without jeopardizing the security of the citizens we want to help. We must also find ways of understanding and addressing the causes of terrorist activity.

There are no easy solutions to reducing our vulnerability to terrorism and we still have much to do, but the greatest challenges often represent our greatest opportunities. Many of us came into geography hoping to make a difference in the world. These are uncertain times, but when I look back over what the world has been able to accomplish in the last fifty years, during times no less uncertain, I am very hopeful for the future.

NOTES

Introduction

1. The opinions in this document are those of the author and do not necessarily represent the position of the National Science Foundation, Yale University, or Haskins Laboratories.

2.2
Urban Vulnerability to Terrorism as Hazard

1. Hot wars are wars in which there is direct overt and lethal violence against an enemy rather than indirect cover and not-necessarily-lethal pressures of other kinds. The distinctions are roughly equivalent to notions of "high intensity" and "low intensity" conflicts that have been prevalent in the literature of strategic studies for many years.

2.3
Emergency Preparedness and Response—
Lessons Learned from 9/11

1. The author would like to thank David Kaufman, Office of National Preparedness, FEMA, and Alan Leidner, Director of Citywide Geographic Information Systems (GIS) for New York City for their reviews of the information contained herein.

3.3
Drug Production, Commerce, and Terrorism

1. The term fourth estate is frequently attributed to the nineteenth century historian Thomas Carlyle, though he himself seems to have attributed it to Edmund Burke (1840): Burke said there were Three Estates in Parliament; but, in the Re-

porters' Gallery yonder, there sat a Fourth Estate more important than they all. It is not a figure of speech, or a witty saying; it is a literal fact.

4.2
Remote Sensing Imagery for Emergency Management

1. The work in this paper was supported by the U.S. Army Corps of Engineers Civil Works Geospatial Research and Development Program (Methods of Rapid Image Processing for Emergency Management), and Headquarters, U.S. Army Corps of Engineers Operations Division Civil Emergency Management Branch's program for remote sensing and GIS emergency management support. The imagery was provided by SPOT Image Corporation, Space Imaging, Earth Data Aviation, RADARSAT, and Litton/WSI/TASC.

8
A Research and Action Agenda

1. Portions of this chapter were previously published by the Association of American Geographers in booklet form (Cutter, Richardson, and Wilbanks 2002), and are used here with permission of the Association of American Geographers.

REFERENCES

Adams, P. C. 2000. "Application of a CAD-based Accessibility Model," in D. G. Janelle and D. C. Hodge (eds.) *Information, Place and Cyberspace: Issues in Accessibility*. Berlin: Springer, pp. 217–39.

Albert, D. P. 2000. "Infectious Disease and GIS," in *Spatial Analysis, GIS, and Remote Sensing Applications in the Health Sciences* by D. P. Albert, W. M. Gesler, and B. Levergood (eds.). Chelsea, MI: Ann Arbor Press, pp. 111–27.

Albert, D. P., W. M. Gesler, and P. S. Wittie. 2000. "Geographic Information Systems in Health Services Research" in *Spatial Analysis, GIS, and Remote Sensing Applications in the Health Sciences* by D. P. Albert, W. M. Gesler, and B. Levergood (eds.). Chelsea, MI: Ann Arbor Press, pp. 55–75.

Alexander, D. 1991. "Information technology in Real-Time for Monitoring and Managing Natural Disasters." *Progress in Physical Geography* 15(3): 238–60.

Alexander, D., 2002. "Nature's Impartiality, Man's Inhumanity: Reflections on Terrorism and World Crisis in a Context of Historical Disaster," *Disasters* 26(1): 1–9.

Ali, T. and R. Matthews. 1999. *Civil Wars in Africa: Roots and Resolutions*. Montreal and Kingston, ON: McGill/Queens University Press.

Alibek, K. and S. Handelman. 1999. *Biohazard*. New York: Random House.

American Association of Veterinary Laboratory Diagnosticians (AAVLD). 2001. National Animal Health Laboratory Network. Available online at http://www.aavld.org/MainMenu2/NAHLN/NAHLNaugust2002.htm

Anderson, S. and S. Sloan. 2002. *Historical Dictionary of Terrorism*. Lanham, MD: Rowman & Littlefield.

Appadurai, A. 2001. "Disjuncture and difference in the Global Cultural Economy," in *The Globalization Reader* by F. J. Lechner and J. Boli (ed.), Oxford, U.K.: Blackwell, pp. 322–30.

Armstrong, K. 2000. *The Battle for God: A History of Fundamentalism*. New York: Ballantine Books.

Armstrong, M. P. 2002. "Geographic Information Technologies and Their Potentially Erosive Effects on Personal Privacy." *Studies in the Social Sciences* 27(1): 19–28.

Armstrong, M. P., P. J. Densham, and G. Rushton. 1986. "Architecture for a Microcomputer-Based Spatial Decision Support System." *Proceedings of the Second International Symposium on Spatial Data Handling.* Columbus, OH: International Geographical Union, 120–31

Aronson, E., P. C. Stern, Commission on Behavioral and Social Aspects of Energy Consumption and Production, National Research Council. 1984. *Energy Use: The Human Dimension.* San Francisco: W. H. Freeman.

Arquilla, J. and D. Ronfeldt. 2001. "Osama bin Laden and the Advent of Netwar." *New Perspectives Quarterly* 18: 4.

Arrighi, G.1994. *The Long Twentieth Century: Money, Power and the Origins of Our Times.* London and New York: Verso Books.

Ashford, D. A., T. M. Gomez, D. L. Noah, D. P. Scott, and D. R. Franz. 2000. "Biological Terrorism and Veterinary Medicine in the United States." *Journal of the American Veterinary Medical Association* 217(5): 664–67 .

Bagley, B. M. and W. O. Walker III, eds. 1994. *Drug Trafficking in the Americas.* Boulder, CO: Lynne Rienner Publishers.

Baldauf, S. 2001. "Afghan Poppies May Bloom Again." *The Christian Science Monitor,* November 23, p. 1.

Ban, J. 2000. "Agricultural Biological Warfare: An Overview." *The Arena* 9: 1–8 http://www.cbaci.org.

Barletta, M., A. Sands, and J. B. Tucker. 2002. "Keeping Track of Anthrax: The Case for a Biosecurity Convention." *The Bulletin of the Atomic Scientists* 58(3): 57–62.

Barnes, S. 2001. "United in Purpose: Spatial Help in the Aftermath." *Geospatial Solutions* 11(11): 34–39.

Barrows, H. H., 1923. "Geography as Human Ecology." *Annals of the Association of American Geographers* 12: 1–14.

Barthell, E. N., W. H. Cordell, H. William, J. C. Moorhead, J. Handler, C. Feied, M. S. Smith, D. G. Cochrane, C. W. Felton, and M. Collins. 2002. "The Frontlines of Medicine Project: a Proposal for the Standardized Communication of Emergency Department Data for Public Health Uses Including Syndromic Surveillance for Biological and Chemical Terrorism." *Annals of Emergency Medicine.* 39(4): 422–29.

Bayardo R. J. Jr., W. Bohrer, R. Brice, A Chichoki, J. Fowler, A. Helal, V. Kanshyap, T. Ksiezyk, G. Martin, M. Nodine, M. Rashid, M. Rusinkiewicz, R. Shea, C. Unruh, and D. Woelk. 1997. "InfoSlueth, Agent-Based Semantic Integration of Information in Open and Dynamic Environments." *Readings in Agents* by M. N. Huhns and M. P. Sing (eds.). San Francisco: Morgan Kaufman Publishers, pp. 205–16.

Bayart, J. F., S. Ellis, and B. Hibou. 1999. *The Criminalization of the State in Africa.* Oxford: James Currey.

Beaird, M. 2001. Northwest Division, U.S. Army Corps of Engineers, Personal Communication, October.

Berdica, K. 2000. *Analyzing Vulnerability in the Road Transportation System,* Licentiate Thesis, Department of Infrastructure and Planning, Royal Institute of Technology, Stockholm, Sweden.

Bergman, A. and J. El-Tahri. 2000. *Israel and the Arabs: An Eyewitness Account of War and Peace in the Middle East.* New York: TV Books.

Biliouri, D. and T. Makarenko. 2001. "U.S. Refusal to Sign Biowar Treaty Threatens World Security." *Jane's Intelligence Review* 13(1): 47–49.

Birkin, M., G. Clarke, M. Clarke, and A. Wilson. 1996. *Intelligent GIS: Location Decisions and Strategic Planning.* Cambridge, U.K.: GeoInformation International.

Blaikie, P., T. Cannon, I. Davis, and B. Wisner, 1994. *At Risk: Natural Hazards, People's Vulnerability, and Disasters.* London: Routledge.

Blair, B. 2002. "Homeland Puzzle—Can Bush Piece Together 170,000 People, 22 Agencies into a Single Department?" *Federal Times* June 10, 2002: 1.

Bolus, R. and A. Bruzewicz. 2002. "Evaluation of New Sensors for Emergency Management," Technical Report ERDC/CRREL TR-02–11. U.S. Army Corps of Engineers, Engineer Research and Development Center, August 2002.

Booth, M. 1996. *Opium: a History.* New York: St. Martin's Griffin.

Borio, L. and 25 others, for the Working Group on Civilian Biodefense. 2002. "Hemorrhagic Fever Viruses as Biological Weapons: Medical and Public Health Management." *Journal of the American Medical Association* 287(18): 2391–405.

Bovine Alliance on Management and Nutrition (BAMN). 2001. *Biosecurity on Dairies.* http://www.aphis.usda.gov/vs/ceah/cahm/Dairy_Cattle/BAMNDairy.pdf

Brams, S. J. 1975. *Game Theory and Politics.* New York: The Free Press.

Braudel, F. 1984. *The Perspective of the World: Civilization and Capitalism, 15th–18th Century.* Volume 3. New York: Harper & Row.

Brown, C. 1999. "Burma: The Political Economy of Violence." *Disasters* 23(3): 234–56.

Brown, C. 2002. "The Interface of Animal and Human Health." Presented at the International Conference on Emerging Infectious Diseases. March 25, 2002, Atlanta, GA. Available online at: http://www.cdc.gov/iceid/webcast/plenary2.htm.

Brown, J. K. M. and M. S. Hovmøller. 2002. "Aerial Dispersal of Pathogens on the Global and Continental Scales and its Impact on Plant Disease." *Science* 297: 537–541.

Brown, M., ed. 1996. *The International Dimensions of Internal Conflict.* Cambridge, MA: MIT Press.

Bruzewicz, A. J., D. M. Pokrzywka, and C. Devine. 1998. "Remote Sensing, GIS, and the Intranet in the U.S. Army Corps of Engineers, ENGLink Interactive for Emergency Management." Presented at International Challenges for the Next Decade, May 19–22, 1998, Washington, D.C.: The International Emergency Management Society Conference, pp. 191–204.

Bulletin of the Atomic Scientists. 2002. "The Center Spread: Battle Stats." *Bulletin of the Atomic Scientists* 58 (5): 38–39.

Bunk, S. 2002. "Early Warning: U.S. Scientists Counter Bioterrorism with New Electronic Surveillance Systems." *The Scientist.* 16(9): 14.

Burns, L. D. 1979. *Transportation, Temporal and Spatial Components of Accessibility.* Lexington, MA: Lexington Books.

Burrough, P. A., 1986. *Principles of Geographical Information Systems for Land Resources Assessment.* New York: Oxford University Press.

Burton, I., R. W. Kates, and G. F. White, 1993. *The Environment as Hazards, 2nd Edition.* New York: Guildford Press.

Bush, G. W. 2001. *Presidential Executive Order 13231 on Critical Infrastructure Protection in the Information Age.* The White House, October 16, 2001.

Bush, G. W. 2002. "President Bush's Address to the Nation, June 6, 2002." Online: www.whitehouse.gov/deptofhomeland/.

Busumtwi-Sam, J. 1999. "Redefining Security After the Cold War: The OAU, the UN and Conflict Management in Africa," in *Civil Wars in Africa*, by T. Ali and R. Mathews (eds.). Kingston, ON: McGill/Queens University Press, pp. 257–287.

Cahan, B. and M. Ball. 2002. "GIS at Ground Zero: Spatial Technology Bolsters World Trade Center Response and Recovery." *GEOWorld* 15(1): 26–29.

Cameron, G., J. Pate, and K. Vogel. 2001. "Planting Fear." *The Bulletin of the Atomic Scientists* 57(5): 38–44.

Camp, D. D. 2000. "Domestic Terrorism," in *Atlas of Crime: Mapping the Criminal Landscape*, by L. S. Turnbull, E. H. Hendrix, and B. S. Dent (eds.). Phoenix: Oryx Press, p. 162–170.

Campbell, G. 2002. *Blood Diamonds.* Boulder: Westview Press.

Carlock, K. 2001. Rock Island District, U.S. Army Corps of Engineers, Personal communication, November.

Carlson, R. A. and R. A. Di Giandomenico. 1991. *Understanding Building Automation Systems.* Kingston, MA: R. S. Means Company, Inc.

Carlyle, T. 1840. *On Heroes, Hero-Worship and the Heroic in History.* London: Chapman and Hall.

Castegneri, J. 1998. "Temporal GIS Explores New Dimensions of Time." *GIS World* 11 (9): 48–51.

Castells, M. 1996. *The Rise of the Network Society.* Malden: Blackwell.

———. 1997. *The Power of Identity.* Malden: Blackwell.

Census Bureau, U.S. Department of Commerce. 2000. *County and City Data Book: 2000, A Statistical Abstract Supplement.* 13th ed. Table B-10. Counties: Farm Population, Farm Earnings, and Agriculture. Washington: Census Bureau.

Center for Nonproliferation Studies (CNS), Monterey Institute of International Studies. 2002. *Agro-Terrorism: Agricultural Biowarfare: State Programs to Develop Offensive Capabilities.* http://cns.miis.edu/research/cbw/agprogs.htm.

Centers for Disease Control and Prevention (CDC). 1993. "Update: Multistate Outbreak of Escherichia Coli O157:H7 Infections from Hamburgers–Western United States, 1992–1993." *MMWR Weekly* 42(13): 258–63.

———. 2000. "Biological and Chemical Terrorism: Strategic Plan for Preparedness and Response. Recommendations of the CDC Strategic Planning Workgroup." *MMWR Weekly* 49(No. RR-4): 1–14.

———. 2002. The National Electronic Disease Surveillance System. Available online at: http://www.cdc.gov/nedss/

Chalk, P. 2000. "The Agroterrorism Threat." *Conference Proceedings, Bioterrorism: Homeland Defense Symposium: The Next Steps.* February 8–10, 2000. Santa Monica, CA.

Choy, M., M.-P. Kwan, and H. V. Leong. 2000. "Distributed Database Design for Mobile Geographical Applications." *Journal of Database Management* 11(1): 3–17.

Chyba, C. 2002. "Toward Biological Security." *Foreign Affairs* May/June 2002: 122–37.

Cincotta, R. P., J. Wisnewski, and R. Engleman. 2000. "Human Population in the Biodiversity Hotspots." *Nature* 404 (27 April): 990–92.

Clark, K. 1999. *Mapping Crime: Principle and Practice.* Washington, D.C.: National Institute of Justice.

Clawson, P. L. and R. W. Lee III, 1998. *The Andean Cocaine Industry.* New York: St. Martin's Griffin.

Clinton, W. 1996. *Presidential Executive Order13010 on Critical Infrastructure Protection.* The White House, July 15, 1996.

———. 1998. Presidential Decision Directive 63, *The Clinton Administration's Policy on Critical Infrastructure Protection (White Paper)*, The White House, May 1998.

Cohen J. E. and C. Small. 1998. "Hypsographic Demography: The Distribution of Human Population by Altitude." *Proceedings, National Academy of Sciences* 95(24): 14009–14.

Comfort, L. B. Wisner, S. Cutter, R. Pulwarty, K. Hewitt, A. Oliver-Smith, J. Wiener, M. Fordham, W. Peacock, and F. Krimgold. 1999. "Reframing Disaster Policy: the Global Evolution of Vulnerable Communities." *Environmental Hazards* 1(1): 39–44.

Commission on National Security. 2001. *Road Map for National Security: Imperative for Change*, Phase III Report of the U.S. Commission on National Security in the 21st Century, February 15, 2001 (Hart-Rudman Commission Report).

Conway, K., D. McArthur, C. Tague, and R. Wright. 2000. "Integrating GIS and Flood Hazard and Risk Modeling in a Cross-Border Data Poor Environment." *Proceedings, Fourth International Conference on GIS and Environmental Modeling.* Banff, Alberta p. 12.

Couclelis, H. and A. Getis. 2000. "Conceptualizing and Measuring Accessibility within Physical and Virtual Spaces," in *Information, Place and Cyberspace: Issues in Accessibility* by D. G. Janelle and D. C. Hodge (eds.). Berlin: Springer, pp. 15–20.

The Countryside Agency, 2001. *Foot and Mouth Disease: The State of the Countryside Report.* http://www.countryside.gov.uk/stateofthecountryside.

Courtwright, D. T. 2001. *Forces of Habit: Drugs and the Making of the Modern World.* Cambridge, MA: Harvard University Press.

Cova, T. J. and R. L. Church. 1997. "Modeling Community Evacuation Vulnerability Using GIS." *International Journal of Geographic Information Science* 11: 763–84.

Crains' 1992. *Chicago Business*, December issue, p. 1

Crenshaw, M. 1981. "Thoughts on Relating Terrorism to Historical Contexts," in *Terrorism in Context* by M. Crenshaw (ed.) University Park, PA: Pennsylvania State University Press, pp. 3–24.

Cresswell, T. 1996. *In Place/Out of Place: Geography, Ideology and Transgression.* Minneapolis, MN: University of Minnesota Press.

Cromley, E. K. and S. L. McLafferty. 2002. *GIS and Public Health.* New York: The Guildford Press.

Curry, M. 1997. "The Digital Individual and the Private Realm." *Annals of the Association of American Geographers* 87(4): 681–99.

Curtis, G. B., R. Stoddard, D. Y. Kim, and J. K. Devasundaram. 2002. "Anthrax: GIS Helps Investigators Hunt for the Deadly Spores." *GeoWorld* 15 (10): 34–37.

Cutter, S. L., 1988. "Geographers and Nuclear War: Why We Lack Influence on Public Policy." *Annals of the Association of American Geographers* 78(1): 132–43.

———. (ed.). 1994. *Environmental Risks and Hazards.* Englewood Cliffs, NJ: Prentice Hall.

———. (ed.). 2001. *American Hazardscapes: The Regionalization of Hazards and Disasters.* Washington, D.C.: The Joseph Henry Press, National Academy of Sciences.

Cutter, S. L., J. T. Mitchell, and M. S. Scott. 2000. "Revealing the Vulnerability of People and Places: A Case Study of Georgetown County, South Carolina." *Annals of the Association of American Geographers* 90(4): 713–37.

Cutter, S. L., D. Richardson, and T. Wilbanks. 2002. *The Geographical Dimensions of Terrorism: Action Items and Research Priorities.* Washington, D.C.: Association of American Geographers.

Cutter, S. L. and W. H. Renwick. 2003. *Exploitation, Conservation, Preservation: A Geographic Perspective on Natural Resource Use.* New York: John Wiley & Sons.

Dangermond, J. 2002a. "Taking the Pulse of the Planet with GIS." *ESRI News, ArcNews,* Spring 2002. http://www.esri.com/news/arcnews/spring02articles/takingthe pulse.html.

———. 2002b. *Geographic Information for Diplomacy, Development, and Homeland Security.* Presentation to the Secretary's Open Forum—Department of State, July 26, 2002.

Dansby, B. 2002. Personal correspondence.

Dao, J. 2002. "The War on Terrorism Takes Aim at Crime." *New York Times,* April 7: Section 4: 5.

Daratech, Inc. 2002. http://www.daratech.com.

Date, C. J., 1975. *An Introduction to Database Systems.* Reading, MA: Addison-Wesley.

Davis, B. 2002. Stennis Space Center, NASA, Personal communication, August.

Densham, P. J., 1991. "Spatial Decision Support Systems," in *Geographical Information Systems and Applications* by P. J. Densham, (ed.) London: Longman Scientific and Technical, pp. 403–12.

Dobkins, L. Harris and Y.M. Ioannides. 2001. "Spatial Interactions among US cities." *Regional Science and Urban Economics* 31: 701–732.

Dobson, J. E. 2001. "Global Data Coverage Makes Progress." *GeoWorld* 14 (5): 26–27.

Dobson, J. E., E. A. Bright, P. R. Coleman, and B. L. Bhaduri. 2003. "LandScan2000: A New Global Population Geography," in *Remotely-Sensed Cities.* by V. Mesev (ed.). London: Taylor & Francis, Ltd, forthcoming.

Dobson, J. E., E. A. Bright, P. R. Coleman, R.C. Durfee, B. A. Worley. 2000. "LandScan: A Global Population Database for Estimating Populations at Risk." *Photogrammetric Engineering & Remote Sensing* 66(7): 849–57.

DoD (U.S. Department of Defense). 1998. *The Critical Infrastructure Protection (CIP) Plan* (draft), November 18, 1998.

Duffield, M. 2000. "Globalization, Transborder Trade, and War Economies," in *Greed and Grievance: Economic Agendas in Civil Wars* by Mats Berdal and D. Malone (ed.). Boulder, CO: Lynne Rienner Publishers, pp. 69–89

Economist. 2002. "A Bumper Crop." *Economist.* October 5: 42.

Enders, W., 1995: *Applied Econometric Time Series*. New York: Wiley & Sons.

Economic Research Service (ERS), US Department of Agriculture. 2001. *U.S. Agricultural Trade Update*. FAU-59. Monthly supplement to Foreign Agricultural Trade of the United States. November 26.

———. 2002. *U.S. and State Farm Income Data*. 20 August (last update). http://www.ers.usda.gov/Data/farmincome/finfidmu.htm.

ESRI. 2000. *Map Book Volume 17: Geography and GIS-Sustaining our World*. Redlands, CA: ESRI Press.

Estrin, D. 1999. "Next Century Challenges: Scalable Coordination in Sensor Networks." Marina del Rey, CA: USC/Information Sciences Institute.

Falk, T. and R. Abler. 1980. "Intercommunications, Distance, and Geographical Theory." *Geografiska Annaler* 62B: 59–67.

Fege, D. 2002. Personal communication, January 7, 2002. Fege is with the U.S. EPA Border Liaison Office in San Diego.

Federal Bureau of Investigation (FBI). 2002. "The Terrorist Threat Confronting the United States." Congressional statement before the Senate Select Committee on Intelligence, February 6. http://www.fbi.gov/congress/congress02/watson020602.htm.

FEMA (Federal Emergency Management Agency). 1996. *State and Local Guide for All—Hazard Emergency Operations Planning*. Washington, D.C.: Federal Emergency Management Agency.

———. 2002a. *Managing the Emergency Consequences of Terrorist Incidents, Interim Planning Guide for State and Local Governments*. Washington, D.C.: Federal Emergency Management Agency.

———. 2002b. *"Tool Kit for Managing the Emergency Consequences of Terrorist Incidents, Interim Planning Guide for State and Local Governments."* Washington, D.C.: Federal Emergency Management Agency.

FGDC (Federal Geographic Data Committee). 2002a. *Geospatial One-Stop*, http://www.fgdc.gov/geo-one-stop (accessed August 15, 2002).

———. 2002b. http://www.fgdc.org.

———. 2002c. "Homeland Security and Geographic Information Systems: How GIS and Mapping Technology Can Save Lives and Protect Property in Post-September 11th America." http://www.fgdc.gov/publications/homeland.html

Feldman, D. L. 1995. "Revisiting the Energy Crisis: How Far Have We Come?" *Environment* 37 (4): 16–20, 42–44.

Fonseca, F. T., M. J. Egenhofer, P. Agouris, and G. Camara. 2002. "Using Ontologies for Integrated Geographic Information Systems." *Transactions in GIS* 6: 231–57.

Forer, P. 1998. "Geometric Approaches to the Nexus of Time, Space and Microprocess: Implementing a Practical Model for Mundane Socio-Spatial Systems," in M. J. Egenhofer and R. G. Golledge (eds.), *Spatial and Temporal Reasoning in Geographic Information Systems*. New York: Oxford University Press, pp. 171–90.

Foresman, T. W. (ed.). 1998. *The History of Geographic Information Systems: Perspectives from the Pioneers*. Upper Saddle River, NJ: Prentice Hall PTR.

Fowler, C. and P. Mooney. 1990. *Shattering: Food, Politics, and the Loss of Genetic Diversity*. Tucson: University of Arizona Press.

Fraser, M. R. and D. L. Brown. 2000. "Bioterrorism Preparedness and Local Public Health Agencies: Building Response Capacity." *Public Health Reports* 115(4): 326–30.

Fuller, G., A. B. Murphy, M. Ridgley, and R. Ulack. 2000. "Measuring Potential Ethnic Conflict in Southeast Asia." *Growth and Change* 31: 305–31.

Fulton, B. 2002. *Leveraging Technology in the Service of Diplomacy: Innovation in the Department of State.* Arlington, VA: E-Government Series, The Pricewaterhouse-Coopers Endowment for The Business of Government, March.

Gahegan, M., B. Brodaric, and M. Takatsuka. 2000. "Designing a Framework to Support the Semantic Interoperability of Geospatial Information." *Proceedings of GIScience 2000 Conference.* October 2000. http://www.geovista.psu.edu/ publications/aag99vr/GIScience2000/102-Gahegan.pdf.

Ganster, P. 1993. "Transborder Linkages in the San Diego-Tijuana Region." *San Diego-Tijuana in Transition: A Regional Analysis,* by N. C. Clement and E. Z. Miramontes (eds.). San Diego: IRSC, pp. 109–18.

———. 1998. "The United States-Mexico Border Region: An Overview." *Photogrammetric Engineering and Remote Sensing* (64)11: 1077–83.

———. 2000. *San Diego-Tijuana International Border Area Planning Atlas.* San Diego: San Diego State University Press and Institute for Regional Studies of the Californias.

Ganster, P. and A. Sweedler. 1990. "The United States-Mexican Border Region: Security and Interdependence." *United States-Mexico Border Statistics Since 1900,* by David Lorey (ed.). Los Angeles: UCLA Latin American Center Publications, pp. 419–441.

Garrison, H. G., C. W. Runyan, J. E. Tintinalli, C. W. Barber, W. C. Bordley, S. W. Hargarten, D. A. Pollack, and H. B. Weiss. 1994. "Emergency Department Surveillance: An Examination of Issues and a Proposal for a National Strategy." *Annals of Emergency Medicine* 24(5): 849–55.

Gatrell, A. C. 2002. *Geographies of Health: An Introduction.* Malden, MA: Blackwell Publishers.

Gedicks, A. 2001. *Resource Rebels.* Cambridge, MA: South End Press.

Geiger, H. J. 2001. "Terrorism, Biological Weapons, and Bonanzas: Assessing the Real Threat to Public Health." *American Journal of Public Health* 91(5): 708–9.

Gelernter, D. 1992. *Mirror Worlds: or The Day Software Puts the Universe in a Shoebox . . . How it Will Happen and What it Will Mean.* London: Oxford University Press.

General Accounting Office. 2001a. *Bioterrorism: Federal Research and Preparedness Activities.*(GAO-01–915, Sept 28, 2001)

———. 2001b. *Combating Terrorism: Selected Challenges and Related Recommendations.* (GAO-01–822, Sept 20, 2001).

———. 2002. *Critical Infrastructure Protection: Federal Efforts Require a More Coordinated and Comprehensive Approach for Protecting Information Systems,* (GAO-02–474), Report to the Committee on Government Affairs, U.S. Senate (July 15, 2002).

GeoCommunity, 2001. "Intergraph's Response and Recovery Efforts in New York City." *Spatial News.* www.geo.com.

Getis, A. and J. K. Ord. 1996. "Local Spatial Statistics: An Overview," in *Spatial Analysis: Modelling in a GIS Environment*, by P. Longley and M. Batty (eds.). Cambridge, UK: Geoinformation International, pp. 261–78.

GC (Gilmore Commission). 2001. *Third Annual Report to the President and the Congress*, Advisory Panel to Assess Domestic Response Capabilities for Terrorism Involving Weapons of Mass Destruction. December 15, 2001 (Gilmore Commission Third Report).

Gleick, J. 1999. *Faster: The Acceleration of Just About Everything*. New York: Pantheon Books.

Goldhaber, M. H. 1997. "Attention shoppers!" *Wired*, 5.12. Available at www.wired. com.

Goldstone, J. 2001. "Demography, Environment and Security," in *Environmental Conflict*, by P. F. Diehl and N. P. Gleditsch (eds.). Boulder, CO: Westview Press, pp. 84–108.

Golledge, R. G. and R. J. Stimson. 1997. *Spatial Behavior: A Geographic Perspective*. New York: Guilford Press.

Goodchild, M. F., 1997. "Towards a Geography of Geographic Information in a Digital World. *Computers, Environment and Urban Systems* 21(6): 377–91.

———. 1997. "What is Geographic Information Science?" *NCGIA Core Curriculum in GIScience*, http://www.ncgia.ucsb.edu/giscc/units/u002/u002.html. Posted October 7, 1997.

———. 2002. "MapFusion for GIS Interoperability." *Geospatial Solutions* 12(4): 48–51.

Goodchild, M. F., M. J. Egenhofer, R. Fegeas, and C. A. Kottman (eds.). 1999. *Interoperating Geographic Information Systems*. Boston: Kluwer Academic Publishers.

Goodson, L. P. 2001. *Afghanistan's Endless War: State Failure, Regional Politics, and the Rise of the Taliban*. Seattle: University of Washington Press.

Gould, P. 1993. *The Slow Plague: A Geography of the AIDS Pandemic*. New York: Blackwell.

Government of Canada. 2002. *Critical Infrastructure Protection Home Page*, Office of Critical Infrastructure Protection and Emergency Preparedness, Government of Canada. www.ocipep.gc.ca/critical/index_e.html (accessed August 1, 2002).

Greene, R. W. 2000. *GIS in Public Policy: Using Geographic Information for More Effective Government*. Redlands, CA: ESRI Press.

———. 2002. *Confronting Catastrophe: A GIS Handbook*. Redlands: ESRI Press.

Greenman, Catherine. 2001. "Mapping the Hazards to Keep Rescuers Safe." *New York Times On Line*. Accessed at nytimes.com, October 4, 2001.

Guillén López, T., and G. Sparrow. 2000. "Governance and Administrative Boundaries." *San Diego-Tijuana International Border Area Planning Atlas*, by P. Ganster (ed.). San Diego: San Diego State University Press and Institute for Regional Studies of the Californias, pp. 41–47.

Hägerstrand, T. 1970. "What About Ppeople in Regional Science?" *Papers of the Regional Science Association* 24: 7–21.

Haggett, P. 1975. *Geography: A Modern Synthesis*. 2d ed., New York: Harper and Row.

Haining, R. 1998. "Spatial statistics and the Analysis of Health Data," in *GIS and Health*, by A. C. Gatrell and M. Lytonen (eds.). Padstow, UK: Taylor & Francis, pp. 29–47.

Harris, S. 2002. "Disconnect." Government Executive Magazine, September 1, 2002. Available www.govexec.com/features/0902/090257.htm

Hardt, M. and A. Negri. 2000. *Empire.* Cambridge, MA: Harvard University Press.

Hart, J. F. 1991. *The Land that Feeds Us.* New York: Norton.

Harvey, D. 2002. "Cracks in the Edifice of the Empire State," in M. Sorkin and S. Zukin (eds.), *After the World Trade Center: Rethinking New York City.* New York: Routledge, pp. 57–67.

Herbst, J. 2000. *States and Power in Africa.* Princeton, NJ: Princeton University Press.

Hegeman, R. 2001. "Terrorism Took a Toll on Kansas." *The Topeka Capital-Journal.* December 30. http://www.cjonline.com/stories/123001/kst_ksterror.shtml

Heidemann, J. 2001. *Using Geospatial Information in Sensor Networks.* Marina del Rey: USC/Information Sciences Institute.

Hewings, G. J. D., and R. Mahidhara. 1996. "Economic Impacts: Lost Income, Ripple Effects and Recovery," in S. Changnon (ed.) *The Great Flood of 1993.* Boulder: Westview Press, pp. 205–17.

Hewings, G. J. D., M. Sonis, J. Guo, P. R. Israilevich and G. R. Schindler. 1998. "The Hollowing Out Process in the Chicago Economy, 1975–2015," *Geographical Analysis* 30(3): 217–33.

Hewings, G. J. D., S. Changnon and C. Dridi. 2000. "Assessing the Significance of Extreme Weather and Climate Events on State Economies." *Discussion Paper* 00-T-6 Regional Economics Applications Laboratory, University of Illinois, Urbana (www.uiuc.edu/unit/real).

Hewitt, K. 1997. *Regions of Risk.* London: Longman.

Hewitt, K. and I. Burton, 1971. *The Hazardousness of Place: A Regional Ecology of Damaging Events.* Toronto: University of Toronto, Department of Geography Research Publication #6.

Hirschfield, A. and K. Bowers (eds.). 2001. *Mapping and Analyzing Crime Data: Lessons from Research and Practice.* New York: Taylor and Francis.

Hodgson, M. E. and S. L. Cutter. 2001. "Mapping and the Spatial Analysis of Hazardscapes," in *American Hazardscapes: The Regionalization of Hazards and Disasters* by S. L. Cutter (ed.). Washington, D.C.: Joseph Henry Press, pp. 37–60.

Hoffman, B. 1998. *Inside Terrorism.* New York: Columbia University Press.

Horiuchi, V. 1997. "I-15 Side Effect: Worry Over Rising Accident Rate." *Salt Lake Tribune,* 11/10/1997, p. D1.

Hughes, J. M. and J. L. Gerberding. 2002. "Anthrax Bioterrorism: Lessons Learned and Future Directions." *Emerging Infectious Diseases* 8(12): 1013–1014.

Huntington, S. P. 1996. *The Clash of Civilizations and the Remaking of World Order.* New York: Touchstone.

Hutchinson, A. 2002. "International Drug Trafficking and Terrorism. Testimony before the Senate Judiciary Committee Subcommittee on Technology, Terrorism, and Government Information, March 13, 2002." Available online at http://www.state.gov/g/inl/rls/rm/2002/9239.htm.

Isaacson, J. and K. O'Connell, 2002. *Beyond Sharing Intelligence, We Must Generate Knowledge.* Rand Review V 26, N 2.

Jacquez, G. M., 1997. "Medical Geography and Disease Clustering," in *1997 McGraw-Hill Yearbook of Science and Technology,* New York: McGraw-Hill, pp. 297–99.

Jankowski, P. 1995. "Integrating Geographical Information Systems and Multiple Criteria Decision-Making Methods." *International Journal of Geographical Information Science* 9: 251–273

Jensen, J. R. and M. E. Hodgson. 2003. "Remote Sensing of Natural and Man-Made Hazards and Disasters," *Manual of Remote Sensing: Human Settlements.* Bethesda, MD: ASPRS, forthcoming.

Jordan, P. 1993. "The Problems of Creating a Stable Political-Territorial Structure in Hitherto Yugoslavia," in *Croatia: A New European State*, by I. Crkvenci, M. Klemencic, and D. Feletar (eds.). Zagreb: Urednici, pp. 133–42.

Kant, E. 2002. "Wireless GIS Solution Aids WTC Rescue Efforts." *ArcUser* 5(1): 13–17.

Kasperson, J. X., R. E. Kasperson, and B. L. Turner II. 1995. *Regions at Risk: Comparisons of Threatened Environments.* Tokyo, New York, Paris: United Nations University Press.

Kasperson, R. E. and J. X. Kasperson (eds). 2001. *Global Environmental Risk.* Tokyo, New York, Paris and London: United Nations University Press and Earthscan.

Kasperson, R. E., O. Renn, P. Slovic, H. S. Brown, J. Emel, R. Goble, J. X. Kasperson, and S. Ratick, 1988. "The Social Amplification of Risk: A Conceptual Framework." *Risk Analysis* 8(2): 177–87.

Katele, I. B. 1988. "Piracy and the Venetian State: The Dilemma of Maritime Defense in the Fourteenth Century." *Speculum* 63(4): 865–89.

Keen, D. 2000. "Incentives and Disincentives for Violence," in *Greed and Grievance: Economic Agendas in Civil Wars*, by M. Berdal and D. Malone (eds.). Boulder, CO: Lynne Rienner, Publishers, pp. 19–41

Kemp, K., and R. Wright. 1997. "UCGIS Identifies GIScience Education Priorities." *GeoInfoSystems* 7: 16–20.

Kemp, Z. and A. Kowalczyk. 1994. "Incorporating the Temporal Dimension in a GIS," in M. Worboys (ed.) *Innovations in GIS, 1.* New York: Taylor and Francis, pp. 89–103.

Kent, R. 1993. "Geographical Dimensions of the Shining Path Insurgency in Peru." *Geographical Review* 83(4): 441–54.

Khaemba, W. M. and A. Stein. 2000. "Use of GIS for a Spatial and Temporal Analysis of Kenyan Wildlife with Generalized Linear Modeling." *International Journal of Geographical Information Science* 14(8): 833–53.

Kitron, U. 1998. "Landscape Ecology and Epidemiology of Vector-Borne Diseases: Tools for Spatial Analysis," *Journal of Medical Entomology* 35: 435–45.

Klare, M. 1995. *Rogue States and Nuclear Outlaws: America's Search for a New Foreign Policy.* New York: Hill and Wang.

Klare, M. T. 2001. *Resource Wars: The New Landscape of Global Conflict.* New York: Metropolitan Books.

Kohnen, A. 2000. *Responding to the Threat of Agroterrorism: Specific Recommendations for the United States Department of Agriculture.* BCSIA Discussion Paper 2000–29, ESDP Discussion Paper ESD-2000–04. Cambridge, MA: John F. Kennedy School of Government, Harvard University. October.

Kuokka, E. and L. Harada. 1998. "Matchmaking for Information Agents," in *Readings in Agents*, by M. N. Huhns and M. P. Sing (eds.). San Francisco: Morgan Kaufman Publishers, pp. 91–97.

Kwan, M.-P. 1997. "GISICAS: An Activity-Based Travel Decision Support System Using a GIS-Interfaced Computational-Process Model," in *Activity-Based Approaches to Travel Analysis*, by D. F. Ettema and H. J.P. Timmermans (eds.). New York: Pergamon, pp. 263–282.

———. 2000. "Interactive Geovisualization of Activity-Travel Patterns Using Three-Dimensional Geographical Information Systems: A Methodological Exploration with a Large Data Set." *Transportation Research C* 8: 185–203.

Lakshmanan, T. R. 1993. "Social Change Induced by Technology: Promotion and Resistence," in N. Akerman (ed.), *The Necessity of Friction*. Boulder, CO: Westview Press, pp. 75–97.

Lane, H. C., J. LaMontagne, and A. S. Fauci. 2001. "Bioterrorism: A Clear and Present Danger." *Nature Medicine* 7(12): 1271–73.

Langewiesche, W. 2002. "American Ground: Unbuilding the World Trade Center, Part One: The Inner World." *The Atlantic Monthly* July/August 2002: 44–79.

Langran, G. 1992. *Time in Geographical Information Systems*. London: Taylor and Francis.

Laqueur, W. 1996. "Postmodern Terrorism." *Foreign Affairs* 75(5): 24–36.

Lazurus, R. K. Kleinman, I. Dashevsky, C. Adams, P. Kludt, A. DeMaria, Jr. and R. Platt. 2002. "Use of Automated Ambulatory-Care Encounter Records for Detection of Acute Illness Clusters, Including Potential Bioterrorism Events." *Emerging Infectious Diseases* 8(8): 753–60.

Le Billon, P. 2001a. "The Political Ecology of War: Natural Resources and Armed Conflicts." *Political Geography* 20: 561–84.

———. 2001b. "Angola's Political Economy of War: The Role of Oil and Diamonds, 1975–2000." *African Affairs* 100(398): 55–80.

Lee, J. 2001a. *A 3D Data Model for Representing Topological Relationships Between Spatial Entities in Built Environments*. Ph.D. Dissertation, Department of Geography, The Ohio State University.

———. 2001b. "A Spatial Access Oriented Implementation of a Topological Data Model for 3D Urban Entities." Paper presented at University Consortium for Geographic Information Science (UCGIS) Summer Assembly. Buffalo, NY, June 21–24.

Levi, M. A. and H. C. Kelly. 2002. "Weapons of Mass Disruption." *Scientific American* 287(5): 76–81.

Lintner, B. 1999. *Burma in Revolt: Opium and Insurgency Since 1948*. Chiang Mai, Thailand: Silkworm Books.

Logan, B. 2002. "The Lessons of 9/11." *Geospatial Solutions* 12(9): 26–30.

Longley, P. A., M. F. Goodchild, D. J. Maguire, and D. W. Rhind. 2001. *Geographic Information Systems and Science*. New York: Wiley.

Lovins, A. and C. H. Lovins. 1982. *Brittle Power: Energy Strategy for National Security*. Andover, MA: Brick House Publishing.

Lum, S. K. S. and B. C. Moyer. 2001. "Gross Domestic Product by Industry for 1998–2000. *Survey of Current Business* (November):17–33.

MacDonald, S. B. 1988. *Dancing on a Volcano: the Latin America Drug Trade*. New York: Praeger.

MacEachren, A. M., C. A. Brewer, and L. W. Pickle. 1998. "Visualizing Georeferenced Data: Representing Reliability of Health Statistics." *Environment and Planning A* 30: 1547–61

Maes, P. 1994. "Agents that Reduce Work and Information Overload." *Communications of the ACM* 37(7): 30–40.

Manion, K. A., W. Dorf and M. Hacvan-Orumieh. 2001. "Deep Infrastructure Group Provides Critical Data for Disaster Relief." *GeoPlace.com.*

Marceau, D. J., L. Guindon, M. Bruel, and C. Marois. 2001. "Building Temporal Topology in a GIS Database to Study the Land-Use Changes in Rural-Urban Environment." *Professional Geographer* 53(4): 546–58.

Mark, D., B. Smith, M. Egenhofer, and S. Hirtle. 2003. "Ontological Foundations for Geographic Information Science," in R. B. McMasters and L. Usery (eds.), *Research Challenges in Geographic Information Science.* New York. John Wiley and Sons.

Martínez, O. 1990. "Border People and Their Cultural Roles: The Case of the U.S.-Mexican Borderlands." *Borders and Border Regions in Europe and North America*, by P. Ganster, J. Scott, and W. Eberwein (eds.). San Diego: San Diego State University Press, pp. 293–98.

Masser, I. 1998. *Governments and Geographic Information.* New York: Taylor and Francis.

Mathewson, K. 1991. "Plantations and Dependencies: Notes on the 'Moral Geography' of Global Stimulant Production," in C. V. Blatz (ed.) *Ethics and Agriculture: An Anthology of Current Issues in World Context.* Moscow, ID: University of Idaho Press, pp. 559–67.

Mauney, T., A. Kong, and D. Richardson. 1993. *Interactive Automated Mapping System.* United States Patent #5,214,757 (Assignee: GeoResearch, Inc.). U.S. Patent and Trademark Office, May 25, 1993. (Continuation of Ser. No. 564,018, August 7, 1990).

McCann, B., B. DeLille, H. Dittmar, and M. Garland, 1999. *Road Work Ahead: Is Construction Worth the Wait?* Washington, D.C.: Surface Transportation Policy Project.

McColl, R. W. 1969. "The Insurgent State: Territorial Bases of Revolution." *Annals, Association of American Geographers* 59: 613–31.

McCoy, A. W. 1991. *The Politics of Heroin: CIA Complicity in the Global Drug Trade.* Chicago: Lawrence Hill Books.

———. 1999. Lord of Drug Lords: One Life as Lesson for US Drug Policy." *Crime, Law & Social Change* 30: 301–31.

McGovern, T. W., G. W. Christopher, and E. M. Eitzen. 1999. "Cutaneous Manifestations of Biological Warfare and Related Threat Agents." *ARCH Dermatology* (American Medical Association) 135(March): 311–22.

McIlraith, S., T. C. Son, and H. Zeng, 2001. "Semantic Web Services." *IEEE Intelligent Systems, Special Issue on the Semantic Web* 16(2): 46–53.

McVittie, T. 2001. "Designing Communications Software for Tactical Wireless Networks." *The Proceedings of the ONR Workshop Series on Collaborative Decision Support Systems "Continuing the Revolution in Military Affairs."* June: 175–91.

Miller, H. J. 1991. "Modeling Accessibility Using Space-Time Prism Concepts within Geographical Information Systems," *International Journal of Geographical Information Systems* 5: 287–301.

————. "Measuring Space-Time Accessibility Benefits within Transportation Networks: Basic Theory and Computational Methods," *Geographical Analysis* 31: 187–212.

Miller, J., S. Engelberg, and W. Broad. 2001. *Germs: Biological Weapons and America's Secret War*. New York: Simon & Schuster.

Mitchell, J. K. (ed). 1999. *Crucibles of Hazard: Mega-Cities and Disasters in Transition*. Tokyo, New York and Paris: United Nations University Press.

————. 2002. "Building Research Capacity to Address Terrorism," Natural Disasters Roundtable Forum, Countering Terrorism: Lessons learned from Natural and Technological Disasters, NRC, Washington, D.C., February 28–March 1.

————. 2003. "The Fox and the Hedgehog: Myopia about Homeland Vulnerability in US Policies on Terrorism." *Research in Social Problems and Public Policy* 11: forthcoming.

Miyao, T. 1995. "Reconstruction boom after the Great Hanshin Earthquake Won't Arise." E*conomist*, 3.7.95, 26–30. (in Japanese)

Modelski, G. 1987. *Long Cycles of World Politics*. London: Macmillan.

Monmonier, M., 1997. *Cartographies of Danger: Mapping Hazards in America*. Chicago: University of Chicago Press.

Monmonier, M. 2003. *Spying with Maps: Surveillance Technologies and the Future of Privacy*. Chicago: University of Chicago Press.

Morris, R. S., J. W. Wilesmith, M. W. Stern, R. L. Sanson, and M. A. Stevenson. 2001. "Predictive Spatial Modeling of Alternative Control Strategies for the Foot-and-Mouth Disease Epidemic in Great Britain, 2001." *The Veterinary Record* 149: 137–44.

Morrison, A. C., A. Getis, M. Santiago, J.G. Rigau-Perez, and P. Reiter. 1998. "Exploratory Space-Time Analysis of Reported Dengue Cases During an Outbreak in Florida, Puerto Rico, 1991–1992," *American Journal of Tropical Medicine and Hygiene* 58: 287–98.

Morrow, B. H. 1999. "Identifying and Mapping Community Vulnerability. *Disasters* 23(1): 1–18.

Murphy, A. B. 1989. "Territorial Policies in Multiethnic States". *The Geographical Review* 79: 410–21.

National Academy of Public Administration (NAPA). 1998. *Geographic Information for the 21st Century—Building a Strategy for the Nation*. Washington, D.C.: National Academy of Public Administration.

National Agricultural Statistics Service (NASS), U.S. Department of Agriculture. 1999. *1997 Agricultural Atlas of the United States*. http://www.nass.usda.gov/census/census97/atlas97.

National Atlas of the United States and the Centers for Disease Control and Prevention. 2002. *West Nile Virus Maps*. http://www.nationalatlas.gov/virusmap.html

National Research Council. 1993. *Toward a Coordinated Spatial Data Infrastructure for the Nation*. Washington, D.C.: National Academy Press.

————. 1997. *Rediscovering Geography—New Relevance for Science and Society*. Washington, D.C.: National Academy Press.

————. 1998. *People and Pixels: Linking Remote Sensing and Social Science*. Washington, D.C.: National Academy Press.

————. 1999. *Distributed Geolibraries: Spatial Information Resources.* Washington, D.C.: National Academy Press.

————. 2002a. *Making the Nation Safer: The Role of Science and Technology in Countering Terrorism.* Washington D.C.: National Academy Press.

————. 2002b. *Community and Quality of Life: Data Needs for Informed Decision Making.* Washington, D.C.: National Academy Press.

————. 2002c. *Down to Earth: Geographic Information for Sustainable Development in Africa.* Washington, D.C.: National Academy Press.

Natural Resources Conservation Service (NRCS), U.S. Department of Agriculture. 2001. *State of the Land.* http://www.nrcs.usda.gov/technical/land/meta/m4964.html.

National Security Strategy of the United States of America. 2002. Washington, D.C.: Office of the President of the United States of America.

New York City Infrastructure Task Force, Emergency Response Sub-Committee. 2001. Minutes of the Meeting, October 3, 2001. New York City.

New York Times, 2002. "Internal Security is Attracting a Crowd of Arms Contractors." *New York Times,* March 20, 2002, p. C1 and C12.

Nicholls, R. J. and C. Small. 2002. "Improved Estimates of Coastal Population and Exposure to Hazards Released." *EOS: Transactions on the American Geophysical Union* 83(28): 301, 305.

NIMA (National Imagery and Mapping Agency) and USGS (U.S. Geological Survey). 2002 (in review). *Homeland Security Infrastructure Program, Phase I Tiger Team, Final Report.*

Noji, E. K. 2002. "Medical and Public Health Consequences of Natural and Biological Disasters." *Natural Hazards Review* 2(3): 143–56.

Nordstrum, C. 1997. *A Different Kind of War Story.* Philadelphia: University of Pennsylvania Press.

Nusser, S. M. 2001. *Challenges in Geospatial Information Technologies for Field Survey Data Collection.* Washington, D.C.: Computer Science and Telecommunications Board, National Research Council.

Oas, I. 2002. *The Spatial Dementia of Geopolitics: Online Agency and U.S. Hegemonic Decline.* Masters Thesis. Department of Geography. University Park PA: Pennsylvania State University.

O'Brien, P. W. 2002. *Institutional Warning Response Following the September 11th World Trade Center Attack.* Quick Response Report #150. Natural Hazards Research and Applications Information Center, University of Colorado Boulder, CO.

Odlyzko, A. 2001. "Internet Pricing and the History of Communications." *Computer Networks* 36: 493–517.

O. G. D. 1998. *The World Geopolitics of Drugs 1997/1998.* Annual Report. Paris: Observatoire Géopolitique des Drogues.

O'Hanlon, M. 2002. "A Flawed Masterpiece." *Foreign Affairs* May/June 2002: 47–63.

OHS (Office of Homeland Security). 2002. *National Strategy for Homeland Security,* July 2002.

Okuyama, Y., G. J. D. Hewings, and M. Sonis. 1999. "Economic Impacts of an Unscheduled, Disruptive Event: A Miyazawa Multiplier Analysis." In G. J. D. Hewings, M. Sonis, M. Madden and Y. Kimura (eds), *Understanding and Interpreting*

Economic Structure, Advances in Spatial Sciences. Heidelberg, Germany: Springer-Verlag, pp. 113–44.

O'Neil, D. J. 2000. *Statewide Critical Infrastructure Protection, New Mexico's Model,* TRW News 211, November-December 2000.

Open GIS Consortium, Inc. 2002. http://www.opengis.org/index.htm.

O'Tuathail, G. 2000. The Postmodern Geopolitical Condition. *Annals of the Association of American Geographers* 90(1): 166–78.

———. 1999. "De-Territorialized Threats and Global Dangers: Geopolitics and Risk Society," in Newman, D. (ed.) *Boundaries, Territory and Postmodernity.* London: Frank Cass, pp. 17–31.

Parr, J. B., G. J. D. Hewings, J. Sohn, and S. Nazara. 2002. "Agglomeration and Trade: Some Additional Perspectives." *Regional Studies* 36: 675–84.

Pate, J. and G. Cameron, 2001. *Covert Biological Weapons Attacks against Agricultural Targets: Assessing the Impact against U.S. Agriculture.* BCSIA Discussion Paper 2001-9, ESDP Discussion Paper ESDP-2001-1-05 ESD-2000-1-04, John F. Kennedy School of Government, Harvard University. August.

Peach, J., and J. Williams, 2000. "Population and Economic Dynamics on the U.S.-Mexican Border: Past, Present, and Future." in *The U.S.-Mexican Border Environment: A Roadmap to a Sustainable 2020,* by P. Ganster (ed.). San Diego: San Diego State University Press, pp. 37–72.

PCCIP. 1997. *Critical Foundations: Protecting America's Infrastructures.* Report of the President's Commission on Critical Infrastructure Protection, October 1997.

Pfaff, W. 2001. "Washington's Call for War Plays into Terrorists' Hands." *International Herald Tribune* September 17, 2001. http://www.iht.com/ihtsearch.php?id=32719&owner=(International%20Herald%20Tribune)&date=000000.

Pickle, L. W., M. Mungiole, G. K. Jones, and A. A. White. 1996. *Atlas of United States Mortality.* U.S. Department of Health and Human Services, Public Health Service, Centers for Disease Control and Prevention, National Center for Health Statistics, Hyattsville, Maryland, DHHS Publication No. (PHS) 97–1015.

Pluijmers, Y. and P. Weiss. 2002. *Borders in Cyberspace: Conflicting Public Sector Information Policies and their Economic Impacts.* http://www.spatial.maine.edu/Govt Records/cache/Final%20Papers%20and%20Presentations/bordersII.htm.

Platt, R. H. 1995. "Lifelines: An Emergency Management Priority for the United States in the 1990s." *Disasters* 15: 172–76.

Powell, R. 1999. *In the Shadow of Power: States and Strategies in International Politics.* Princeton: Princeton University Press.

Pohl, J. 2001. *Information-Centric Decision Support Systems: A Blueprint for "Interoperability."* The Proceedings of the ONR Workshop Series on Collaborative Decision Support Systems "Continuing the Revolution in Military Affairs." June 2001. pp. 35–47.

Pollock, J. 2002. "The Web Services Scandal: How Data Semantics Have Been Overlooked in Integration Solutions." *eAI Journal,* August 2002. Online www.eajournal.com.

Pratt, R. H. and T. J. Lomax. 1996. "Performance Measures for Multimodal Transportation Systems," *Transportation Research Record* 1518: 85–93.

Putnam, R. D. 2000. *Bowling Alone: The Collapse and Revival of American Community.* New York: Simon and Schuster.

Radke, J., T. Cova, M. Sheridan, A. Troy, M. Lan, and R. Johnson. 2000. "Application Challenges for Geographic Information Science: Implications for Research, Education, and Policy for Emergency Preparedness and Response." *Journal of the Urban and Regional Information Systems Association,* by G. Elmes and R. Wright (eds.) (special UCGIS issue) (12)2: 15–30.

Renner, M. 2002. "Breaking the Link Between Resources and Repression," in *State of the World 2002,* Linda Starke (ed.). New York: W.W. Norton, pp. 149–73

Rhind, D. W. (ed.). 1997. *Framework for the World.* New York: Wiley.

Richards, P. 2001. "Are 'Forest' Wars in Africa Resource Conflicts? The Case of Sierra Leone," in *Violent Environments,* N. Peluso and M. Watts (ed.). Ithaca, NY: Cornell University Press, p. 81.

Richardson, D. 1991. "GeoLink Unites GPS and GIS Technologies." *GIS World* 4(6): 43–44.

———. 1994. "Managing with Maps: The Convergence of GPS and GIS Technologies (Plenary Session)," in *Federal Geographic Technology Conference.* Ft. Collins, CO: GIS World Books, pp. 9.

———. 2001. "Creating a Central Place for Geography in Society and the University: An Historic Opportunity," in Tobin G. A., B. E. Montz, and F. A. Schoolmaster (eds.) *Papers and Proceedings of the Applied Geography Conferences.* Denton, TX, University of North Texas: 24: 311–15.

———. 2002. "Building a Research Agenda on the Geographical Dimensions of Terrorism: an On-Going Process. *Transactions in GIS* 6: 225–229.

Ritchie, R. C. 1986. *Captain Kidd and the War Against the Pirates.* Cambridge, MA: Harvard University Press.

Rogers, P., S. Whitby, and M. Dando. 1999. "Biological Warfare against Crops." *Scientific American* 280(6): 70–75.

Roitman, J. 2001. "New Sovereigns? Regulatory Authority in the Chad Basin," in *Interventions and Tansnationalism in Africa,* by T. Callaghy, R. Kassimir and R. Latham (eds.), Cambridge, U.K., Cambridge University Press. pp. 240–263.

Rosenzweig, C. and W. Solecki. 2002. "Metropolitan East Coast Assessment: Climate Change and a Global City." http://metroeast_climate.ciesin.columbia.edu/credits.html

Rotberg, R. 2002. "Failed States in a World of Terror." *Foreign Affairs* 81(4): 127–40.

Rotz, L. D., A. S. Khan, S. R. Lillibridge, S. M. Ostroff, and J. M. Hughes. 2002. "Public Health Assessment of Potential Biological Terrorism Agents." *Emerging Infectious Diseases* 8(2): 225–30.

Rushton, G., G. Elmes, and R. McMaster. 2000. "Considerations for Improving Geographic Information Research in Public Health." *URISA Journal* 12(2): 31–49.

Sanabria, H. 1992. *The Coca Boom and Rural Social Change in Bolivia.* Ann Arbor: University of Michigan Press.

Savitch, H. V. and G. Ardashev. 2001. "Does Terror Have an Urban Future?" *Urban Studies* 38(13): 2515–33.

Schutzberg, A. 2001a. "IS in the Trenches." *GIS Monitor* (www.gismonitor.com). September 26, 2001.

———. 2001b. "GIS ASPs: Ready for Action?" *Directions Magazine.* Volume 6. http://www.directionsmag.com/article.asp?ArticleID=109.

Shepherd, I. D. H. 1991. "Information integration and GIS," in D. J. Maguire, M. F. Goodchild, and D. W. Rhind (eds.), *Geographical Information Systems: Principles and Applications, vol. 1.* Harlow, U.K.: Longmann Scientific and Technical, pp. 337–60.

Showstack, R. 2001. "GIS Plays Key Role in NYC Rescue and Relief Operation." *EOS: Transactions, American Geophysical Union* 82(40): 1.

Small, C., V. Gornitz, and J. E. Cohen. 2000. "Coastal Hazards and the Global Distribution of Human Population." *Environmental Geosciences* 7: 3–12.

Small, C. and T. Naumann. 2001. "The Global Distribution of Human Population and Recent Volcanism." *Environmental Hazards* 3(3–4): 93–109.

Smith, M. L. (ed.). 1992. *Why People Grow Drugs.* London: Panos Publications.

Smith, N. 2002. "Scales of Terror: the Manufacturing of Nationalism and the War for U.S. Globalism," in M. Sorkin and S. Zukin (eds.), *After the World Trade Center: Rethinking New York City.* New York: Routledge, pp. 97–108.

Somers-St. Claire, R. 1997. *Framework, Introduction and Guide.* Washington, D.C.: The Federal Geographic Data Committee.

Spencer, M. 1998. *Separatism: Democracy and Disintegration.* Lanham, MD: Rowman and Littlefield.

Springer, N. 1999. "Designing Dynamic Maps." *Cartographic Perspectives* 33: 60–62.

Stein, A. A. 1990. *Why Nations Cooperate: Circumstance and Choice in International Relations.* Ithaca, NY: Cornell University Press.

Steinberg, M. K. 2000. "Generals, Guerillas, Drugs, and Third World War-Making." *Geographical Review* 90(2): 260–267.

Thomas, D. S. K., S. L. Cutter, M. Hodgson, M. Gutekunst, and S. Jones. 2002. *Use of Spatial Data and Geographic Technologies in Response to the September 11 Terrorist Attack.* Quick Response Report #153. Natural Hazards Research and Applications Information Center University of Colorado, Boulder, CO, http://www.colorado.edu/hazards/qr/qr153/qr153.html.

Thompson, J. E. 1994. *Mercenaries, Pirates, And Sovereigns: State-Building and Extraterritorial Violence In Early Modern Europe.* Princeton: Princeton University Press.

Tobin, G. A. and B. E. Montz. 1997. *Natural Hazards: Explanation and Integration.* New York: Guilford Press.

Torpey, J. 2000. *The Invention of the Passport: Surveillance, Citizenship and the State.* Cambridge, U.K.: Cambridge University Press.

Torvalds, L., and D. Diamond. 2001. *Just for Fun: The Story of an Accidental Revolutionary.* London: Harper Business.

Tsou, M-H. 2001. *A Dynamic Architecture for Distributing Geographic Information Services on the Internet.* Unpublished doctoral dissertation. Boulder, Colorado: University of Colorado Department of Geography.

Tucker, J. B. 2000. "Introduction," in J. B. Tucker, (ed.) *Toxic Terror: Assessing Terrorist Use of Chemical and Biological Weapons.* Cambridge, MA: MIT Press, pp 1–14.

Tucker, J. B. and R. P. Kadlec. 2001. "Infectious Disease and National Security." *Strategic Review* 29(2): 12–20.

United Nations International Strategy for Disaster Reduction (ISDR). 2002. *Living with Risk: A Global Review of International Disaster Reduction Strategies.* New York: United Nations. http://www.unisdr.org/unisdr/Globalreport.htm.

University Consortium for Geographic Information Science (UCGIS). 1996. "Research Priorities for Geographic Information Science." *Cartography and Geographic Information Systems* 23(3): 115–27.

United Nations Development Program. 2002. *1ˢᵗ Annual World Vulnerability Report.* Geneva: Forthcoming.

U.S. Department of Transportation. 2001. Personal Communication with Angélica Villegas, August 24, 2001. Villegas is a researcher with the Institute for Regional Studies of the Californias, San Diego State University.

U.S. Environmental Protection Agency. 2001a. *Binational Prevention and Emergency Response Plan Between Douglas, Arizona and Agua Prieta, Sonora.* San Francisco: U.S. Environmental Protection Agency, Region IX.

———. 2001b. *San Diego: Hazardous Material Commodity Flow.* San Francisco: US/Mexico Border Program, Chemical Emergency Prevention and Preparedness Office, U.S. Environmental Protection Agency, Region IX.

U.S. Office of Management and Budget. 2002 *Homeland Security Budget. 2003.* Washington, D.C.: The White House. http://www.whitehouse.gov/homeland/homeland_security_book.html.

van Creveld, M. 1991. *The Transformation of War.* New York: The Free Press.

Vine, M. F., D. Degnan, and C. Hanchette. 1998. "Geographic Information Systems: Their Use in Environmental Eidemiologic Research." *Journal of Environmental Health* 61(3): 7–16.

Volpini, L. 2002. Personal communication, January 9, 2002. Volpini is with EPA Region IX and coordinates development of border sister city emergency response plans.

Wachowicz, M. 1999. *Object-Oriented Design for Temporal GIS.* London: Taylor and Francis.

Walker, J., D. Simerlink, C. Rodarmel, and L. Scott 2002. "Technical Aspects of Multi-Sensor Fusion over the World Trade Center Disaster Site." CADD/GIS Symposium, San Antonio, TX.

Wang, Z. and Wang, Z. 2002. "Study on Spatial-Temporal Features of Land Use/Land Cover Change Based on Technologies of RS and GIS." *Journal of Remote Sensing* 6(3): 228–231.

Weber, R. T., D. A. McEwen, and R. J. Robinson. 2002. *Public/Private Collaboration in Disaster: Implications from the World Trade Center Terrorist Attacks.* Quick Response Report #155. Natural Hazards Research and Applications Information Center University of Colorado Boulder, CO.

Weiss, P. 1999. "Stop-and-Go Science," *Science News* 156: 8–10

Weisburd, D. and T. McEwen. 1997. *Crime Mapping & Crime Prevention.* Monsey, NY: Criminal Justice Press.

West, C. T. and D. G. Lenze. 1994. "Modeling the Regional Impact of Natural Disaster and Recovery: A General Framework and an Application to Hurricane Andrew." *International Regional Science Review* 17: 121–50.

Whitby, S. M., 2002. *Biological Warfare against Crops.* Basingstoke, UK: Palgrave.

White, G. F., 1964. *Choice of Adjustment to Floods.* Chicago, IL: University of Chicago, Department of Geography Research Paper No. 93.

White, G. W. 2000. *Nationalism and Territory: Constructing Group Identity in Southeastern Europe.* Boulder, CO: Rowman & Littlefield.

White House, 2002. The Department of Homeland Security. Online: www.white house.gov/news.

WHO Group of Consultants. 1970. *Health Aspects of Chemical and Biological Weapons.* Geneva, Switzerland: World Health Organization.

Wilbanks, T., 1982. "Location and Energy Policy," in J. Frazier, (ed.), *Applied Geography: Selected Perspectives.* Englewood Cliffs, NJ: Prentice-Hall, pp. 219–232.

Wilford, J. N. 2000. *The Mapmakers.* New York: Alfred A. Knopf.

Wixman, R. 1995. "Ethnic and Territorial Conflicts in Eastern Europe," in *The Challenge of Ethnic Conflict to National and International Order in the 1990s: Geographical Perspectives.* Washington, D.C.: United States Government Printing Office, RTT 95–10039, pp. 25–41.

Wood, W. 1999a. "Geo-analysis for the Next Century: New Data and Tools for Sustainable Development," in G. Demko and W. Wood (eds.), *Reordering the World: Geopolitical Perspectives on the 21st Century, Second Edition.* Boulder, CO: Westview Press, pp. 192–205.

———. 1999b. "Geography: A Lesson for Diplomats." *The Fletcher Forum of World Affairs* 23(2): 5–20.

Worboys, M. F., 1995. *GIS: A Computing Perspective.* London: Taylor and Francis.

World Wide Web Consortium Architecture Domain: Web Services Activities. 2002. http://www.w3.org/2002/ws/.

Wright, J. K. 1936. "A Method of Mapping Densities of Population with Cape Cod as an Example." *Geographical Review* 26: 103–110.

Wright, R., E. Nelson, and H. Johnson, 1997. "Visualizing the Tijuana River Watershed for Environmental Research and Education." *Proceedings, GIS/LIS '97.* Cincinnati, OH: GIS/LIS, pp. 275–83.

Wright, R., and A. Winckell, 1998. "Harmonizing Framework and Resource Data Across Political Boundaries." *GIS Solutions in Natural Resource Management,* by S. Morain (ed.). Santa Fe, NM: Onward Press, pp. 71–93.

Wright, R. K. Baron, K. Conway, and R. Warner, 2000. "Flood Hazard and Risk Assessment Modeling with GIS in the Transborder Tijuana River Watershed." *Proceedings, Watershed 2000.* Vancouver, B.C. p. 15.

Wu, Y-H. and H. J. Miller. 2001. "Computational Tools for Measuring Space-Time Accessibility Within Dynamic Flow Transportation Networks." *Journal of Transportation and Statistics* 4(2/3): 1–14.

Zeiler, M. 1999. *Modeling Our World: The ESRI Guide to Geodatabase Design.* Redlands, CA: ESRI Press.

Zwerdling, D. 2001. "Terrorism and the Food Supply," Report for National Public Radio's *All Things Considered.* December 13. http://discover.npr.org/features/featue.jhtml?wfld=1134769.

CONTRIBUTORS

Frederick Abler is a Research Associate at the Collaborative Agent Design Research Center (CADRC) in the College of Architecture and Environmental Design at California Polytechnic State University in San Luis Obispo (Cal Poly). For the past six years, he has been the Project Manager of the Integrated Computerized Deployment System, an agent-based spatial decision support system for maritime logistics used by the United States Department of Defense. He is also Principal Investigator for the Objective Networks Project. His interests lie in human-computer interaction, virtually embodied autonomous agents, symbolic systems, digital design and simulation environments, and in the process of effective design.

Andrew J. Bruzewicz is director of the U.S. Army Corps of Engineers' Remote Sensing/GIS Center and Associate Technical Director for Geospatial Research and Development. He manages the Corps' civil works geospatial research and development program area (survey and mapping, remote sensing, and GIS), and is responsible for remote sensing and GIS support during disasters. His primary professional interests are the integration of remote sensing and GIS into the Corps' mission areas with particular emphasis on emergency management, data sharing within and between agencies, and remote sensing and GIS education. He has an A. B. (Economics) and an A.M. (Geography) from the University of Chicago where he is a Ph.D. Candidate in Geography.

Susan L. Cutter is a Carolina Distinguished Professor and Director of the Hazards Research Lab in the Department of Geography, University of South Carolina. She is a past President of the Association of American Geographers and a Fellow of the American Association for the Advancement of Science (AAAS). She serves on the National Research Council's Division on Earth and Life Studies (DELS) Advisory Board. Dr. Cutter has been working in the risk and hazards fields for more than 25 years and has authored or edited eight books and more than 50 peer-reviewed articles. Her most recent book, *American Hazardscapes* (Joseph Henry Press), chronicles the increasing vulnerability to natural disaster events in the United States during the past 30 years. Dr. Cutter is also the co-founding editor (along with James K. Mitchell) of *Environmental Hazards.* She has a B.A. from California State University, Hayward and a M.A. and Ph.D. in geography from the University of Chicago.

Jack Dangermond is Founder and President of Environmental Systems Research Institute, Inc. (ESRI), headquartered in Redlands, California, USA. Founded in 1969, ESRI is the leading Geographic Information Systems (GIS) company in the world, providing software like ArcInfo, ArcView GIS, and ArcExplorer to clients in 90 countries. Mr. Dangermond is recognized in both academia and industry as a leader of and an authority on the GIS field. Over the last thirty years, Jack has delivered keynote addresses at numerous international conferences, published hundreds of papers on GIS, and given thousands of presentations on GIS throughout the world. He is the recipient of a number of medals, awards, lectureships, and honorary degrees, including the 2000 LaGasse Medal of the American Society of Landscape Architects, the Brock Gold Medal of the International Society for Photogrammetry & Remote Sensing, the Cullum Geographical Medal of the American Geographical Society, the EDUCAUSE Medal of EduCause, the Horwood Award of the Urban and Regional Information Systems Association, the Anderson Medal of the Association of American Geographers, and the John Wesley Powell Award of the U.S. Geological Survey. He is a member of many professional organizations and has served on advisory committees for as NASA, EPA, NIMA, the National Academy of Sciences, and the NCGIA. Jack was educated at California Polytechnic College-Pomona, the University of Minnesota, Harvard University's Laboratory for Computer Graphics and Spatial Design. Mr. Dangermond holds three honorary doctorate degrees from Ferris State University in Michigan, the University of Redlands in California, and City University in London.

Ray J. Dezzani is an Assistant Professor of Geography and the Center for Transportation Studies at Boston University. He was educated at the University of California at Berkeley and Riverside. His research interests include the political inequality of location, regional growth theory, the world-systems perspective in geography, as well as stochastic models of economic convergence and spatial statistics. He has published a number of papers addressing these topics.

Jerome E. Dobson is a Research Professor at the University of Kansas (2001-present), President of the American Geographical Society (2002-presnt), and Contributing Editor of *GeoWorld* magazine (1990-present). Previously he was a member of the Distinguished Research and Development Staff of Oak Ridge National Laboratory (ORNL) where he worked from 1975–2001. Dr. Dobson led ORNL's LandScan Global Population Project from 1997 to 2001. He served as President of the University Consortium for Geographic Information Science (UCGIS) from 1997 to 1998. In the mid-1980s, he proposed and successfully worked with the White House and Congress to provide funding to the National Science Foundation for the National Center for Geographic Information and Analysis, subsequently co-located at the University of California in Santa Barbara, University of Buffalo, and the University of Maine. Dobson has authored more than 130 publications with contributions to geographic methodology, and to the understanding of lake acidification, continental drift, and human evolution.

David Dow has taught courses in GIS and lectured on cartography in the Department of Geography and the San Diego State University Foundation's GIS Certificate Program between 1994 and the present. His areas of topical proficiency and expertise include GIS, cartography, visualization, and spatial knowledge acquisition. Since 1999 he has acted as technical coordinator for the San Diego State University Foundation's GIS Certificate Program.

Colin Flint is Assistant Professor of Geography at the Pennsylvania State University. He is the co-author (with Peter Taylor) of *Political Geography: World-Economy, Nation-State, and Locality* and has published articles in *Political Geography, Geopolitics, Progress in Human Geography*, and the *Annals of the Association of American Geographers*. His research interests include geopolitics, the geography of war and peace, terrorism, hate groups, and electoral geography.

Gerald E. Galloway (PE, Ph.D.) is Secretary, U.S. Section, International Joint Commission, U. S.-Canada. A geographer and a civil engineer, he was head of the Department of Geography and Environmental Engineering at West Point where also served as Dean of the Academic Board. His 38-year military career included extensive work in development of battlefield information systems and their geographic components. He retired from the military in 1995 as a Brigadier General. The views in this paper are those of the author and do not necessarily reflect the position of the International Joint Commission.

Paul Ganster is director of the Institute for Regional Studies of the Californias and Associate Director of International Programs at San Diego State University. He is an historian with a specialty in Latin America. For the past twenty years his efforts have been directed toward policy questions of the U.S.-Mexican border region, and the comparative study of border regions around the world. Ganster's current research interests include border environmental issues, transborder governance issues, ecosystems management within the context of human systems, quality of life indicators in the border region, and comparative border region analysis. He serves on a number of regional advisory boards dealing with the border region and is the current Chairman of the Southwest Center for Environmental Research and Policy. In addition to teaching at San Diego State University, Ganster has been visiting professor at the School of Economics of the Universidad Autónoma de Baja California in Tijuana, Mexico.

Arthur Getis is the Stephen and Mary Birch Foundation Chair of Geographical Studies at San Diego State University. Currently, he is president of the University Consortium for Geographic Information Science (UCGIS). Together with Professor Manfred Fischer of Vienna he edits the *Journal of Geographical Systems*. Currently, with the support of NIH, he is doing research on the transmission of dengue fever. He has received the Walter Isard Distinguished Scholarship award from the North American Regional Science Association and Distinguished Scholarship Honors from the Association of American Geographers. His Ph.D. is from the University of Washington and his M.S. and B.S. degrees are from the Pennsylvania State University.

Michael F. Goodchild is Professor of Geography at the University of California, Santa Barbara; Chair of the Executive Committee, National Center for Geographic Information and Analysis (NCGIA); Associate Director of the Alexandria Digital Library Project; and Director of NCGIA's Center for Spatially Integrated Social Science. He received his B.A. from Cambridge University in Physics in 1965, and his Ph.D in Geography from McMaster University in 1969. He was elected member of the National Academy of Sciences and Foreign Fellow of the Royal Society of Canada in 2002. His current research interests center on geographic information science, spatial analysis, the future of the library, and uncertainty in geographic data. He is author of over 350 scientific papers and books.

Lisa M. Butler Harrington is an Associate Professor of Geography at Kansas State University. Her primary areas of interest include natural resources (particularly biotic resources), human-environmental relations, environmental change, and rural geography. Harrington has degrees from Colorado State University (B.S.), Clemson University (MRPA), and the University of Oklahoma (Ph.D). She has served as Chair of the Contemporary Agriculture and Rural Land Use specialty group of the Association of American Geographers (AAG) and of the AAG Research Grants Committee. Harrington has over 40 publications.

Geoffrey J. D. Hewings is a professor in the departments of Geography, Economics and Urban and Regional Planning and Director of the Regional Economics Applications Laboratory (REAL) at the University of Illinois. His main research areas are in the fields of urban and regional analysis, with a strong emphasis on the development and application of large-scale models. He has taught and conducted research in the United States, England, Canada, Australia, China, Japan, Korea, Brazil, Chile, Colombia and Indonesia. His recent interests have been modeling the changes in national and regional economies associated with the development of free trade agreements. Current work focuses on the role of interstate trade among the states of the Midwest. REAL maintains comprehensive impact and forecasting models for each Midwest state and for the Midwest as a whole; in addition, a monthly forecasting index for Chicago is featured in Crain's Chicago Business. His publications include 6 books, over 30 chapters and 100 articles in major professional journals; he has supervised 25 doctoral dissertations He is currently President of the Regional Science Association International for 2001–2002.

John A. Kelmelis is Chief Scientist for Geography at the U.S. Geological Survey (USGS). He leads program development and research for Cooperative Topographic Mapping, Land Remote Sensing, and Geographic Analysis and Monitoring. With the other members of the Bureau Program Planning Committee he is responsible for strategic and annual planning, integrated science, and the health of the scientific disciplines in USGS. He has managed the U.S. Antarctic Mapping Program, integration of advanced cartographic systems into USGS, and the USGS Global Change Research Program. He was director of the Scientific Assessment and Strategy Team for the White House, a visiting scientist at the Smithsonian Institution, a science consultant with the U.S. House of Representatives, a cartographer with the Defense Mapping Agency, and administrator of the Inland Wetlands and Watercourses Act for the State of Connecticut. Dr. Kelmelis represents the United States in a number of international organizations. He has written numerous scientific articles, book chapters, and reports. He received his B.A, in earth science from Central Connecticut State College, M.S. in engineering management from the University of Missouri at Rolla, and his Ph.D. from the Pennsylvania State University.

Mei-Po Kwan is Associate Professor of Geography at the Ohio State University and holds a Ph.D. in Geography from the University of California, Santa Barbara. She is currently an associated faculty of the Center for

Urban and Regional Analysis and the John Glenn Institute for Public Service and Public Policy at OSU. Dr. Kwan is an Associate Editor of *Geographical Analysis* and serves on the International Editorial Advisory Board of *The Canadian Geographer*. She has also served as the guest editor of special issues for *Gender, Place and Culture, Journal of Geographical Systems,* and *Cartographica*. Her research interests include GIS-based geocomputation and 3D geovisualization, qualitative GIS, gender/ethnic issues in transportation and urban geography, new information technologies, feminist methodologies, and cybergeography. Her recent project explores the impact of Internet use on women's activity patterns in space-time and the gender division of household labor.

T. R. Lakshmanan is Professor of Geography, the Director of the Center for Transportation Studies, and Executive Director of the Center for Energy and Environmental Studies at Boston University. In 1994 Dr. Lakshmanan was appointed by President Clinton as the founding director of the Bureau of Transportation Statistics in the U.S. Department of Transportation. In this role, he used the state of the art information technology in developing and widely disseminating a transportation knowledge base and decision support system for transportation management in states and metropolitan areas in the United States. Dr. Lakshmanan was editor of the *Annals of Regional Science* from 1988 to 1994. He served as Chairman of the Working Group on Energy Resources and development of the International Geographic Union from 1980 to 1988 and was Vice President of the International Regional Science Association from 1981 to 1983. Dr. Lakshmanan has served on the Executive Committee of NRC's Transportation Research Board and on the NRC Panel on Technologies for Affordable Housing. In 1985 he was elected a Life Member of Clare Hall College, Cambridge University and in 1989 was awarded the Anderson Medal of the American Association of Geographers. He holds a Ph.D. (1965) from Ohio State University, and a M.A. (1953) and B.Sc. (1952) from the University of Madras.

Scott A. Loomer is the Science Advisor for Geospatial Sciences at the National Imagery and Mapping Agency (NIMA), Washington, D.C. He serves as a senior advisor to the Director of NIMA as well as leading NIMA's research and development efforts in geospatial science. Prior to joining NIMA in 2001, Dr. Loomer was Professor of Geospatial Information Science and Deputy Head of the Department of Geography and Environmental Engineering at the United States Military Academy, West Point, New York. Dr. Loomer received his Ph.D in Geography from the University of Wisconsin, Madison in 1987. His B.S. and M.S. degrees are in Civil and Environmental Engineering, also at the University of Wisconsin. He is a registered Professional Engineer in Wisconsin.

John H. Marburger III is the Director, White House Office of Science and Technology Policy (OSTP) and Science Adviser to President George W. Bush. The Senate confirmed Dr. Marburger as OSTP Director in October 2001. He also co-chairs the President's Committee of Advisers on Science and Technology (PCAST) and supports the President's National Science and Technology Council. From 1980 to 1994 Marburger was President of the State University of New York at Stony Brook. In 1994 he returned to the faculty and also became President of Brookhaven Science Associates, a partnership between SUNY Stony Brook and Battelle Memorial Institute, which won the contract to operate the U.S. Department of Energy's Brookhaven National Laboratory. He also chaired the Universities Research Association, which operates the Fermi National Accelerator Laboratory. Prior to SUNY Stony Brook, Marburger was dean of the College of Letters, Arts and Sciences at the University of Southern California where he was a professor physics and electrical engineering. He has a B.A. with a major in physics from Princeton and a Ph.D. in Applied Physics from Stanford University.

Kent Mathewson is Associate Professor of Geography and Anthropology at Louisiana State University. His teaching and research specialties are cultural and historical geography, cultural ecology, and history of geography. His regional interests include Latin America and the American South. He has authored and/or (co) edited articles and books in these fields, including: *Irrigation Horticulture in Highland Guatemala* (Westview 1984); *ReReading Cultural Geography* (University of Texas 1994); *Concepts in Human Geography* (Rowman & Littlefield 1996); and *Dangerous Harvest: Drug Plants and the Transformation of Indigenous Landscapes* (Oxford 2003). He has held various positions in the Association of American Geographers and currently serves as National Councilor. He also serves as the AAG representative to the AAAS section H (Anthropology). Mathewson has a B.A. in geography from Antioch College, and holds M.S. and Ph.D. degrees in geography from the University of Wisconsin-Madison.

Harvey J. Miller is Professor of Geography at the University of Utah. His research and teaching interests include transportation and communication systems, geographic information science, and spatial analysis. He is author (with Shih-Lung Shaw) of the *Geographic Information Systems for Transportation: Principles and Applications* (Oxford University Press) and editor (with Jiawei Han) of *Geographic Data Mining and Knowledge Discovery* (Taylor and Francis). He is currently North American Editor of *International Journal of Geographical Information Science*.

James K. Mitchell grew up in Northern Ireland where he experienced the effects of terrorism and the complexities of related public policymaking. Since receiving a Ph.D. from the University of Chicago (1974) Ken has specialized in hazards research and is author of more than 100 professional publications including *Crucibles of Hazard: Megacities and Disasters in Transition* (United Nations University Press, 1999). He has served on disaster-related committees of the National Research Council and chaired the Council's ad hoc committee on the International Decade for Natural Hazard Reduction. He has also chaired the International Geographical Union's Study Group on the Disaster Vulnerability of Megacities, founded the Association of American Geographers Hazards Specialty Group and the international journal *Global Environmental Change*, as well as co-founding the more recent quarterly *Environmental Hazards*.

Alexander B. Murphy is Professor of Geography at the University of Oregon, where he also holds the James F. and Shirley K. Rippey Chair in Liberal Arts and Sciences. He specializes in cultural and political geography. Murphy is the incoming President of the Association of American Geographers and a Vice-President of the American Geographical Society. He is an editor of both *Progress in Human Geography* and *Eurasian Geography and Economics*. Murphy is the author or co-author of more than fifty articles and several books, including *The Regional Dynamics of Language Differentiation in Belgium* (University of Chicago, 1988); *Cultural Encounters with the Environment*, Rowman and Littlefield, 2000 (With Douglas Johnson); and *Human Geography: Culture, Society, and Space*, 7th ed., John Wiley, 2002 (with Harm de Blij).

Yasuhide Okuyama is currently a Research Associate in the Regional Research Institute of West Virginia University. He earned his Ph.D. in Regional Planning from the University of Illinois, in 1999. He also obtained the master's degrees in Urban and Regional Planning from the University of Wisconsin at Madison (1994) and in Environmental Science from the University of Tsukuba, Japan (1986). He taught in the Department of Urban and Regional Planning in the University at Buffalo, the State University of New York, from 1999 to 2002. His research interests include regional economic analysis and modeling, transportation modeling and policy, and modeling economic impacts of disasters. He has published a number of papers in academic journals, book chapters, and conference proceedings

Harlan Onsrud is Professor of Spatial Information Science and Engineering at the University of Maine. His research focuses on the analysis of legal, ethical, and institutional issues affecting the creation and use of digital spatial databases and the assessment of the social impacts of spatial technologies. He teaches courses in information systems law, cadastral and land information systems, and information ethics. Onsrud is Chair of the U.S. National Committee (USNC) on Data for Science and Technology (CODATA). He currently serves on the Mapping Science Committee within the National Research Council, and is co-chair of the Global Spatial Data Infrastructure (GSDI) Legal and Economics Working Group. He is immediate past-president of the University Consortium for Geographic Information Science (UCGIS) and is Editor-in-Chief of the *Journal of the Urban and Regional Information Systems Association* (*URISA Journal*). He is a licensed engineer, surveyor, and attorney.

Douglas B. Richardson is Executive Director of the Association of American Geographers. Dr. Richardson was founder and president of GeoResearch, Inc., which pioneered the development of real-time interactive GPS/GIS mapping and management technologies from 1980 through 1998, when he sold the firm and its patents. Doug currently also co-directs the AAG's National Science Foundation project on *The Geographical Dimensions of Terrorism: A Research Agenda for the Discipline,* which has developed a set of recommendations related to this topic for Federal Agencies and the geographic research community. He holds a Ph.D. in geography from Michigan State University.

Philip Rubin is Director of the Division of Behavioral and Cognitive Sciences at the National Science Foundation, where he is responsible for a wide variety of fields including archaeology, cultural and physical anthropology, geography and regional science, environmental behavioral and social sciences, child development, human cognition and perception, cognitive neuroscience, linguistics, and social psychology. At NSF he is a member of the Science and Technology Centers (STC) working group and co-chair of the new Human and Social Dynamics priority area. He has served as the NSF *ex officio* representative to the National Human Research Protection Advisory Committee (NHRPAC) and co-chairs the interagency National Science and Technology Council (NSTC) Human Subjects Research Subcommittee, Non-Biomedical Working Group, under the supervision of the President's Office of Science and Technology Policy (OSTP). He is also a member of the NSTC SBE Working Group on Terrorism. Rubin is also the Vice President and Senior Scientist at Haskins Laboratories in New Haven, a Professor Adjunct in the Department of Surgery, Otolaryngology, at the Yale University School of Medicine, and a Research Affiliate in the Department of Psychology at Yale University. He is a Fellow of the American Association for the Advancement of Science (AAAS) and a Fellow of the Acoustical Society of America (ASA). Rubin received his B.A. from Brandeis University in psychology and linguistics and his M.A. and Ph.D. from the University of Connecticut in experimental psychology.

Marilyn O. Ruiz is a Clinical Assistant Professor in the Veterinary Diagnostic Laboratory, College of Veterinary Medicine, University of Illinois at Urbana-Champaign. Her research interests are in the areas of cartographic visualization techniques, implementation of GIS in public health, and GIS and spatial analysis for improved understanding of disease ecology, disease mapping and ecosystem health. She held positions with the Army Corps of Engineers Construction Engineering Research Laboratory and the Florida State University before coming to the University of Illinois.

Marilyn Silberfein is a professor of Geography and Urban Studies at Temple University. She has specialized in rural development issues in Africa and has published two books and several articles on the subject. She has also been a rural development practitioner, serving for two years as an IPA with USAID and carrying out fieldwork in Tanzania, Kenya, and Sierra Leone among other countries. As a result of the current reality in Africa, she has shifted her interests to spatial and environmental aspects of resource-based conflicts.

Michael Steinberg is an Assistant Professor of Geography at the University of Southern Maine. He is the author and editor of articles and books on cultural and political ecology, including indigenous peoples and drug plant production in Latin America. He is the lead editor of the volume *Dangerous Harvest: Drug Plants and the Transformation of Indigenous Landscapes*, to be published by Oxford University Press in 2003. His articles have appeared in journals such as the *Professional Geographer*, *Geographical Review*, and *Economic Botany*.

Mike Tait is currently Director of the Internet Solutions Division at ESRI, Inc. His current responsibilities include management and oversight of ArcWeb Services and ArcLocation Solutions product development, as well as, implementation and operation of the Geography Network. Prior assignments at ESRI include managing the development of ArcIMS, ESRI's Internet mapping software product. Recent special assignments include leading ESRI's 9/11 support team for the City of New York's Emergency Operations Mapping Center, and program manager for the CENTCOM GIS deployment at the National Imagery and Mapping Agency. Prior to joining ESRI Mike was an Urban Planner for the City of Austin, Texas, and a Field Artillery Officer in the U.S. Marine Corps. He has an M.S. in Planning and B.A. in Geography from the University of Texas at Austin.

Deborah S. K. Thomas is an Assistant Professor of Geography at the University of Colorado at Denver. She has over tens years of research and application experience working with GIS in a variety of areas including hazards management, environmental health, and crime mapping. Dr. Thomas participated in the quick response analysis of the use of geographical information technologies in the rescue and relief period following the collapse of the World Trade Center in New York City. She has several book contributions and has published in the *Journal of Geography*, the *International Journal of Mass Emergencies and Disasters* and *Social Science Quarterly*. Dr. Thomas also serves as a social and behavioral science associate editor for *Natural Hazards Review*.

Thomas J. Wilbanks is a Corporate Research Fellow at ORNL and leads the Global Change and Developing Country Programs of the Laboratory. He is also an Associate of the Belfer Center for Science and International Affairs at Harvard University and an Adjunct Professor of Geography at the University of Tennessee. He is a past President of the Association of American Geographers (AAG), and received AAG Honors in 1986, the Distinguished Geography Educator's Award of the National Geographic Society (NGS) in 1993, and was awarded the James R. Anderson Medal of Honor in Applied Geography in 1995. He is a member of the Board on Earth Sciences and Resources of the National Research Council, NRC's Committee on Human Dimensions of Global Change, and the Science Steering Group for the U.S. Carbon Cycle Program.

William B. Wood is Deputy Assistant Secretary for Analysis and Information Management, Bureau of Intelligence and Research, U.S. Department of State. He oversees the work of offices covering Global Issues, African Affairs, and Information Services. He also serves as the Geographer for the Department of State, supervising the depiction of international boundaries on U.S. government maps, and the use of GIS and remote sensing for foreign affairs applications. He has published numerous articles on sustainable development, forced migration, humanitarian crises, and war crimes; co-edited (with G. Demko) *Reordering the World: Geopolitical Perspectives on the 21st Century*. He received the AAG's Anderson Award for Applied Geography in 2001.

Richard Wright is Professor Emeritus of Geography at San Diego State University. He is a specialist on geographic information systems (GIS), cartographic visualization, and watershed analysis. He has been a consultant to private industry and public agencies on a variety of mapping and geographic information systems projects. During the past ten years he has been involved with GIS education, the use of GIS in land use and water quality modeling, and transborder geo-spatial data integration in the United States-Mexico border region. He is a past member of Association of American Geographers Council, a current member of the International Geographic Information Foundation Board, and the recipient of the Anderson Medal in Applied Geography for 2002.

INDEX